Contents

List of plates page vii

List of maps and diagrams vii

List of tables viii

Acknowledgements ix

List of abbreviations and conventions xii

INTRODUCTION

1 Diary-keeping in seventeenth-century England 3

PART I
The political, ecclesiastical and economic world

2 Ralph Josselin's early life and his political and ecclesiastical career 15

3 Josselin's economic activities (i): income, expenditure and saving 33

4 Josselin's economic activities (ii): farming, weather and prices 68

PART II
The life-cycle

5 Birth and childhood 81

6 Adolescence, marriage and death 92

PART III
The social world: family, kin and neighbours

7 Husband–wife, parents–children 105

8 Other kinship ties 126

9   Ties with godparents, servants and friends   144

10 The relative importance of kin and neighbours   153

PART IV

The mental world

11 Attitudes to pain, sin and God   163

12 Dreams, imagery and the structure of thought   183

APPENDIXES

A   The fertility of Ralph Josselin's wife   199

B   Children and servants: the problem of adolescence   205

C   Extracts from records relating to the Josselin family   211

    Bibliography   224

    Index   235

THE FAMILY LIFE OF
RALPH JOSSELIN

A portrait believed to be of Ralph Josselin. Another portrait reputed to be of Josselin is in the possession of Colonel G. O. C. Probert

THE FAMILY LIFE OF RALPH JOSSELIN

A SEVENTEENTH-CENTURY CLERGYMAN

AN ESSAY IN HISTORICAL ANTHROPOLOGY

BY

ALAN MACFARLANE

The Norton Library
W·W·NORTON & COMPANY·INC·
NEW YORK

Books That Live
The Norton imprint on a book means that in the publisher's
estimation it is a book not for a single season but for the years.
W. W. Norton & Company, Inc.

First published 1970.
Reprinted by permission of Cambridge University Press.
First published in the Norton Library 1977.

Library of Congress Cataloging in Publication Data

Macfarlane, Alan.
    The family life of Ralph Josselin, a seventeenth-
century clergyman.

    (The Norton library)
    Reprint of the ed. published by the University
Press, Cambridge, Eng.
    Bibliography: p.
    Includes index.
    1. Josselin, Ralph, 1617-1683. 2. Church of
England—Clergy—Biography. 3. Clergy—England—
Biography. I. Title.
BX5199.J66M3   1977   283 '.092 '4 [B]   77-440
ISBN 0-393-00849-5

2 3 4 5 6 7 8 9 0

List of plates, maps and diagrams, and tables

PLATES

A portrait believed to be of Ralph Josselin *frontispiece*
Reproduced by permission of Mrs S. Sherwood:
print provided by F. G. Emmison, County Archivist, Essex Record Office

An extract from Ralph Josselin's Diary *facing p.* 22
Reproduced by permission of Colonel G. O. C. Probert

An extract from Earls Colne parish register *facing p.* 23
Reproduced by permission of the Rev. A. S. J. Holden:
print provided by F. G. Emmison

MAPS AND DIAGRAMS

1	County of Essex, showing location of Earls Colne and other places mentioned in Josselin's Diary	*page* x
2	Parish of Earls Colne, showing location of Josselin's landholdings	xi
3	Josselin's income between 1641 and 1683	36
4	Josselin's expenses	41
5	Expense of maintaining Josselin, his wife, servants and children, 1641–83	47
6	Josselin's debts and loans, 1645–70	56
7	Growth in the value of Josselin's estate, 1640–83	58
8	Josselin's landholdings in Earls Colne	62
9	Disposal of Josselin's lands	66
10	Distribution of those of Josselin's kin whose residence is known	142

11 Noted and lamented deaths in Josselin's
    environment   156

12 Josselin's intimate, effective and peripheral kin 157

    Ralph Josselin's kin and family   *facing* p. 234

TABLES

    I   Sources of Josselin's income, 1641–83   *page* 39

   II   Items of Josselin's expenditure, 1641–83   54

  III   Josselin's land acquisitions   60–1

   IV   Transmission of Josselin's wealth   65

    V   Vital statistics of Josselin's family   82

   VI   Movement of children away from home   93

  VII   Josselin's contacts with his cousins   138

 VIII   Josselin's contacts with his affinal kin   141

   IX   Comparison of Josselin's recognition of kin with
        that of two modern families   158

    X   Incidence of death in Josselin's family   164

   XI   Dreams of Josselin   184

  XII   Fertility of Josselin's wife   200

 XIII   Birth intervals (in months): Josselin and Colyton
        compared   201

  XIV   Weaning and conception dates in Josselin's family 202

Acknowledgements

This work is the result of co-operative effort and owes an enormous amount to Iris Macfarlane, the author's mother. She not only re-wrote a major portion of the original draft, but also added references and fresh ideas. Any stylistic merit that parts of the book may possess is entirely the result of her labours. Without her help the work could not have been completed.

A number of others have kindly read various sections of the work and I would like to thank them for their helpful comments: Lady Rosalind Clay, Dr Joan Thirsk, Professor Trevor-Roper and Dick Smethurst, all of Oxford University, and Dr E. A. Wrigley of Cambridge. Mary McCullough and my wife Gill, both of them social workers skilled at unravelling emotional relationships within the family, also made some extremely valuable comments and criticisms. Arthur Searle of the Essex Record Office added to many kindnesses by reading practically the whole typescript and commenting on it. To him and Keith Thomas, who read the various drafts with his usual vigilance and suggested many ways in which they could be improved, I am especially grateful. My thanks also go to the staff of Cambridge University Press for the trouble they took in preparing the text for publication during my absence in Nepal.

Finally, I would like to thank Colonel G. O. C. Probert, in whose possession the manuscript Diary of Ralph Josselin is at present, for permission to quote from it. The Essex Record Office also kindly gave the author permission to quote from documents in their custody and the staff, once again, made research doubly pleasant and fruitful by their willing assistance. I thank the County Archivist and all at Chelmsford.

A. M.

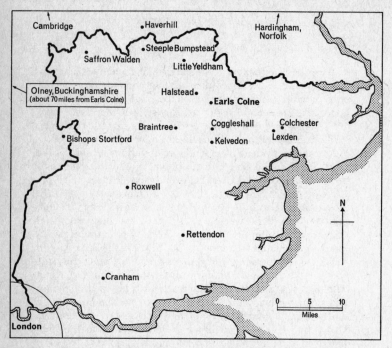

Fig. 1. The county of Essex, showing the location of Earls Colne and of other places mentioned in Josselin's Diary.

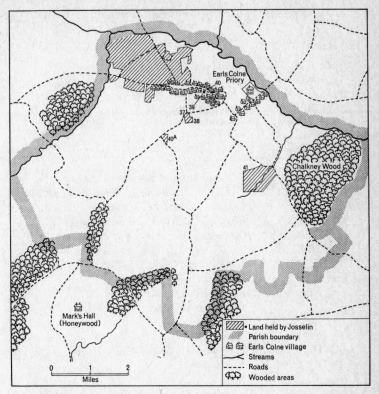

Fig. 2. The parish of Earls Colne, showing the location of Josselin's landholdings. Numbers refer to holdings in table III, pp. 60–1.

List of abbreviations and conventions

Agric. Hist. Rev.	*Agricultural History Review*
Am. Anth.	*American Anthropologist*
Am. Jour. Soc.	*American Journal of Sociology*
Arch. Ael.	*Archaeologia Aeliana*
Ass. Arch. Soc.	Associated Architectural Societies' Reports and Papers
Brit. Jour. Soc.	*British Journal of Sociology*
B.M.	British Museum
B.R.O.	Buckinghamshire Record Office
Bull. Inst. Hist. Res.	*Bulletin of the Institute of Historical Research*
Cam. Soc.	Camden Society Publications
Chet. Soc.	Chetham Society Publications
Comp. Stud. Soc. & Hist.	*Comparative Studies in Society and History*
D.N.B.	*Dictionary of National Biography*
Econ. Hist. Rev.	*Economic History Review*
Eng. Hist. Rev.	*English Historical Review*
E.R.O.	Essex Record Office, County Hall, Chelmsford
Ess. Rev.	*Essex Review*
H.R.O.	Hertfordshire Record Office
Hist. & Th.	*History and Theory*
Hum. Biol	*Human Biology*
L.P.	*The Lismore Papers*
Northants. Rec. Soc.	Northamptonshire Record Society
P. & P.	*Past and Present*
Pop. Stud.	*Population Studies*
P.R.O.	Public Record Office
Q.R.	*Quarterly Review*
Soc. Rev.	*Sociological Review*
Sur. Soc.	Surtees Society
Suss. Arch. Coll.	*Sussex Archaeological Collections*

Trans. Cumb. & *West. Ant. &* *Arch. Soc.*	*Transactions of the Cumberland and Westmor-* *land Antiquarian and Archaeological Society*
Trans. Hist. Soc. *Lancs. & Ches.*	*Transactions of the Historic Society of Lanca-* *shire and Cheshire*
Univ. Birm. Hist. *Jour.*	*University of Birmingham Historical Journal*

Place of publication of books referred to is London, unless otherwise indicated.

All references to unpaginated material are to the *recto* side, unless 'v' for *verso* is specifically indicated.

All dates are in new style with the year commencing 1 January.

All references to dates in the original Diary of Ralph Josselin appear in the body of the text in brackets, abbreviated from the form 12.10.1646 to 12.10.46—in other words, all years commence 16--. An italicized date means that the reference comes from among the miscellaneous notes in the front pages of the manuscript Diary, and not from under the appropriate date in the Diary itself.

Spelling and punctuation in quotations from the Diary have not been substantially altered, although capitals and occasional punctuation marks have been added to improve the sense: 'j' has been substituted for 'i' where necessary, and likewise 'th' for 'y' (as in 'the' for 'ye' etc.). Josselin's use of the '&' symbol has been copied; and he sometimes uses a 'c' instead of a 'ti' (as in 'porcons' meaning 'portions').

Inflation, both in the seventeenth and twentieth centuries, makes it impossible to give more than a very rough estimate of the comparative value of money, but £1 was probably worth more than twelve times as much in Josselin's time as it is now (1969).

Introduction

I

Diary-keeping in seventeenth-century England

The search for answers to new questions usually coincides with the discovery of new sources of information. The recent shift of interest from political and constitutional to economic and social history has been accompanied by the increased utilization of the vast deposits of local records scattered throughout Europe and North America. The major intellectual advances in the next few years will be made by combining the problems suggested by the social sciences, particularly sociology and social anthropology, with the documents stored in regional archives.[1] Yet there are a number of dangers inherent in this exciting synthesis. One of these is the tendency for individuals and their attitudes to be overlooked in the search for statistical facts. Another bias is towards the material and outward aspects of human life, the physical conditions of the past. The fundamental problems of attitudes and assumptions, of the mental life of people living long ago, are ignored because local records are peculiarly silent—except indirectly—about large sectors of past thought. The following study of the life of a seventeenth-century clergyman is a partial attempt to restore the balance.

This analysis of Ralph Josselin's life deals with the problems of a demographic and sociological kind which currently intrigue many historians. But the use of a diary as a prime source, rather than the parish registers or probate inventories upon which most social history is at present based, allows us to make a more personal and intimate study. It enables us to probe a long-vanished mental world, as well as to describe the social characteristics of a previous civilization. It is an attempt to test Eileen Power's belief that 'social history lends itself particularly to what may be called a personal treatment'.[2] The advantages of such a biographical approach are excellently summarized by Robert Redfield in his description of the 'Little Community as a typical biography':

[1] Keith Thomas, 'History and Anthropology', *P. & P.*, vol. 24 (1963), provides a brilliant summary of the possible contributions of social anthropology; there is nothing as good for sociology and history. Two useful outlines of local records are W. G. Hoskins, *Local History in England* (1959), and John West, *Village Records* (1962).

[2] *Medieval People* (university paperback edn, 1963), p. vii.

3

As soon as our attention turns from a community as a body of houses and tools and institutions to the states of mind of particular people, we are turning to the exploration of something immensely complex and difficult to know. But it is humanity, in its inner and more private form; it is, in the most demanding sense, the stuff of the community. While we talk in terms of productivity, or of roles and statuses, we are safely and easily out in the light, above ground, so to speak, moving among an apparatus we have ourselves built, an apparatus already removed, by our own act of mind, from the complicated thinking and feeling of the men and women who achieve the productivity or define and occupy the roles. But it is the thinking that is the real and ultimate raw material; it is there that the events really happen. And the choice of a human biographic form for describing the whole turns us to it . . . this inner stuff of the villagers' minds.[1]

Although there have been many biographies of members of the gentry and ruling classes in seventeenth-century England, there are few of less wealthy people.

From the late sixteenth century onwards there is a steadily expanding amount of historical material for English history in the form of correspondence, diaries and autobiographies,[2] and other family papers. The standard bibliography of British diaries lists some 363 surviving diaries up to the year 1699, and over 100 autobiographies are listed elsewhere by the same author, again before 1699.[3] This indicates how extensive the surviving records are. Yet even these numbers represent incomplete lists. Other diaries are omitted by Matthews,[4] and it seems more than likely that many more are slowly decomposing in various country houses. If this study makes anything clear, it is the urgent need for an intensified hunt by archivists and a greater awareness, on the part of the general public, of the value of old personal documents. Given such an awareness it may be possible to recover many valuable diaries. Many of the original manuscripts from which transcripts were made and published have now been lost

[1] *The Little Community* (Paperback edn, Chicago, 1960), p. 59.

[2] Henceforth, the term 'diary' is used as an all-embracing word and includes autobiographies. Often a 'diary' is nothing more than some personal observations scribbled in the margins of an almanack.

[3] William Matthews, *British Diaries* (Cambridge, 1950) and *British Autobiographies* (Berkeley, 1955). Arthur Ponsonby, *English Diaries* (1923) and *More English Diaries* (1927), prints extracts from a number of diaries and discusses why people kept diaries.

[4] For example, the extremely detailed diary of Nicholas Blundell (partially printed in *Blundell's Diary*, ed. T. E. Gibson (Liverpool, 1895)) and that of Leonard Wheatcroft (discussed in Wallace Notestein, *English Folk* (1938), ch. 8). It is also clear that not all the diaries in the B.M. manuscript collections have been noted by Matthews. The task of finding them is made more difficult by the fact that they are often described as 'commonplace' or 'letter' books.

or destroyed.[1] Since the transcripts are often only partial selections, this is a very serious matter.[2] In other cases we have only one out of several diaries—for instance, this is true of Adam Eyre's surviving manuscript.[3] It is therefore to be hoped that a considerable number of detailed diaries will be salvaged before it is too late.[4]

To account for the rapid growth of diary-keeping after the Reformation, and particularly during the second half of the seventeenth century, would require a long analysis of the whole religious and cultural background of the period; of the changes in education, of the shift from an oral to literary culture, of the growing stress on introspection in religious exercises, of the increased interest in household accounting. Broad changes in methods of communicating ideas were obviously behind the new literary form. David Riesman tried to summarize such changes by arguing that 'The diary-keeping that is so significant a symptom of the new type of character may be viewed as a kind of inner time-and-motion study by which the individual records and judges his output day by day. It is evidence of the separation between the behaving and the scrutinizing self'.[5] In this discussion, however, we will restrict our attention to three types of motive for keeping diaries which seem to have resulted in three types of diary, or, in exceptional cases, in three strands within a single diary.

Many of the documents listed in bibliographies as 'diaries' are really account books. For instance, that of Richard Stapley of Sussex is largely a list of his purchases and disbursements.[6] This makes many of the diaries particularly valuable to economic historians.[7] Another motive for writing diaries was to provide an aid to

---

[1] Examples are F. R. Raines (ed.), *The Journal of Nicholas Assheton of Downham, Lancs.*, Chet. Soc., vol. XIV (1848), p. v; *The Diary of Sir Henry Slingsby of Scriven, Bart*, ed. D. Parsons (1836); Rev. E. Turner, 'Extracts from the Diary of Richard Stapley, Gent.', *Suss. Arch. Coll.*, vol. II (1849), p. 108.

[2] For example, it would be valuable to have the much fuller original of 'The Journal of Lady Mildmay, circa 1570–1617', extracts from which were published by R. Weignall in *Q.R.*, vol. CCXV (1911), pp. 119–38.

[3] *Adam Eyre, A Dyurnall*, ed. H. J. Morehouse, Sur. Soc., vol. LXV (1875), pp. 62, 115. Also known to be incomplete are *The Note Book of the Rev. Thomas Jolly, 1671–1693*, ed. H. Fishwick, Chet. Soc., new series, vol. XXXIII (1894), p. vi, and *The Diary of John Rous*, ed. M. Green, Cam. Soc., vol. LXVI (1856), p. x. As we shall see, Josselin's own Diary is also incomplete.

[4] A number of other diaries, mentioned in contemporary biographies or funeral sermons, but no longer known to exist, are listed in William Haller, *The Rise of Puritanism* (New York, 1957), pp. 97–8.

[5] *The Lonely Crowd* (abridged edn, New Haven, 1961), p. 44.

[6] Stapley, 'Diary', *passim*.

[7] Other diaries which would be of particular value to economic historians are R. W. Blencoe, 'Extracts from the Journal and Account Book of Timothy

memory. Walter Powell kept a diary with all the ages of his friends and children and notes of important events 'to helpe my memorie concerning those things and upon all occasions'.[1] The events which it was thought should be remembered obviously depended on the interests of individual diarists. In many cases it was the exciting political events which were noted; in others, details of visits, friends, family life, and strange local happenings were selected. Many noted the weather. Another type of event which might need remembering were the blessings received from God. An anonymous relative of Oliver Cromwell started her diary 'for the Help of my Memorie, concerning the Worke of God on my Soule, which I desire thankfully to commemorate'.[2] This merged into the third major motive prompting people to keep diaries, the religious one.

The desire to examine one's soul and to attempt to correct subsequent behaviour in accordance with God's directions is the 'time-and-motion study' motive of which Riesman wrote. The flavour of this approach is indicated in a letter received by Ralph Thoresby from his father, a letter which first impelled the son to keep a diary:

take a little journal of any thing remarkable every day, principally as to yourself as, suppose, Aug. 2. I was at such a place; [or] I omitted such a duty . . . I have thought this a good method for one to keep a tolerable decorum in actions, &c. because he is to be accountable to himself as well as to God, which we are too apt to forget.[3]

Such an attitude was formalized and widely propagated in the 1650s by two books. In 1650 Isaac Ambrose published a section on diary-keeping. The utility of diaries, he said, was as follows:

1. Hereby he [the diarist] observes something of God to his soul, and of his soul to God. 2. Upon occasion he pours out his soul to God in prayer accordingly, and either is humbled or thankful. 3. He considers how it is with him in respect of time past, and if he have profited, in grace, to find out the means whereby he hath profited, that he may make more constant use of such means; or wherein he hath decayed, to observe by what temptation he was overcome, that his former errors may make him more wary for the future.

Burrell', *Suss. Arch. Coll.*, vol. III (1850); 'Extracts from the Journal and Account Book of the Rev. Giles Moore', *ibid.* vol. I (1847); and, especially valuable, *L. P.* (1st series), ed. A. B. Grosart (5 vols, 1886)—the family papers of the earl of Cork.

[1] *Diary of Walter Powell, 1603–1654*, transcribed J. A. Bradney (Bristol, 1907), p. xi.

[2] 'Anonymous religious diary, 1690–1702', B.M. Add. MS. 5858, fol. 213ᵛ.

[3] *The Diary of Ralph Thoresby*, ed. J. Hunter (2 vols, 1830), vol. I, p. xv.

He then proceeded to give excerpts of spiritual meditation from his own, imaginary, diary.[1] Ambrose's work was very popular, especially in Lancashire where many of the best nonconformist diaries were kept during the later seventeenth century.

Another recommendation of diary-keeping, this time a whole book on the subject entitled *The Journal or Diary of a Thankful Christian*, was published in 1656, written by John Beadle, an Essex minister.[2] The author first pointed out that

We have our State Diurnals, relating the National affaires. Tradesmen keep their shop books. Merchants their Accompt books. Lawyers have their books of presidents. Physitians their Experiments. Some wary husbands have kept a Diary of dayly disbursements. Travellers a Journall of all they have seen, and hath befallen them in their way. A Christian that would be exact hath more need, and may reap much more good by such a Journall as this. We are all but Stewards, Factors here, and must give a strict account in that great day to the high Lord of all our wayes, and of all his wayes towards us.[3]

Then follow some 184 pages of instructions on how to keep a diary; what to put in it, how to peruse it. For instance, chapter three describes 'What personall and private passages of Providence those are which ought to be recorded in our Journall or Diary'. The psychological advantages to be gained from diaries modelled on Beadle's precepts have already been explored by a historian of Puritanism, William Haller. He suggested that they were a substitute for the Roman Catholic confessional, a mechanism for ridding the conscience of guilt.[4] This helps to explain the existence of many of the spiritual autobiographies of the period, but it clearly does not account for the more prosaic account books, travellers' journals, and other types of 'diary' listed by Beadle.

Even if we are able to explain the general reasons for the genesis of diary-keeping, there is still the problem of deciding why particular people kept diaries. This is especially important since we need to know whether those who kept diaries were exceptional or representative; is it safe to generalize from particular diaries, especially about the religious attitudes of the period? Only occasionally do specific writers explain why they kept a diary. Thomas Isham, a boy of fourteen at the time, was promised £6 a year if he kept a journal in

[1] Isaac Ambrose, *Complete Works* (1674), p. 118.
[2] Beadle was a minister of Barnston, some fifteen miles away from Ralph Josselin's parish, but there is no indication that they directly influenced each other.
[3] Beadle, *Journal or Diary*, sig. bᵛ.
[4] *Rise of Puritanism*, pp. 38, 96–100.

Latin describing 'whatever happened on each day'.[1] Elias Pledger was motivated by the desire to emulate: 'In September '83. I read John Drapers life which did much affect and made me set about writing this account of Gods various providences to me, and my Carriage to him'.[2] Henry Newcome, also, began keeping his diary inspired by the desire to imitate, but he soon found its value as a spiritual 'tribunal'.

> It [i.e. the diary] was chiefly begun upon the occasion of hearing that Dr Ward ... had left a diary ... And certainly this great advantage it was unto me, that several passages that I had quite forgotten, I found there after set down ... My scrutiny at night, would have awed me from idleness, and some other youthful vanities ... this fear of my own tribunal (as Seneca calls it) made me that I was a prisoner in my sin, and I had no pleasure in it.[3]

In the absence of such personal statements as these we can only guess from the diaries themselves at the character and motives of the writers. There can be little doubt that if we used diaries on their own we would receive a picture of Tudor and Stuart England that was biased towards the more methodical and the more introspective sides of life. It is therefore important that they should be studied alongside all the other sources for the period. Only then will it appear how far their authors were unrepresentative.

The possible value and the overall number of pre-1699 diaries has already been suggested. Yet their importance can be over-estimated. Many of the 'diaries' listed for Britain during the sixteenth and seventeenth centuries are very short, often consisting of only a few dozen entries or covering only a few months.[4] Others are exclusively devoted to only one aspect of contemporary life; for example, the more than 40,000 pages of the countess of Warwick's diary mention little about anything except prayers and thanks to God.[5] Most diaries contain something of interest to every brand of historian, but there are only a very few which combine, over a number of years, the three strands outlined above, the economic, personal and political, and the religious. Only from a few diaries, therefore, are we able to

---

[1] *The Journal of Thomas Isham of Lamport, Northants, 1671–3*, ed. W. Rye (Norwich, 1875), p. 17.

[2] 'The Diary of Elias Pledger of Little Baddow, Essex', unpublished manuscript in Dr Williams's Library, London, fol. 8.

[3] *The Autobiography of Henry Newcome*, ed. R. Parkinson, Chet. Soc., vol. XXVI (1852), pp. 14–15.

[4] For example, the diary of Rev. John More, 1694–1700, as extracted in B.M. Add. MS. 25463, fols. 197–9, is extremely brief.

[5] 'The Diary of Mary Rich, Countess of Warwick 1666–72', B.M. Add. MS. 27351-5 and 27358.

obtain a rounded picture of the 'total' life of a family in the past. Until new diaries are discovered, there are probably only half a dozen or so which are sufficiently detailed to enable us to make the full analysis attempted in this book.[1] The number of first-class diaries increases very markedly in the eighteenth and, especially, the nineteenth centuries and it should be possible to make a series of biographical studies of individuals who illustrate the change of attitudes during these centuries.

Although such sources have not been completely neglected by previous writers, it seems certain that historians of pre-industrial England will increasingly use evidence from diaries. Mildred Campbell in her book on the *English Yeoman* used some fifteen diaries to good effect.[2] Wallace Notestein made some use of the diaries of Adam Eyre and Ralph Josselin in his *English People on the Eve of Colonization* and made a series of biographical studies based on diaries in two other books.[3] Yet it is surprising to find, for example, that R. H. Tawney made only one reference to a diary, apart from the 'lives' of Newcastle, Clarendon and Colonel Hutchinson, in his study of protestantism and capitalism.[4] There is a similar neglect by social and local historians. For example, W. G. Hoskins in his authoritative survey of the sources for *Local History in England* stresses their importance for nineteenth-century historians, but fails to include Matthews, *British Diaries*, the standard bibliography, in his 'suggested reading' or to point out the value of diaries for earlier periods.[5] Perhaps most surprising of all is the fact that a recent pioneering discussion of birth, marriage and death, subjects which form the core of diary accounts, should have used this source so little. This work is Peter Laslett's *The World we have lost* which appears to refer to only one diary (that of Robert Furse), apart from the Rector's Book of Clayworth and John Locke's diary, both of which the author had used as the basis for earlier work. The otherwise sensitive and encompassing work of Philippe Ariès, translated as *Centuries of*

---

[1] The only two diaries which really seem to be as detailed and as wide-ranging as Josselin's are *Rev. Oliver Heywood's Diary, 1630–1702*, ed. J. Horsfall Turner (4 vols, Brighouse, 1882), and *The Diary of Samuel Pepys*, ed. H. B. Wheatley (8 vols, 1904). Any suggestions of other diaries as good as these would be gratefully received.   [2] Published at New Haven, 1942.

[3] *English People on the Eve of Colonization* (New York, 1954): *English Folk* (1938); *Four Worthies* (1956). The biographical studies are useful, but tend towards an impressionistic and sentimental treatment.

[4] Tawney refers to the diary of Thomas Burton on p. 320 of *Religion and the Rise of Capitalism* (Pelican edn, 1961).

[5] *Local History*, p. 35. A. L. Rowse's use of a diary in *Tudor Cornwall* (1941), pp. 426–33 is commended as 'most effective', it is true. If the diary used by Rowse had covered more than a few months we might have learnt even more.

Childhood, also appears to have missed almost completely a source which would have yielded so much.[1]

One reason for the apparent neglect by historians becomes clear when we turn to the particular diary upon which the following study is based. The Diary of Ralph Josselin, vicar of Earls Colne in Essex from 1641 to his death in 1683, is extremely detailed. The original, in minute handwriting, covers some 185 small pages; when typed out in double-spacing it occupies some 600 pages of foolscap paper.[2] There is an entry for almost every day in the period between 1644 and 1665 and thereafter at least one entry a week. When the manuscript came to be published in 1908, however, the editor was forced to cut out over half of the original entries. In accord with the political and ecclesiastical interests of his contemporaries he sacrificed what he described as 'many entries of no interest whatsoever . . . trivial details of every day life, records of visits of his friends etc'.[3] Such has been the shift of historical interest during the last few years that it is precisely such 'trivial details' which interest many historians most of all. Consequently, anyone who uses only the edited versions of sixteenth- and seventeenth-century diaries may not realize their true value, especially for social history.

Ralph Josselin provides us with little evidence as to why, in the first place, he intended to keep a diary. The heading of his Diary does indicate, however, that it falls into the 'remembering God's blessings' category. It reads: 'A Thankfull Observacon of Divine Providence & Goodness Towards Mee and a Summary View of my Life'. This summary of major events up to 1644 was expanded in that year, for, at the age of twenty-seven, Josselin wrote, 'Many things I have omitted that may be found in my notes, almanack &c. But now henceforwards I shall be more exact and particular' [8. 8. 44].[4] During the rest of his life he kept a wide-ranging account of his many activities. In the next chapter we will see the picture the

[1] P. Laslett, *The World we have lost* (university paperback edn, 1965); P. Ariès, *Centuries of Childhood* (translated, 1962).

[2] See opposite p. 22 for a sample page of the Diary. The original Diary is in the possession of Colonel G. O. C. Probert of Bevills, Bures, Suffolk, who was kind enough to show it to the author. A complete microfilm and transcript are available at the E.R.O. (ref: T/B 9/1 and 2). Much time and effort was saved by the existence of the painstaking and substantially accurate transcript, and it is to be hoped that a complete edition of the Diary will soon be published.

[3] *The Diary of the Rev. Ralph Josselin, 1616–1683*, ed. E. Hockliffe, Cam. Soc., 3rd series, vol. xv (1908), p. v. Hockliffe's work is nevertheless extremely useful, it is also almost 100% accurate.

[4] Like many others, Josselin's Diary is incomplete and the 'notes, almanack &c' to which he refers, as well as account books referred to elsewhere in the Diary, cannot now be traced.

Diary gives us of the yeoman farmer and officiating clergyman, the supporter of parliament during the Civil War and a man who sustained a continual interest in political events. Within this framework of national politics, Puritan religion, mixed farming and a harsh physical existence with primitive methods of heating, drainage, lighting and supplying water, Ralph Josselin and his family lived out their domestic life. This domestic life, revolving around the three 'life crises' of birth, marriage, and death, receives much attention in the Diary. It is analysed in part II below. In part III the same events are looked at in a different perspective: the relationships within the nuclear family,[1] between more distant kin, and between friends and neighbours are examined. In the final part a preliminary analysis is made of some of Josselin's attitudes and beliefs.

Through the description it will be obvious that much has been omitted. Some of the omissions are the fault of the present writer, others reflect gaps in the evidence. In a sense it is the things that are unmentioned by the sources, the unmentionable, or assumptions that are too basic or obvious to need stating, which are of paramount interest to the historian. A list of topics that rarely, if ever, appear in Josselin's Diary suggests itself; toilet habits, sexual relations between husband and wife, weaning methods, sleeping arrangements. We learn very little of contemporary attitudes to night and day, to animals, to the structure of time and space. We are given few glimpses of the physical layout of Josselin's house, of his furniture, of the way he brought up his young children. Nevertheless, the range of topics covered by the Diary—dreams, suicide, pain and death, dates of conception and dates of weaning among them—and the very fact that it was written at all, makes Ralph Josselin's Diary remarkable. Through Josselin's efforts we are able to step back 300 years and to look out through the eyes of an Essex vicar of the mid seventeenth century. Much will be screened from us, as it was from him, but much, also, will be revealed. Yet, until further studies based on an anthropological approach to similar material have been made, we will not be certain how far Josselin was a representative figure. It is essential always to bear in mind that the very fact that he kept a diary suggests that he was slightly exceptional. Josselin's position as a clergyman, and as a wealthy yeoman farmer, may also mean that his outlook was very different from that of the majority of his seventeenth-century fellows. Every generalization in the following pages needs comparative testing.

[1] The 'nuclear' family consists of father, mother and their children.

PART I

The political, ecclesiastical and economic world

2

Ralph Josselin's early life and his political and ecclesiastical career

EARLY YEARS

Ralph Josselin was born at Roxwell in Essex on 26 January 1617. He was the first son but third child. His paternal grandfather was a wealthy yeoman who, in 1632, left more than £1,000 by his will.[1] Yet little of this reached the diarist, eldest son of his eldest son John. Josselin's father sold his patrimony in 1618 and retired to Bishops Stortford. There, by unsuccessful farming and attempts to build up an estate for his son, he proceeded to lose most of the £800 he had been left by his father.[2] When he died intestate on 28 October 1636 he left his nineteen-year-old son only £20. He had, however, left his heir one important legacy; a sound education. Josselin's mother Anne died on 29 November 1624 when her son was approaching his eighth birthday:[3] Josselin's father then gave his son a 'good educacon, by his owne instruction, example and in schooles as I was capeable'. In the Diary there is a description of these early schooldays:

In the schoole I was active & forward to learne which contented my master & father ... I remember not that I ever was whipt ... I made it my aime to learne & lent my minde continually to read historyes ... when I was exceeding yo[u]ng would I project the conquering of kingdoms & write historyes of such exploits. I was much delighted with Cosmography taking it from my Father. I would project wayes of receiving vaste estates and then lay it out in stately building, castles, libraryes, colledges & such like.

This early interest in books and in building up estates helps to explain much in Josselin's later life. Clearly, as in his interest in cosmography, it was partly stimulated by his father. It is less certain where he derived his early resolve 'to the worke of the Lord in the Ministry'. Josselin naturally ascribed it to God; there was clearly

[1] There is an abstract of this will on p. 215 below. The genealogical table facing p. 234 will help to indicate family connexions. The following account of Josselin's childhood is based on the introductory pages of narrative in the Diary.
[2] It seems that he had, for a time, been a 'maultster'; see next note.
[3] 'Anne Joslyne, wife of John Joslyne, maultster' was buried on 29 November 1624, according to the Bishops Stortford register in the H.R.O.

some family opposition at first. 'I hope I shall never forgett Gods fitting mee for a scholler', he wrote, 'and giving mee a spirit for the same, from which nothing would divert mee; at last God putt it into my fathers head to listen to me'. Other, more wordly, reasons are also given for the choice of career. As a child Josselin had wanted to emulate ministers: 'I confesse my childhood was taken with ministers and I heard with delight & admiracon & desire to imitate them from my youth, & would be acting in corners'. His interest in history had naturally developed alongside study of the bible; 'I had a singular affection to the historyes in the bible, being acquainted with all those historyes in very yo[u]ng dayes'. Finally, when his mother died, it became clear that his father's diminishing estate might never come to Josselin, but might go to a step-mother if his father re-married, and 'therefore I desird to bee a scholler; so should I make the better shift if from home, & bee able to live of my selfe by Gods blessing'.[1]

John Josselin did, in fact, re-marry when his son was aged fourteen or fifteen and the 'disrespect' of the new step-mother towards the boy probably encouraged the father to send his son off to Jesus College, Cambridge. There he was entered pensioner in Michaelmas 1633, received his B.A. in 1636–7, and his M.A. in 1640.[2] Shortage of money meant that Josselin was 'forced to come from Cambridge many times for want of meanes & loose my time in the co[u]ntry', but he also profited from these country visits. The minister in his father's town, Steeple Bumpstead, was a Mr Borradale whom Josselin listened to 'with delight'.[3] He described how 'when I heard him, my use was to walke home alone not with other boys or company, & stay not in the churchyard but immediately away, & meditate upon the sermon & example my self by the same'. There is no evidence that he was ever as deeply influenced at Cambridge, for though he was 'close & diligent' in his studies, 'the supersticons of the Church were a perplexity' to him. When his father died in 1636 he was still uncertain about his future career; without money

---

[1] A precedent for Josselin's choice of career was provided by his father's brother Nathaniel, who was a minister at Hardingham in Norfolk until ejected at the Restoration (A. G. Matthews, *Calamy Revised* (Oxford, 1934), p. 299). Another of Josselin's uncles, Ralph, was also an active and left-wing participant in religious affairs: he was an elder in the Braintree classis (W. A. Shaw, *A History of the English Church During the Civil Wars and Under the Commonwealth* (1900), vol. II, p. 375).

[2] J. and S. A. Venn (comp.), *The Book of Matriculations and Degrees ... in the University of Cambridge* (Cambridge, 1913), p. 393.

[3] John Borradale, at Steeple Bumpstead from 1622 to 1649 (Harold Smith, *The Ecclesiastical History of Essex* (Colchester, no date—about 1930), p. 395).

or influential patrons he did not know how to proceed. 'Sometimes I thought upon my fathers farme, then upon the law, but God and the perswasions of Mr Borradale & Mr Thornlecke settled mee againe upon Cambridge.' He completed his course and obtained his B.A. Then he set out to hunt for a job.

For the next three years Josselin moved from place to place in search of a satisfactory post. He had to borrow horses and small sums of money from his friends to ride to an offer of an usher's job in Bedfordshire, but their humiliating loans were in vain for the position was already filled when he arrived. He then stayed with one of his uncles for a while. Finally, hearing of another vacancy in Bedfordshire, he sold most of his clothes, borrowed some money on another uncle's credit, and began a two-year career as a school-master. Although he received only a small amount in fees, he managed to buy some books and clothes and to save a little money. He preached his first sermon at Michaelmas 1639 at the age of twenty-two and in October of the same year was invited over to be a curate at Olney in Buckinghamshire.

Josselin, with a curacy and some £20 in cash after his debts had been paid, was now in a slightly more secure position. This position was further enhanced when he took his Master's degree at Cambridge. He could even begin 'to thinke of marrying' and became engaged to a girl he had seen in Olney church soon after his arrival. In September 1640 he moved to Cranham in Essex where an earlier sermon he had delivered had impressed his uncle and other residents. The living was worth £44 p.a., in which sum was included a £10 p.a. contribution by his uncle. Shortly after his arrival he married. But he found that teaching at Upminster was 'great trouble, but no great advantage to me' and, though he liked his parishioners, he suffered continual bad health. Various offers for his services came from other parishes and he finally accepted that made by a north Essex village, Earls Colne, 'a place in a very good ayre'. He visited the impropriator, Richard Harlakenden of Earls Colne Priory, and it was agreed that he should receive a total of £80 p.a., half of it from tithes, the other half from voluntary contributions. He moved to Earls Colne with his wife in March 1641. He remained vicar of the town until his death in August 1683.

POLITICAL OPINIONS

Josselin's early life and religious activities were set against a back-ground of political and ecclesiastical changes which had a profound influence on them. Occasionally Josselin was swept into active participation in contemporary politics; usually he was an interested observer and commentator. Almost all his descriptions of political events are included in the published edition of his Diary. They constitute over half the printed text and present a unique 'worm's eye' view of contemporary events. The overall impression from the narrative is of a man who became a moderate Cromwellian, very well informed both about national and international affairs, closely in touch with events in London. Since his reflections are already readily available, only a few samples will be given here. These are intended to indicate the main contours of events and to illustrate the constant state of political insecurity within which the Josselins lived.

Josselin's search for a living had occurred against a background of impending civil war. If we arbitrarily divide up the political events during his years at Earls Colne, the first phase could be seen to last until the execution of King Charles I in 1649. These years were dominated by the military events of the Civil War. In autumn 1642 Josselin described how he 'provided for my self Sword, Halbert (halberd), Powder and Match; the drums now also began to beate up; for my part I endeavoured to encourage others to goe forth'. After the battle of Edgehill he sent off a fully-armed man with a month's pay. There are month-to-month reports of parliamentary victories and set-backs; for instance, 'things were now sad with us, Waller routed, & Fairfax, & Bristol lost, & Hull like to be betrayed, the City divided' [July 1643]. In July 1644 he rode for a brief visit to a regiment in Northamptonshire, but his real involvement in active fighting did not occur until the summer and autumn of 1645.[1] As a chaplain to the troops he marched to Hertfordshire and then returned 'home safe with our troops: no damage to any man, one horse shott in the legge through a mistake'. Then during a two-week campaign in September he marched through the midlands and East Anglia. A typical entry reads 'Wee marched through Rutlandshire . . . wee quarterd that night at Houghton at a poore house; pitiful blacke bread; I gott a white loafe crust; o[u]r lodging was upon straw & a quilt, in o[u]r clothes'. Three days later he marched into Derbyshire; 'lost 2 men: one shott in the breeches & yett no hurt; killed one of the Cavaliers'. Meanwhile, he preached to the troops, for instance at Stamford. After the defeat of the king things were quieter for a while although the quartering of parliamentary soldiers in Earls Colne and the neighbourhood caused some resentment [e.g. on 5. 4. 47]. Then the king escaped from the hands of the army and the second phase of fighting began.

[1] The whole account is printed on pp. 27–9 of the Cam. Soc. edition of the Diary (August–September 1645, in the original Diary).

It was during this latter period of war that Earls Colne, for the first time, suffered directly. On 10 June 1648 enemy troops marched to Braintree. Two days later 'the enemy came to Colne, were resisted by our towne men. No part of Essex gave so much opposicon as wee did; they plundered us, and mee in particular, of all that was portable, except brasse, pewter, and bedding; I made away to Coggeshall, and avoyded their scouts through providence.' The following day 'I returned home, mett with danger by our owne men, who by some suddaine accident mistaking mee, fought for mee, but I escaped their hands through Gods mercy'. Two months later Colchester surrendered and the local fighting was over.

Yet there was still the problem of what to do with the obstinate king. Josselin viewed the trial of the king as 'strange, extraordinary', but thought that 'if the worke bee of God it will prosper, if not it will come to nothing' [31. 12. 48]. A month later he wrote, 'I was much troubled with the blacke providence of putting the King to death; my teares were not restrained at the passages about his death; the Lord in mercy lay it not as sinne to the charge of the kingdome, but in mercy doe us good by the same' [4. 2. 49]. Despite his grief, he refused to subscribe to a petition of Ministers 'against the present proceedings . . . and a dissent in the matter of the King' for he thought that it was wrong for 'Ministers to intermedle thus in all difficulties of state' [19. 2. 49].

The next phase covered the years of the Commonwealth and protectorate until the return and restoration of Charles II in 1660. Throughout these years Josselin pursued a moderate, parliamentarian course. He feared the Levellers and recorded the news of their 'quashing' as a 'glorious rich providence of God' [18. 5. 49], but he was the first minister in Essex to subscribe to the 'Engagement or oath of loyalty to the Commonwealth' [18. 12. 49]. Throughout the 1650s he gave yearly summaries of the political situation, both within England and on the continent. A full quotation of one of these, that made in January 1652, indicates their quality.

All the threats of o[u]r enemies ended in the ruine of the Scotch designe at Worcester, and the flight of their King into France; all Scotland even reduced by force, and disbanded on treaty; our forces also prospered in Ireland, where the sword, famine and pestilence hath made a great waste. Wee are not in good terms with Holland; the new hopes of the enemies are that these 2 states will fall out to eithers ruine and make way for the Spaniard and Stuard [sic] to recover their owne againe in both.

France is likely to fall into flames by her owne divisions; this summer shee hath done nothing abroad. The Spaniard hath almost reduced Barcelona, the cheife city of Catalonia, and so that kingdome; the issue of that affaire wee waite. Poland is free from warre with the Cossacks but feareth them. Dane and Suede are both in quiet, and so is Germany, yett the peace at Munster is not fully executed: the Turke hath done no great matter on the Venetian, nor beene so fortunate and martial as formerly, as if that people were at their height and declining rather.

The Iles of Silly, Jersey, and Guernsey, Man and all the proper possessions of England now reduced, and no great feare of any power within; God prevent breaches among our selves, o[u]r fleetes are strong at sea.

There have been great inundacions in Spain at Bilboa, and in Italy; letters from Silly mention an earthquake their [sic] on Decemb. 25, past.[1]

The awareness of the issues in foreign policy is considerable.

Josselin was also interested and active in local politics, especially the election of representatives for Cromwell's various parliaments. Particularly good accounts of such elections are given in the Diary for June and July 1654 and there are also lively descriptions of the seditions and plots against Cromwell. There were rumours in 1657 that the protector had been proclaimed king, but soon after this he died and, after a brief interval, Charles II was restored. At first there were local disturbances and rumours: 'at night wee were alarmd; the enemy up in Norfolke . . . the country filled with very strange amazing reports' [16 & 20. 8. 59]. But Josselin seems to have reconciled himself easily enough to the return of monarchy: 'I preacht at Greenwich & prayed by name for K. Charles' he wrote [13. 5. 60], and the following month he rode to Colchester to claim the king's pardon.

Throughout the final political phase, which covered almost all of Charles II's reign, Josselin retained his strong interest in both domestic and foreign events. Particularly worrying to him were the Dutch and French wars. For example, he noted on 6 June 1667 'the Dutch on Harwich coast, Thursday; June 12, Wednesday, they attempt Chatham river to destroy o[u]r great ships with successe & continued there their pleasure; June 27, they came up near Gravesend, they put a stop to all trade, and forced us to defend the whole shore, to o[u]r charge & amazement'. After some early optimism Josselin became increasingly alarmed by Charles II's fondness for France and for the Catholics. By the late 1670s it seemed that 'The Court partie prevaile in Parl[iamen]t' [4. 3. 77] and Josselin could only hope that 'the crisis we apprehended to our religion & liberty

---

[1] Josselin's considerable interest and expertise in foreign affairs are further illustrated in five pages of commentary entitled 'Certaine remarkable things that fell out in my remembrance', which precede the Diary proper and which have not been included in either the typed or published transcripts.

may admitt a longer putting of[f]' [2. 6. 78]. There are references to fresh elections in which the king was reported to have said that 'the contry would choose a dog if he stood ag[ain]st a courtier' [16. 2. 79], and to Titus Oates's denunciations of the Popish plot. Although the new parliament was 'wonderfull couragious' it was soon prorogued and Josselin thought that 'the Courts designe is to make parliam[en]t useles, or rid the crowne of them' [12. 17. 79].

Almost the final entry on political events summed up the great changes which had occurred during Josselin's years at Earls Colne.

The Parl[iament] should have satt this day; its petitiond for, but if they may not sitt for Gods interest, he will stand up for it. Parl[iament] broke Monarchy, perhaps God will have Parl[iament] broken by Monarchicall; time was, no addresses to the King by subjects; now the K[ing] will admitt no addresses to him; we will [sic] to God, who will heare. [26. 2. 80].

These political commotions formed a particularly important background to Josselin's life, for his ecclesiastical living was affected by changes in government. He showed his appreciation of the significance of political events both in the entries in his Diary and even in his dreams, a large proportion of which were political in content.[1]

RELIGIOUS ACTIVITIES AND ECCLESIASTICAL CAREER

The recent discussions of 'Puritanism' and its effects on daily life and attitudes provide a number of interesting hypotheses with which to approach the Diary of Ralph Josselin, a 'typical' Puritan it would seem at first sight.[2] In this first part of the book emphasis will be laid on Josselin's ecclesiastical career and on his ministerial activities. Later, an attempt will be made to probe behind this fairly conventional analysis in order to see how he actually thought and felt about God, sin, death and other problems.[3] The fact that Josselin was a practising vicar throughout the period when he kept his Diary was clearly of fundamental importance in conditioning the kind of observations he made. His view of life was largely determined by his social and economic position, which fluctuated with the fortunes of the Anglican Church.

[1] There is an analysis of his political and other dreams on pp. 183–7.

[2] The following are only a few of the most recent contributions to the vast literature on 'Puritanism': P. Collinson, *The Elizabethan Puritan Movement* (1967); Haller, *Rise of Puritanism*; Christopher Hill, *Society and Puritanism in Pre-Revolutionary England* (Mercury edn, 1966); M. Walzer, *Revolution of the Saints* (1966). While they try to build up a picture of an 'ideal type' Puritan, all the above authors stress how much variation there actually was between 'puritan' and 'puritan'.

[3] See ch. 11 below.

We have already seen that, from his youth, Josselin had wanted to be a minister. There is no evidence of any religious crisis, despair followed by salvation; rather he seems to have always been a moderately left-wing and religiously-minded person. At Cambridge, as earlier noted the 'supersticons of the Church were a perplexity' to him [1632] and when he was ordained a minister by the bishop '& 6 ministers' he 'would not bowe towards the Altar as others did' [Feb. 1640]. His radical streak is apparent in the way in which he describes how 'upon an order of the House of Commons to that purpose' he was able to take down 'all images & pictures & such like glasses' [Michaelmas 1641]. It is natural that he should have rejoiced at the execution of Archbishop Laud, 'that grand enemy of the power of godlynes, that great stickler for all outward pompe in the service of God, left his head at Tower hill London, by ordinance of parliam[en]t' [10. 1. 45]. He was also relieved when a further ordinance removed the 'heavy burthen of the booke of Common prayer' [23. 3. 45].

He shows what we might consider conventional radical features in a number of his other activities. He tried to moderate Christmas celebrations; on one occasion he 'made a serious exhortacon to lay aside the jollity & vanity of the time customs hath wedded us unto' [22. 12. 44] and on another he noted with partial satisfaction that, though 'people hanker after the sports and pastimes that they were wonted to enjoy . . . they are in many families weaned from them' [25. 12. 47]. Likewise he tried to preserve the sanctity of the Sabbath. He lamented after the Restoration that 'This day, a day of holy rest, is now the sport and pleasure day of the generall rout of people' [12. 6. 64] and that some villagers were 'digging this sabbath morning' which would lead to 'flat atheism' [1. 3. 63]. It was a tide he could not stem, although earlier he had had his victories: 'This day I heard and then saw the youth openly playing at catt [catch] on the green; I went up, rowted them; their fathers sleeping in the chimny corner' [10. 3. 61]. It is clear from his descriptions of his own amusements that he was not against pleasure and games and sport as such: it was only when they clashed with the Lord's day. Another attitude he shared with a number of his fellow minister was enthusiasm for the spreading of the gospel. On 25 November 1652 he received the 'act for propagation of the Gospell in New England among the heathen; I resolve to give £5 my self & wife and children, and to promote it unto the utmost'. So enthusiastic was this promotion that he managed to gather over £50 from Earls Colne for this cause [2. 1. 53].

Josselin's interest in books partly reflected his desire to be an

An extract from Ralph Josselin's Diary, September–October 1647

An extract, in Josselin's hand, from the Earls Colne parish register. The baptismal entries for 1651 include John, son of Ralph Josselin, 'pastor of Earls Colne' effective Christian minister, but it is also obvious that he loved reading for its own sake. Throughout his life he had collected books. As a young man he had had to use Lord Mandeville's library [1637], but later he had bought a library for £16 [16. 7. 46] and he frequently mentions other purchases such as that of a 'good bargain of bookes' [1. 10. 44]. A list of the books he mentioned as having read indicates both the width and radical flavour of his purchases.[1] For long periods no books are mentioned in the Diary and we therefore do not know how sustained were his occasional bursts of energy such as that recorded between October and December 1648.

In the latter end of October I begun to reade Bell: de 15 staires or ladder steps to God, a prettie discourse; it containes 418 pages in 16. I also read in mornings Feri Specimen, a learned discourse, it contained p. 559: I observed the most materiall things in him . . . Wee begun this morning to rise early, and to spend some time by fire and candle; I intend in morning to read over the liberall arts, and began with Vossius Rhet. Tom. 1. in 4. It containes 433 p.; ceptis aspira nostris, domine, that hereby, being more skild in the tongue and arts, I may be more usefull in my generacon [6 Nov.] . . . This night I perfected the reading of Ferrius Specimen. Begun the reading, and noting the principal things, out of 2 treatises concerning church govermt by Mr Hooker, called a survey of the sum of church discipline; the second treatise by Mr Cotton, called The way of congregational churches, cleared in 2 treatises, one historicall, against

<hr>

1 It is not possible to discover all the works referred to by Josselin; those which cannot be placed are left in his original words. Dates indicate when he referred to reading the book in the Diary. [1637] Daniel Chamier, *De Oecumenico Pontifice*; [19. 3. 48] Joseph Mede, *Clavis apocalyptica*, and James Ussher, *De Ecclesiasticum Xtianorum successione et statu*; [30. 10. 48] Roberto Bellarmino, *Scale ad deum* and 'Feri Specimen' [? Paul Feri, Protestant divine and preacher]; [6. 11. 48] Gerardus Vossius, *Vossii rhetorices contractae, editia altera*; [13. 11. 48] Richard Hooker, *Of the lawes of ecclesiastical politie*, and John Cotton, *The way of Congregational churches cleared*; [16. 11. 48] *The Centuries of Magdeburg* [compilation by Lutheran scholars]; [11. 12. 48] Sir Richard Baker, *A chronicle of the Kings of England*; [15. 1. 49] 'Smalcius the Socinian, against the incarnacon of Christ, in latine' [James Smalcius]; [16. 1. 49] Sixtinus Amama, *Grammatica Ebraea*; [17. 1. 49] Leonard Lessius, *Hygiasticon: or, the Right course of preserving life and health unto extream old age* [also; *A Treatise of Temperance and Sobrietie*, written by Lud. Cornarus, translated by Mr George Herbert]; [26. 5. 49] Joannes Philippson [Sleidanus], *A famous cronicle of our time*; [26. 5. 49] 'Mr Medes discourses on several texts' [Joseph Mede, *Diatribae, Discourses* ?]; [18. 7. 49] Joannes Philippson [Sleidanus], *De quatuor summis imperiis*; [3. 10. 49] Daniel Sennert, *The institutions or fundamentals of . . . physick*; [3. 10. 49] Flavius Josephus, *The famous workes of Josephus*; translated by T. Lodge; [9. 12. 50] Thomas Brightman, *A revelation of the apocalypse*; [29. 11. 54] Sir George Wharton, *Almanack*. Among the most radical works listed here were those by 'Smalcius the Socinian' and Sennert's *Fundamentals of physic*. Sennertus was accused of blasphemy for teaching that the souls of beasts were not material.

Baylie disswasive, the other polemical. The time I allotted for this was in the forenoone togither with my Hebrew studdies; viz what time I could picke before dinner, having read Vossius ante solem, and being to learne every morning in the Heb. Gram [13 Nov.] ... This night I made an end of reading Bellarmines scale ad Deum, a booke that containeth divers sweet meditacons in it, and now I intend on nights to reade ov[e]r the ecclesiastical history [15 Nov.] ... This night I began by candle light to reade the ecclesiastical history, called the Centuries of Magdeb: This I intend, if God give mee strength, to read on nights, that therby I may understand the state and affayre of that body whereof Christ is the head, and observe from history the witnesse of the several gratious preservacons of Gods truths, and servants in all ages [16 Nov.] ... I finisht the reading of Vossius his first tome [18 Nov.] ... Finisht the reading of Vossius Rhetoricke. I read Bakers Chronicles of England now and then for my recreation, and the Archb[isho]ps triall [11 Dec.]. [He finished reading Baker on 4 Jan.]

Five years before writing the above account Josselin had started to practise his Hebrew and Greek so that he could better understand his authorities [24. 10. 44]. He also decided, just after the preceding description, to 'collect the places of Scripture, that seeme different one from another, and the reconciling of them' [4. 1. 49]. At first sight it may seem surprising that there are so few references to biblical studies though, as we will see, the Diary is full of imagery from the Authorized Version. Perhaps daily bible reading was too integral a part of life to be commented on. Josselin was clearly delighted when he was able to buy a bible for his son for 3s. 2d. and remarked that 'this booke is now very cheap' [18. 7. 49]. He seems in the early 1650s to have been especially absorbed in the apocalyptic portions of the New Testament and was encouraged to continue his 'apocaliptique studies' by his uncle.[1]

The information he received from his reading was disseminated and discussed at monthly meetings with his more zealous parishioners. For example, on 20 April 1647 he 'Mett in conference with divers of my christian friends and neighbours at the widdow Clarke' and two months later there was another meeting 'where we had good discourse' [21. 6. 47]. The topics for discussion are only occasionally mentioned; on one occasion, for instance, the group discussed baptism [10. 4. 48]. Another vitally important mechanism for the propagation of the true gospel was the sermon. It is clear that Josselin was a good preacher; he was invited to preach the assize sermons [5. 8. 46] and preached at St Paul's Cross in London [5. 10. 51]. He was also a lengthy preacher. On one occasion he 'expounded, prayed, and preached about 5 houres' [25. 8. 47], and

[1] Josselin's interest in current millenarianism is described on p. 189 below.

on another he preached until the 'sun was sett', the service having commenced at 11 a.m.[1] [25. 11. 46] He often noted the text of these sermons; 'this day afternoon I went down to church preacht, Eccl. 9. 5. a great audience' [5. 1. 72], but nowhere in the Diary does he copy out such a sermon. The contemporary obsession with sermons makes this a curious omission; perhaps he had a separate book for the purpose. Fortunately, however, two of his sermons have been preserved; one in a contemporary book of sermons summarized in an Essex diary, the other as a published pamphlet.[2]

On 11 November 1669 Josselin noted briefly in his Diary: 'Went to preach a funeral; I r[eceive]d 20s. paire of gloves'. This was the sermon 'preached at the Buriall of Old Mistriss Porter by Mr Joslin' recorded for this date in the diary mentioned above. As may be seen in appendix C, it started as a conventional commentary on a biblical text, but was later invigorated by practical advice drawn from Josselin's own experience. The words he used in the sermon, for instance his advice to children to cheer up their parents in their 'gray haires', were sometimes precisely those he used in his own Diary about his own children [16. 11. 50]. The problems of insubordination to parents and the meaning of pain, two of the subjects he dwelt on in this sermon, were those which, as we can see in his contemporary Diary, he was himself trying to resolve. Similarly, in the sermon preached at the funeral of Mrs Smythee Harlakenden in 1651, for which he received thirty shillings [5. 11. 52], he drew on his own experiences of loss and suffering. In the preface he even referred directly to his own grief at the recent death of his own daughter. He used sermons as an occasion on which to work through his own doubts. He probably helped a number of his listeners by dealing with such personal and directly-felt problems.[3]

We may wonder how a man of Josselin's religious temperament fared during the many ecclesiastical changes that characterized this period. During the first twenty years of his incumbency, up to the Restoration, he seems to have felt that the main threat was from the left, from the religious radicals. He was happy to abandon the prayer book, prepared to help justices of the peace with civil marriages [10. 4. 56], ready even to be an 'Asssistant in Ejecting of Ministers &

[1] His one surviving printed sermon, partly transcribed on p. 222 below, occupied forty-three small pages.
[2] See appendix C, p. 220 below, for the location of, and abstracts from, these sermons. I am grateful to Mr Arthur Searle for bringing the 1669 sermon to my attention.
[3] Obedience to parents was also the theme of a sermon preached on 12 January 1671 when Josselin 'endeavoured to stir up young persons to bee good'.

schoolem[aste]rs for insufficiency' [8. 1. 58]. He was prepared to discuss the possibility of introducing a new system of church government incorporating the Presbyterian principle of 'elders' [31. 3. 48]. But, as in politics, he was a moderate reformer. As he pointed out in a discussion with 'Oates the Anabaptist',[1] the various separatist sects 'had no ministry, and that particular Christians out of office has no power to send ministers out to preach . . . I showed him it was contrary to Scripture' [29. 6. 46]. His troubles with religious extremists began soon after his arrival at Earls Colne. In September 1641 one Thomas Harvy, a weaver of Earls Colne, was examined at the quarter sessions and recounted how, after hearing 'one Mr Joslyn preach' at morning service, he came back to church later in the day and 'tooke the Common prayer booke and threw it into a pond thereby, & the next day in the morning he went to the pond & tooke out the sayd booke Cutt it in peices: p[ar]te thereof he did burne, some he threw away & some he kept in his pocket'.[2] It is perhaps to this and similar incidents that Josselin referred when he noted in his Diary under 1641/2 'I began a little to be troubled with some in matter of separacon'.

Of all the separatists who troubled him, however, it was the Quakers who undoubtedly worried Josselin most. As early as 23 June 1650 he noted 'the unreverent carriage of divers in sitting with their hatts on when the psalme is singing is strange to me'. His alarm grew as the Quaker ethos was formulated. His first few reactions to this new phenomenon illustrate his anxiety.

Preacht at Gaines Coln, the quakers nest, but no disturbance; God hath raised up my heart not to feare, but willing to beare, & to make opposicon to their wayes in defence of truth; it is an evill that runs much in all places [3. 7. 55] . . . Those called Quakers, whose worke is to revile the ministry made a disturbance at Cogshall, and were sent to goale; oh, many feare the Quakers to ruine Cromwell [15. 7. 55] . . . This corner begins to feel the Quakers; some of their heads its said are among us, the Lord bee our refuge; an infallible spirit once granted them, what lies may they not utter, and what delusions may not poor men bee given unto? Lord I see trialls, let me be fitted for them, and saved through them [29. 7. 55] . . . Great noise of people called Quakers; divers have fits about us. and thereby come to bee able to speake; the Lord helpe us to stand fast against every evill and error [10. 2. 56] . . . Heard for certain that one Wade, a Quaker as called, come to our toune [16. 2. 56] . . . Heard & true that Turners daughter was distract in this quaking busines; sad are the fits at Coxall like the pow wowing among the Indies

[1] This was Samuel Oates, father of the notorious Titus Oates of the Popish plot (*D.N.B.*).

[2] E.R.O., Q/SBa 2/43 (11th document, no foliation), midsummer, 1641.

[9. 4. 56] . . . Heard this morning that James Parnel the father of the Quakers in these parts, having undertaken to fast 40 dayes & nights, was die. 10, in the morning found dead; he was by Jury found guilty of his own death, and buried in the Castle yard . . . Its said in the contry that his partie went to Colchester to see his resurrection again [11. 4. 56] . . . Rob: Abot senior in the street told Tho. Harvy,[1] 'there cometh your deluder'. Lord, wee are a contempt and scorne, looke upon it, oh Lord, and heale it; he sat on the horse blocke as people came to church; Mr H[arlakenden?] spoke to him; the Lord help us against thes growing evills [31. 8. 56] . . . In the lane sett upon by one called a quaker, the Lord was with my heart that I was not dismayed; I had some discourse with him, the Lord bee my helpe [31. 10. 56].

Josselin mentioned the Quakers on six further occasions;[2] the second from last of these references suggests his continued mixture of fear and confidence:

Quakers increasd; John Garrod their head in o[u]r town, building them a meeting place, appointing to meet once a week; I am not ov[e]r solicitous of the effect, having seen Abbotts meeting house left, expecting God will appear for his truth, and I hope in perticular for mee in this place who truly desire to feare his name. I doe not determine why, but this morning viz 26, Garrods wife died, within 6 weeks of the use of that house; I onely desire to feare and tremble, but doe not question the downfall of that sect under the feet of Christ & his servants. [15. 12. 74]

Despite Josselin's hopes that divine vengeance would be on his side, the Quakers had established themselves sufficiently by the late 1670s for there to be a special Quaker burial ground. Thus the parish register records, among others, 'Benjamin Newman buried in the Quakers ground, 2 September 1679'.[3] It was clearly very distressing for Josselin to find a militant rival religious community within his village, to be accused of being a 'deluder', and to realize that instead of being regarded as a progressive reformer, he had become part of the 'Establishment'. Yet the threats from within his own village and, possibly, his own conscience, gave way before a different type of threat in the years after the Restoration of Charles II—the power wielded by the restored bishops and their courts.

Josselin's support for both the political and ecclesiastical policy

[1] This may be the same Thomas Harvy whom we have just noted as tearing up the common prayer book some fifteen years previously. Robert Abbott was a notorious non-attender at church and, along with four other men, was summoned and excommunicated at the archdeacon's court in 1663-5 for not attending church and for not receiving communion (E.R.O., D/ACA/55, pp. 59, 60).
[2] On the following dates: 28.1.58; 21.8.59; 30.6.61; 7.7.61; 3.1.64; 25.1.80. Some of these references are published in Smith, *Ecclesiastical History*, pp. 221-2.
[3] E.R.O., D/P/209/1/3 under this date.

of the Commonwealth and protectorate and his continued refusal to subscribe to the Restoration settlement would lead us to expect that he would have been suspended from his living. He was included in a list of nonconformists in 1663,[1] and even, as we shall see, appears to have been formally suspended. But somehow he managed to avoid deprivation. Later historians of nonconformity have found this a puzzling phenomenon.[2] Even Josselin was surprised, for among the blessings of the year 1663 he included 'my publiq libertie strangely continued unto mee & people' [30. 1. 64]. The fact that the Diary provides a unique description of the way in which a man might squeeze through the Restoration attempts to induce conformity, and the impression that Josselin remained in a protracted state of insecurity because of his nonconformity justifies a close analysis of his entries on this subject.

Soon after the return of the king, Josselin noticed 'Ministers pittifully put out of their livings while others advanced' [22. 7. 60], and there was 'talke as if the honest partie were in hazard of a massacre' [29. 8. 60]. At the end of 1660 'Gospell liberties and freedom [were] yet continued', but 'feares' were widespread and it was rumoured that 'lists are taken of the fanatique, and all honest men that are not as formal as others are so accounted' [2. 12. 60]. Mid-way through the following year it was said that 'Bishops and their courts are coming in again' and Josselin asked the Lord 'to helpe us to walke humbly & wisely' [23. 6. 61]. Almost exactly a year later 'I had the Act of Uniformity sent mee' [1. 6. 62]. He had noticed its passage through parliament on the previous 19 May[3] and realized that 'its a sad case that men are likely to bee put in by this Act of Uniformity' [16. 8. 62]. For the rest of the year there are frequent references to the insecurity of the position:

The last Sabbath of our liberty by the Act [17. 8. 62] . . . Preacht last lecture at Castle-Hedingham [19. 8. 62] . . . Some hopes given as if there would bee indulgence given to ministers for the present until the return of the parliament. The London Ministers nigh 80, generally declined

[1] According to Smith, *Ecclesiastical History*, p. 223.

[2] Smith, *Ecclesiastical History*, p. 223, suggested that he may have merely kept on 'till told to stop', and so have got 'overlooked', or that the living may have been treated as a 'donative' of the Harlakendens. Neither suggestion fits in entirely with Josselin's own account. Calamy in the 1702 edition of his work gave him as ejected, but withdrew his name in 1713 (Matthews, *Calamy Revised*, p. 299). Mr Ian Green of Worcester College, Oxford, kindly provided the writer with information on this topic.

[3] 'An Act for the Uniformity of Publick Prayer, and Administration of Sacraments', its main provision was that all ministers, 'on oath and on pain of suspension, should use the Book of Common Prayer'.

preaching [24. 8. 62] ... All hopes of suspension of the Act of Uniformity taken away; God good to mee in my freedome to preach, three ministers & multitudes of our christian neighbours hearing [31. 8. 62] ... God good to us in many mercies, the continued liberty of his words & w[orshi]p, no interrupcon or disturbance [28. 9. 62] ... Cited this day to the Archdeacons visitation; our professors[1] had rather I should lay down than conforme as J. Day told mee, but I had it onely from him; the Lord direct mee. I appeared not [10. 10. 62] ... The booke of common prayer laid in the deske for mee. 19th, laid again & used in part in the morning, but in the afternoon taken away. 26th, brought again, but picht & abused [12. 10. 62] ... Mr Crosman, preaching, actually sent to prison & some others in danger thereof, yett through mercy I am quiett [2. 11. 62] ... New Ministers this day Colne Engain, Mr Symonds & at Cogshall Mr Jessop; both of good report; and now I am left alone of the non-conformists, what God will doe with mee I know not [9. 11. 62] ... I went to the Court at Colchester, cited for procuracons[2] ... I paid & returned well ... none of the nonconformists being cited appeared but onely my selfe; I reckon that day a good day to mee [12. 11. 62] ... God good to mee & mine in manifold mercies, liberty of his Sabbath; I baptized with the Common Prayer publiquly, Wm. Fossets child [23. 11. 62].

So the year 1662 ended with Josselin still, somehow, clinging on. He had made some compromises—paying procurations and using the book of common prayer—and perhaps the authorities considered this to be enough for the time being.

In 1663 Josselin continued to use the prayer book and retained his living 'although Mr Layfield tells me (who was judge at this visitacon)[3] that I am suspended' [17. 5. 63]. Half-way through the following year he was summoned to the archdeacon's court because 'he hath not administered the Sacrament of the Supper the whole year and the parishioners want [i.e. lack] it'.[4] His worry increased as the bishop of London's visitation approached and he thought that his sermon on 11 September 'might be my last', but, when he attended, for some unknown reason he 'mett with no rubbs, but my

---

[1] A 'professor' was one who 'professed' the word, in other words a zealous Christian, not an academic.

[2] Procurations were ecclesiastical taxes, to be paid at a bishop's or archdeacon's visitation.

[3] 'Visitation' was the word for a visit or enquiry by the bishop or archdeacon to whose court all the clergy were summoned. Edward Layfield, archdeacon of Essex 1634–80, was wrongly stated to be rector of Josselin's neighbouring parish of Wakes Colne by Joseph Foster in his *Alumni Oxonienses* (Oxford, 1891–2), according to J. and S. A. Venn, *Alumni Cantabrigiensis* (4 vols, Cambridge, 1922–7).

[4] E.R.O., D/ACA/55, pp. 118, 151, 183. The case appears to have lapsed after this.

path clear so that I hope I may serve my Master with freedom awhile longer' [14. 9. 64]. Perhaps there had been another compromise, for on 30 October Josselin administered communion.[1] It is difficult to know whether his reference to being 'at the visitacon, with respect' [8. 5. 65] during the following year means that he was treated with respect, or himself behaved respectfully, but certainly there do not seem to have been any further troubles for nearly two years. Then, suddenly, 'going to preach, H.Morly of my parish deliv[er]d mee a note of receipt of my procurations, and there in notice I was suspended. I forbore to preach in the afternoon' [28. 4. 67]. This unexpected message apparently had no effect, for though there were continued 'threats of severity against nonconformists' [13. 3. 70], Josselin survived. He was summoned to court for not wearing the surplice, [9. 7. 69] but the following year he 'Rid to the visitacon, & found no trouble' [10. 10. 70].

A detailed account of Josselin's relations with Quakers and church authorities illustrates the insecurity of his position. In the first ten years of his ministry the anxieties had been primarily political; wars were being fought in England and new forms of government devised; in the second decennium the political worries continued but were now flavoured with increasing threats from extremist religious sects. The following ten years, between 1660–9, were dominated by fears of losing his living. As we shall see, the final period of fourteen years was characterized, in the absence of any particularly strong political, ecclesiastical, or economic threats, by increasing ill health and increasing anxiety about his wife and children. Behind all these difficulties lay Josselin's daily activity as a minister. His constant minor religious duties as vicar are less often mentioned than his clashes with sectarians and church authorities, yet they shaped his life just as much.

Josselin's sermons, meetings with godly neighbours to discuss the scriptures, presence at funerals and weddings and at Holy Communion have already been alluded to. These were his more formal duties, although they might blend with his other interests as in the delightful entry 'Cow calved; administred the sacrament, only 14 present' [3. 4. 70]. But there were other informal activities which a country parson was also expected to perform.[2] Many of these are illustrated in the Diary. He acted as an arbitrator in village quarrels,

---

[1] It cannot have been too difficult for Josselin to start holding communion again, for, as described on p. 180 below, he had earlier found the communion service a great spiritual blessing.

[2] There is a delightful summary of many of these duties in George Herbert, *A Priest to the Temple* (1652; Everyman edn, 1908), pp. 258–61.

trying to mediate between hostile interests [e.g. 3. 10. 44]. Another sort of mediation he practised even more frequently was in match-making for marriages. For example, he 'Made a motion againe in Mr Thompsons suite to Mrs Elizabeth Little; I consider he may be welcomd, I acquainted him therewith by letter, & desired him to come over againe to her' [29. 10. 46]. On another occasion he was resentful when two neighbours to whom he had 'shewn great love and care in ripening marriage resolucons' proceeded to marry without informing him [12. 5. 47].[1] Another duty he seems to have carried out conscientiously was that of dispensing charity and hospitality.[2] He also, as far as we can tell from the occasional reference in the Diary [e.g. 29. 4. 46], appears to have taken seriously his task of visiting the sick and comforting the depressed. It is difficult to tell how much he was liked by his parishioners; some-times he records full congregations, sometimes there were few in church. Sometimes the impression is that he was not popular: 'not one person spake to mee, coming out of the church: Lord I am despised' [8. 10. 71]; 'there are [those] that wait for my hurt' [27. 7. 50]; 'most scurrilously abused by old William Adam' [1. 4. 51].[3] On other occasions, for instance when he threatened to leave Earls Colne and 'some of the womenkinde of the parrish desire mee not to goe away, and Mr Elliston' [24. 8. 48], we feel he must have had some appeal.

If the Diary provided no more information on Josselin's religious views and activities than that assembled in the preceding pages we might be justified in believing that Josselin was a 'typical', middle-of-the-road, Puritan; a man who read godly books, discussed with his zealous neighbours and preached long and intense sermons. We might too easily infer from these activities that he was intolerant and bigoted, prepared to threaten those who opposed him with hell fire, full of an apparent arrogance based on an extensive stock of apt biblical quotations. That he was far from this austere stereotype will emerge when, at the end of this book, we turn to an examination of the structure of his thought. For the moment, however, we may leave his ecclesiastical affairs as he left them, by way of his will. In the introduction to this document we see the, possibly stereotyped,

[1] Other references to marriage-making activities are contained in the Diary under the following dates: 4.8.57; 13.3.61; 25-6.5.75.

[2] There is a discussion of the amount of his charitable benefactions on pp. 51–2.

[3] His unpopularity seems to have been greatest in the early 1650s when his acquisition of the lands of the rich spinster Mary Church, and of other copy-hold tenures through his influence with the lord of the manor and his own 'cousin' the steward, brought him into competition with other villagers. His quarrel with the Quakers has already been described.

Calvinist formula in which Josselin commended his soul 'into the hands of God that gave it, trusting assuredly through the meritts of my blessed Saviour Jesus Christ to enjoye an Inheritance in Glory among his sanctifyed ones'.[1] After nearly forty-three tempestuous years as vicar of Earls Colne he had certainly earned such an inheritance.

[1] The whole of the will is transcribed on pp. 211-13 below.

3

Josselin's economic activities (i): income, expenditure and saving

Against the previously sketched background of political and ecclesiastical change, Ralph Josselin lived out his economic life. His Diary provides as full an account of this aspect of his existence as it does of contemporary politics and religion. Without fail between 1650 and 1664 he kept a detailed yearly account of his receipts, disbursements and debts, usually entered in the Diary at the beginning of the ecclesiastical year, 26 March. These accounts, as well as other references to land purchases, debts, and expenses scattered throughout his Diary enable us, with the help of local manorial records,[1] to piece together much of his financial and farming life. There are, naturally, dangers and difficulties in using such accounts. As Dr Bowden has pointed out, speaking generally of such sources, 'no allowance is made for the depreciation of capital assets; farming and non-farming expenditures are occasionally lumped together; little or no attempt is made to allocate overheads to different parts of the enterprise ... while the value of home-consumed produce is also frequently omitted'.[2] Consequently, much of what follows will be guess-work, an attempt to fill in gaps.

Josselin seems to have been a çareful and accurate accountant, probably more reliable, if less specific, than his obvious rival in this field, the Berkshire yeoman Robert Loder.[3] From his Diary we gain a unique picture of the way in which a seventeenth-century yeoman built up his estate and then bequeathed it to his wife and children.[4]

[1] These documents are at the E.R.O. Most useful among them are D/DPr/42, 100, 113, 619, and an extremely good map of the parish made in 1598 and re-copied in 1810, D/DSM P2.

[2] Bowden in Joan Thirsk (ed.), *The Agrarian History of England and Wales* (Cambridge, 1967), vol. IV, pp. 649–50.

[3] G. E. Fussell, the editor of Loder's accounts, criticizes them for their inaccuracy. (*Robert Loder's Farm Accounts, 1610–1620*, ed. G. E. Fussell, Cam. Soc., 3rd series, Vol. LIII (1936), p. xxiv).

[4] Probably the best comparisons with Josselin are afforded by the works of W. G. Hoskins, especially *Provincial England* (1963), ch. VIII; *The Midland Peasant* (Papermac edn, 1965), chs. VI and VII. Alan Simpson, *The Wealth of the Gentry, 1540–1660* (Cambridge, 1963) and M. E. Finch, *The Wealth of Five Northamptonshire Families, 1540–1640*, Northants. Rec. Soc., vol. XIX (1956) have

In the process we learn how it was that a vicar whose officially assessed income was only £28 p.a.[1] managed to leave his son an estate worth over £50 p.a., and dower his daughters with land and money to the total value of approximately £1,250. The Diary shows Josselin constantly pre-occupied with the building up of his landed estate; the impression of economic insecurity, combined with the urge to acquire and re-invest in order to ward off disaster is very strong. The man who wrote the Diary was clearly shaped by the farming life not merely because he was the son of a yeoman, but because he himself lived the life of a yeoman-priest.

INCOME

Josselin had three major sources of annual income. He derived some of his wealth from his position as vicar of Earls Colne; some from the profits from farming and leasing land; and some from fees for eight years of teaching at Earls Colne school. Late in his life Josselin assessed that 'Halfe I have gained hath not been from Colne [i.e. his ecclesiastical living] but on other occasions' [12. 9. 48]. This estimate is entirely borne out by a detailed analysis of his income from various sources.

The 'half' which he thought came from his living can again be subdivided into three. There was, firstly, the amount he received under the original agreement made with the parishioners before his arrival in Earls Colne. Although, as mentioned above, the parliamentary surveyors in 1650 put the value of the living at £24, plus £4 glebe, Josselin came to the town hoping to receive £80 p.a. This 'Agreement for Earls Colne Living' was divided up by Josselin as follows:

Tithes they would make good at	£40. 0s.	
Mr. Rich: Harlakenden: wood & money	£20. 0s.	
His tenants in contribucon	£2. 0s.	
Mr. Tho: Harlakenden	£3. 0s.	
And the towne contribucon	£15. 0s.	[1640]

The 'House, close, churchyard and the dues that accrewed to the Ministery' were valued at a further £10 p.a. It is clear that the total revenues were never reached. Although the Harlakendens paid their share, many parishioners defaulted on tithes and in the town's contribution. Looking back over the previous three years, Josselin

---

made analyses of gentry families similar to that attempted here for a yeoman household.

[1] This was the estimate of the parliamentary surveyors in 1650 (Smith, *Ecclesiastical History*, p. 309).

complained that in 1641 'with all my toyle, I thinke that I could make them [i.e. tithes] amount not above £33, and since they are come to lesse' [1641]. Although he had some 'private gifts' to make up for the 'towne losses', and thought that he might get up to £70 p.a. [19. 10. 44], it seems likely that the normal position during his residence is summed up in the calculations for 1648:

First my case in reference to maintenance is this: first for tithes, the general maintenance, the last year I received in from the Towne, at several times, with much calling upon, £25 6s. 9d. and perhaps this yeare may afford thus much: then Mr. Jacob is to pay £4 which perhaps he will continue to pay: Mr. R. Harlakenden he its likely will performe his £20 per annum: so there is about £49., if the tithes bee gotten in: for the other £31 pound I have not received £4; but suppose their [sic] should £8 or 9 of it be paid, this amounts not unto £60 p.a. [12. 9. 48]

The balance of £2 or £3 to make the sum up to £60 would probably have been made up by ecclesiastical fees for performing baptisms, weddings, funerals, and preaching sermons. In the following diagram (fig. 3), therefore, Josselin's basic income from his living has been averaged out at a steady £60 p.a. Obviously, in reality, it fluctuated from year to year.[1]

Another source which fell short of expectations was the augmentation to Josselin's living made by the Committee for Plundered Ministers.[2] In 1646 Josselin heard that he had been promised money to add to the value of his living [23. 12. 46]. Originally this was supposed to be £50 p.a., but in 1650, when he received his first small sum of £6 from this source, Josselin heard that it had been reduced to £43 p.a. [17–8. 3. 50]. But even this diminished sum was only partly paid. If it had been fully paid throughout the period 1646–59 when it was due, Josselin would have received just over £600. As it is, we only learn, from the Diary, that he received some £113 3s. 8d.; most of this came in the years 1651–3.[3] These stated acquisitions have been included in figure 3, and it has also been assumed that he received a small proportion of this augmentation, on average some £5 6s. 0d. p.a., in the 5 years 1654 and 1656–9, when there is no evidence on the subject. This would make his total up to a round £150, a quarter of what he should have received.

[1] Many of the items of income and expenditure have had to be averaged out over long periods, although it is the short-term fluctuations which were perhaps most significant to Josselin and hence to us.
[2] The work of this committee in Essex is described in Smith, *Ecclesiastical History*, pp. 200 ff. Basically it re-allocated funds which had previously been in the hands of royalist laymen and clergy back to the poorer clergy.
[3] There is a detailed discussion of Josselin's receipts and struggles over the augmentation in Smith, *Ecclesiastical History*, pp. 202–5.

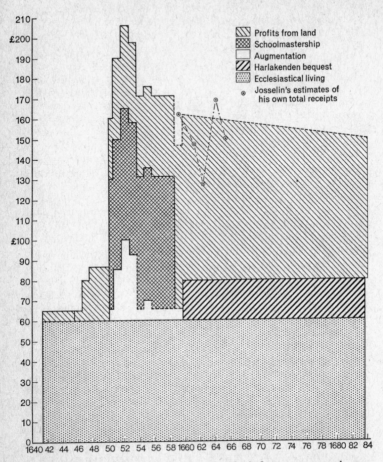

Fig. 3. Josselin's income between 1641 and 1683. Yearly figures are averaged out; broken lines (–––) indicate uncertain totals. As stated in the text, this method of averaging out is unsatisfactory in a number of ways and will give a distorted picture of Josselin's finances, not accounting, for example, for the effects of fluctuations in the weather. Yet, in the present state of almost total ignorance about the finances of the large proportion of the population below the level of the gentry, it has seemed better to give an indication, however rough, rather than nothing at all.

Just at the point at which any money received from the augmentation was about to dry up at the king's restoration, Josselin's living
was supplemented in another way. Mr Richard Harlakenden, the
impropriator (owner) of the living, hearing that Josselin was contemplating a move to a richer parish, offered him an extra £20 p.a.
if he would stay. This was more than a vague offer, for he called at
Josselin's house in February 1659 and left £50 'as mine if he or I
died, but if wee lived as an engagement for 2 yeares and halfe until
Sept: 29.61 and then if he did not purchase £20 yearly and adde to
my means, if living, he would raise and pay out of his estate £20
yearly' [1. 2. 59]. A few months later 'Mr R. H. made a bequest of
the great tithes to mee & the ministers of Colne' [4. 6. 59]. It seems
reasonable to assume that these were worth approximately £20 p.a.,
as promised, and to deduce that he received this extra payment
from 1659 on, although the grant was only formalized by a deed in
1673.[1] Josselin's gratitude is shown in the entry he made in the
parish register at the burial of Richard Harlakenden: 'the good
Harlakenden who by deed gave the great tithes of most of the parish
to the Church frendes'.[2]

As lucrative per annum as the ecclesiastical living, yet held for
only a fifth of the time, was the schoolmastership at Earls Colne.
Josselin himself estimated that the school was 'worth neare £70
yearly to mee', besides the 'comfort to teach my [own] children'
[1. 2. 57]. Earlier he had assessed the school rents at £62 3s. 4d. p.a.
[3. 12. 50]. He taught at the school between 10 January 1650 and
12 July 1658, except for a short gap from March to June 1650. He
thus had just over eight full years of teaching, with a consequent
profit of about £520, if we average out his receipts at just under
£65 p.a. As will become clear later, this was the period of maximum
growth in Josselin's capital assets and the period when he acquired
the bulk of his land. The money from his teaching was undoubtedly
of fundamental importance in this rapid expansion. Nor does Josselin
seem to have found the extra work too much of a strain: 'I find I goe
through the matter of the schoole without any extraordinary
burthen; the times of schoole I make my times of studdy' [23. 6. 50].
He was clearly sorry to lose it.

The third major source of income was the profit from land, both
land he leased and that he farmed himself. The detailed analysis of

[1] According to Philip Morant, *The History and Antiquities of the County of Essex*
(2 vols, 1816), vol. II, p. 214, where the deed is printed.
[2] E.R.O., D/P/209/1/3 (Earls Colne register) under the date 17.9.77. 'Great
tithes' were those which went to the rector or owner of the living; 'small tithes'
to the vicar. Tithes were, in theory, a tax of one-tenth of all produce.

how much Josselin drew from each piece of land, and how he accumu-
lated his estate, will be made later (see below, pp. 57–64). Here we
are only interested in the overall revenue from landholding. This
can be estimated by combining a knowledge of how much land
Josselin held each year with his own, occasional, estimate of income
from his land. The total is again illustrated in figure 3. During the
first five years his glebe land and land obtained with his wife at
marriage brought in about £5 p.a. Then in 1646 he bought a farm,
and the following year partly bought, partly inherited, a property
from an uncle. With the earlier property this brought his annual
income from his landholdings to £27 p.a. [27. 3. 50]. It increased
to about £40 p.a. from 1651 onwards when he was left property by
a friend and leased and bought other property which more than
compensated for the sale of his 1646 purchase. Then in 1657 he
received as his own the second part of the legacy mentioned above,
which he had up till then been hiring. The following year he
completed the purchase of an estate with a capital value of £310.
A detailed assessment of the annual value of his land at this point
gave the total of £84. 14s. 0d. p.a. [5. 4. 59]. Further minor purchases
were made in the 1660s, together with sales and purchases in the
1670s, which probably more or less cancelled each other out. In his
will, Josselin handed over land worth some £80 p.a. to his son, wife,
and daughter Mary. It therefore seems reasonable to assume that
throughout the period between 1659 and his death in 1683, he was
receiving between £80 and £90 p.a. income, either in money or in
produce, from his land.

A number of minor sources of income are also indicated in the
Diary. Early in his career Josselin seems to have invested money in
the hop trade. He noted 'I have bought a part in a shippe: it cost
me £14. 10s. God send mee good speed with the same; I have sent
my part in a bagge of hops to Sunderland' [5. 8. 44]. Unfortunately,
we do not know the returns on this investment; nor do we know
how long Josselin continued to be a small-time investor in trade.
Perhaps he was scared off when two years later, 'I heard by Major
Hanes that our shippe wherein my part was about £18 was cast
away, three men drowned', even though the 'merchants saved their
goods' [24. 10. 46]. Other small sums of money came from his
activities as chaplain during the Civil War: for instance he was paid
£2 10s. 'for waiting as preacher' on Colonel Harlakenden's regiment
at Walden [10. 8. 45].

From the above calculations there emerges a rough statement of
Josselin's approximate income each year. In the 1640s it was in the
region of £65 to £110; in the 1650s between £160 and about £205;

in the 1660s it had dropped back to about £160 p.a. It is only for this last period that we have Josselin's own estimates of his total income with which to check our calculations. As indicated in figure 3, in 1661 he estimated his income at £146 16s. 0d. [31. 3. 61]; in 1662 at £117 15s. 9d. [30. 3. 62]; in 1664, having omitted 1663, he put the total at £168 18s. 4d. [March 1664]; in 1665 the total was £139 4s. 8d. [5. 4. 65]. It is probable that there was some disguised income in the form of food and fuel from his estate and this would account for the discrepancy of some £15 p.a. between Josselin's estimates and the calculations of what he *ought* to have been getting in the later years.

Josselin's income from land sales needs separate treatment for these capital transactions, though contributing to his total life's income, were not part of his regular, annual, flow of receipts. Three land sales in 1651 (£250), 1661 (£57) and 1673 (£123) brought in a total of £430.

From the preceding calculations there emerges the following, approximate, table of the amount of income which Josselin derived from each major source over his whole life.

TABLE I. *The sources of Josselin's income from 1641–83*

Source	Probable total income	%
Ecclesiastical living (at £60 p.a. to 1659; £80 p.a. thereafter)	£3,000	49
Augmentation from plundered ministers	c. £150	2.5
Teaching	£520	8.5
Profits from leasing/farming land	£2,000	33
Sales of land	£430	7
	£6,100	100

The table shows that just about half of Josselin's £6,000 plus of income, both from annual receipts and capital transactions, came from sources other than his ecclesiastical living. We may now turn to the way in which this money was spent.

EXPENDITURE

It is even more difficult to deduce how Josselin spent his growing income than to assess how much he earned. There are many more forms of expenditure than sources of income, and the diarist is less particular in noting individual items here than he is when accounting for his income. For instance, he never mentions how much he spent on rearing his children and sending them to school, or on feeding himself, his wife, and his servant; yet these would, clearly, be large items in his total budget. Moreover the topic is further complicated by the fact that we are not merely interested in expenditure of money, actual purchases, but also in the equally significant, but less easily measured and less frequently recorded, allocation of time and labour. Clearly, for example, the 'cost' of children cannot be measured solely in terms of food, clothing and medicine; the periods of ill-health and hard labour by the mother would also, ideally, be assessed. Despite these difficulties, the interest of learning how a villager invested his available resources some 300 years ago is so great, that it justifies, we believe, the following highly tentative analysis. It is hoped that these crude calculations will be refined by future historians.

It is convenient to group the main items on Josselin's expense sheet into three sections, though these are obviously, far from water-tight compartments. Firstly there are external expenses on his estate, both secular and ecclesiastical. These consist of expenses of farm equipment and labour and of taxes, ecclesiastical, national, and manorial. Capital transactions, the purchase of land and housing, will be discussed at the end of the section. Secondly there are the costs of his own family, servants and kin. Finally there is a miscellaneous category which may, broadly, be subsumed under the heading of 'leisure and ritual' expenses. This includes the purchase of books, charitable gifts, and hospitality, and what has been termed the 'ceremonial fund'[1]—principally, in Josselin's case, payments for festivities at baptisms, weddings and funerals.

Before we turn to particular items, however, we may gain an overall picture, from Josselin's own assessments. His totals are shown in figure 4. In 1657 Josselin noted 'my expenses far deeper than divers yeares formerly' [25. 3. 57] and the following March he gave his first yearly total; he stated that he had spent £110 over the preceding twelve months [26. 3. 58]. In 1661, at his next assessment, his expenses had climbed to £233 9s. 6½d. [31. 3. 61], it was possibly the most expensive year of his life. Thereafter his recorded total dropped year by year; in 1662 his 'layings out' were £199 4s. 11d. [30. 3. 62],[2] in 1664 his expenses were £160 13s. 2d. [March 1664],

[1] The term and the concept are discussed in E. R. Wolf, *Peasants* (New Jersey, 1966), pp. 7–9.

[2] He made another calculation for the same date of £192 19s. 11d. The choice of the higher sum is arbitrary, though it seems more likely that Josselin under-estimated than over-estimated his income.

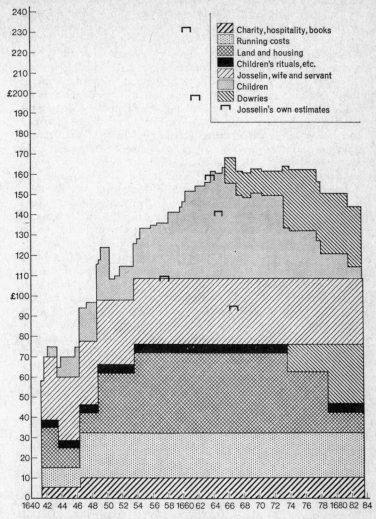

Fig. 4. Josselin's expenses. The categories are fully explained in the text; totals have been averaged out over several years.

the following year they were £141 4s. 9d. [5. 4. 65], and by March 1667 they had sunk to £95 15s. 4d. It seems likely that they remained at this level or lower over the next 15 years, for it was over these years that he managed to save some £700 in cash as dowries for his daughters.

The amount invested in keeping both his ecclesiastical and landed estates running, quite apart from the value of his own labour, was probably between £900 and £1,000 over his life. This went on taxes and on re-stocking and working his farm. As both a yeoman and vicar, Josselin was being double-taxed. He never added up the totals of such taxes, but on one occasion he made the following estimate of his payments on his ecclesiastical living. Out of a total £60 p.a. 'I am to pay taxes, which will amount to £3 p.a.: tenths to the Parliament, and reparacons, which will bring it downe to a matter of £50 a yere' [12. 9. 48]. It seems likely that, if anything, the burden of taxes on his landed estates increased as his landholding grew larger. The civil taxes included the hearth tax, which he paid at 12s. p.a. after 1662 when he had moved to his smaller house of six hearths,[1] and the poll tax. Of the latter he wrote, 'this day I paid £1 12s. 6d. for my pole tax. I paid it once formerly in £4 as I remember. This rate unusuall twice in an age' [11. 10. 60]. It would seem fair, therefore, to average out his taxation payments, both to ecclesiastical and secular authorities, at £10 p.a. over his time at Earls Colne. This would mean a total payment of just over £420.

On top of the general taxes were local payments to the lord of the manor. Most of Josselin's land was copyhold, and on this he had to make two types of payment to the Harlakendens, lords of the manors of Earls Colne and Colne Priory. He paid an entry fine or 'relief' when he took over the property, in Josselin's case a sum equalling one year's rent, and also a smaller, yearly, 'quitrent'. Many of these reliefs and yearly rents are recorded in contemporary manorial records and enable us to make a rough estimate of the total payments.[2] When Josselin's son John inherited a large part of his father's land he paid a relief of £80: this, with the detailed sums alluded to above, suggests that Josselin paid something like £100 in entry fines. A rental, or list of rents, for 1671 gives his total rents due that year as £4 4s. 1d.;[3] probably this was about the sum he was paying throughout the period 1659–83. This £100 or so of rent was probably

---

[1] For the one year 1662 he should have paid 22s. for the 11-hearth vicarage. The hearth taxes of 1662 and 1671 with his name on are at the E.R.O., D/RTh/1 and 5.

[2] These are listed in table III, pp. 60–1 below.

[3] E.R.O., D/DPr/113, printed on p. 220 below.

increased by no more than £10 by rents before 1659. If we add together all taxes, fines and rents, we find that Josselin paid up to £630 in all. If, as occasionally happened his tenants paid tithes and lords rent, this was deducted from the rent paid to Josselin.

Then there was the cost of running the farm; buying stock and seed, manuring, ditching, weeding and harvesting, replacing farm implements and repairing farm buildings. Only occasionally, except in the purchase of livestock, do we get a glimpse of these expenses. In May one year we learn that 'Seaver tooke of mee all the bushes ... to stubbe up by the rootes & to pull all the broome; he is to cleare the grounds; for this I am to give him 10s. & the broome, which I doe account to bee 13s. 0d.' [30. 5. 51]. The same autumn 'William Webb and his brother tooke my ditching, to throw the marle [i.e. a mixture of lime and clay] into the field, to cutt the hedge ... I am to give them 3½d. per rod, and where worth it 4d' [26. 11. 51]. Only once do we learn of the extra expense of labour at harvest: 'made an end of haying for this yeare, and my hay very good ... it cost mee the least of any yeare, mowing & making & inning not above 40s. besides my own helpe' [10. 7. 69]. We also only occasionally discover the cost of seed; for example he planted three bushels of white wheat which he had just bought for 10s. [12. 10. 64]. With so little information it needs a considerable amount of guess-work to arrive at an estimate of how much Josselin had to plough back into his land to keep it productive.

The problem is simplified by Dr Bowden's model table of expenditure per acre on a small arable farm, without outside labour, over the years 1600–20.[1] If we deduct from his table the cost of rent which, in Josselin's case, has been accounted for separately, we are left with a total cost of 11. 86s. per acre. As will be seen in a later section, Josselin leased out the larger proportion of his land and probably farmed himself only between 10 and 20 acres.[2] As he made explicit in his leases, his tenant was to pay the running costs of this leased land. If we assume he had an average personal holding of 15 acres over the 30 years from 1651 onwards, Josselin must have spent something like £270 in all, at Bowden's rate; some £9 p.a. Some corroboration for this figure is obtained from Josselin's own account of the amount of money he was investing each year in land acquired in 1650. Throughout the 1650s he was 'improving' it at the cost of £4 p.a., or just over. For instance, in 1652–3 he had laid out £4 5s. on it [26. 3. 53], and the following year some £4 9s. 0d. [24. 3. 54]. It is impossible to be certain, but it is probable that this

[1] Bowden in Thirsk (ed.), *Agrarian History*, pp. 652–3.
[2] See p. 69 below.

would not include, for example, the cost of harvest labour. In general it seems safe to conclude that at least £270 of his £2,000 receipts from land went back onto the farm in the form of seed, livestock, labour, farm equipment and repair of buildings. At least £900 had been spent in maintaining his land and paying taxes.

The second major item of expenditure was the family. Included here was not only the cost of Josselin himself, his wife, and his children, but also of keeping a domestic servant to help with the household work. We may exclude from consideration, however, the small sums spent on other kin, either his own or his wife's, since these were never large; they probably averaged less than £1 p.a. over his 43 years at Earls Colne, at the most. Josselin never wrote down an estimate of the total cost of food, clothing, medicine, fuel, and other necessities in his household. The nearest he came to an assessment occurred in 1648 when he claimed that his ecclesiastical income of £50 could not even keep 'my self, wife, 3 children, mayde, my wife a childing woman' in 'a very lowe manner' [12. 9. 48]. It would appear from the fact that he paid £5 a quarter for board and lodging with Mr Cressner for his wife and himself during their first few years at Earls Colne [April 1641], and that he had paid £10 p.a. 'for his diet' in 1637 [25. 3. 37] and in 1639 [July 1640], that it cost about £10 p.a. per person for the basic necessities of life. This estimate is the one adopted later in the chapter.

To test the validity of the £10 p.a. estimate, and to make a calculation of the expense of raising children, necessitates a short methodological digression. Surprisingly little has been written by historians on how much it cost per annum to keep children, adolescents and adults, both male and female, alive. The cost will obviously vary from year to year and at different social levels. Before reconstructing the yearly expenditure on the family it is necessary to state the assumptions upon which the calculations are based. They are as follows. It is assumed that it would cost £5 p.a. to maintain boys and girls for their first 5 years; £7 p.a. for the next 5. They would probably then consume almost the same amount as adults—indeed their needs in terms of medicine, protein and clothing might even be greater. But only the boys are then placed at the £10 p.a. adult sum; the girls are put at £6 p.a. It seems likely that, in Josselin's case, in the few years between the age of 10 and leaving home, the girls acted as part-time domestic servants, thus repaying some of their keep. The boys, however, probably continued to be educated and there is no evidence that they helped about the farm. These rates of expenditure last until the children left home, the girls at between 10 and 13 years of age, the boys at between 15 and 16. The cost of raising children, however, did not end abruptly when they left home. Yet, since Josselin sometimes noted the major part of the money he spent hereafter, there is not such a necessity to guess at totals. As mentioned before, it is also assumed that it cost £10 p.a. per adult, for the necessities of life. Although Josselin himself probably consumed more food than his wife, the extra costs incidental to her 10 live births probably compensated for this.

All the above estimates are undoubtedly minimum rates, possibly lower than reality. They are based on calculations made for people in an inferior position to Josselin's family. Though, to a certain extent, Josselin had the advantage of living off his own, home-grown, food, the following calculations represent the lowest possible sums Josselin could have spent on himself and his family. Some idea of the cost of raising children in Essex in the seventeenth century is given by the payments that were believed to be able to support a bastard child: these usually ran at between £5 and £6 6s. 0d. p.a. for children up to the age of 10 or 14, on top of the labour of the mother.[1] Another clue is provided by a scheme for setting up a foundling hospital in London in 1687. In this, people were to be entitled to redeem children up to the age of 5 years for £25; 'being of that age, or under the age of seven years, for forty pounds; and from seven to ten, for fifty pounds; but after the age of ten years, every year it continues in the house, shall advance ten pounds in the price of its redemption'.[2] This would represent the cost of keeping the child and, in all likelihood, a small profit for the institution. Obviously Josselin's children were treated better than bastards or foundlings, but, as argued above, their father's farm lightened their cost.

Some of our best estimates of the cost of clothing and feeding adults also come from the lowest strata of society, from the payments to labourers and servants. Robert Loder, we are informed, calculated his servant's keep, when they lived in, as an extra charge 'averaging £10 a year more or less' and the 'total cost of food for each person in the family, calculated on an arithmetical average, ranged about £10 per annum'.[3] Dr Everitt has written of another yeoman-farmer

---

[1] Dr Quintrell writes that 'The weekly imposition on fathers varied from ... 1s. 4d. to 2s. 2d. for ten to fourteen years ... Mothers rarely paid more than 6d. a week unless the father's contribution was very small ... they were always sent to the house of correction ... they were able in theory to help to support the child from their earnings' (Brian Quintrell, 'The Government of the County of Essex, 1603–1642' (Unpublished Ph.D. thesis, 1965, London University Library), pp. 210–11).

[2] Mrs E. Cellier, 'A Scheme for the Foundation of a Royal Hospital', *Harleian Miscellany*, vol. IX (1810), pp. 196–7.

[3] *Loder's Farm Accounts*, ed. Fussell, pp. xxviii, xxx.

as follows: 'Nicholas Toke allowed one of his sheep-lookers in Romney Marsh £10 a year for his board and £36 a year for the diet of two men and two boys'.[1] Again it is obvious that Josselin and his wife lived at a higher standard than farm labourers and that the rate of £10 p.a. for an adult applied to his household is a minimum rate.[2] Yet even at these low estimates, Josselin's expenditure on his family was very considerable. It is shown in diagrammatic form in figure 5 below.

On these assumptions it is easy enough to calculate Josselin's total expenditure on himself and his wife; during his 43 years at Earls Colne he must have spent at least £850 on this. This would have been fairly evenly distributed throughout his residence in the village, though his standard of living probably went up with his income. On top of this came the expense of a servant who helped with domestic work. Josselin appears to have had such a servant from a few months after his arrival until his death. Although he paid such servants, on average, only about £2 10s. 0d. p.a. each, this came on top of the same minimum £10 adult living expenses. The servants would therefore, have cost something like £525 over his life.[3] If we add some £25 on to these totals for adults for miscellaneous small unrecorded expenses, we discover that altogether Josselin must have spent at least £1400, or nearly a quarter of his income, on himself, his wife and servant. The cost of the children requires a much more detailed analysis since both the incidence of the expenses during Josselin's life, and the variations between the different children, need to be specified.

An attempt to estimate the cost of each of Ralph Josselin's children, except the child who died at the age of ten days, is given in figure 5. These calculations are based on the previously stated assumptions about the cost of children until they left home and then on Josselin's statements about where the children went and the date at which they left.[4] Analysis is only made possible by Josselin's meticulous notes on

[1] In Thirsk (ed.), *Agrarian History*, p. 437. *The Household Account Book of Sarah Fell of Swarthmoor Hall, 1673–8*, ed. N. Penny (Cambridge, 1920), p. 253, states that a mower's allowance for board in Westmorland in 1674 was 8d. per day, or just over £12 p.a.
[2] William Stout, for example, boarded and lodged out with others at £12 p.a. (*The Autobiography of William Stout of Lancaster, 1665–1752*, ed. J. D. Marshall (Manchester, 1967), p. 205).
[3] For a discussion of Josselin's attitude towards, and payments to, domestic servants, see p. 147 below. He first notes employing one on 20.10.41 and, as we can see from his lamentations when he was without one for a few days, employed one, at least, almost continuously.
[4] Analysed in table VI, p. 93 below.

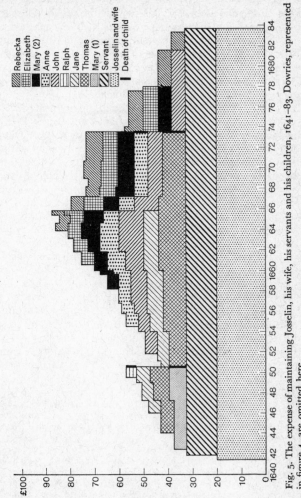

Fig. 5. The expense of maintaining Josselin, his wife, his servants and his children, 1641–83. Dowries, represented in figure 4, are omitted here.

Legend:
Rebecka
Elizabeth
Mary (2)
Anne
John
Ralph
Jane
Thomas
Mary (1)
Servant
Josselin and wife
Death of child

47

these facts, and by knowing the dates of birth, marriage or death of each child.[1] To the objection that these calculations overlook the rewards Josselin received through the children's labour in early adolescence we can only make the answer that there is no evidence that the children worked for their parents. It has often been suggested that pre-industrial societies are characterized by child-labour, that children are a productive investment.[2] This may have been true in other areas of England,[3] and even within the lower social strata in Josselin's own village; but there is, as yet, no reason for supposing that this was so in the Josselin household except for some help by the girls with domestic labour, as allowed for above.

Figure 5 needs little explanation. Perhaps the most debatable part of the calculations concerns the expenses of children after they left home and before they married, so we may turn to these in further detail. Otherwise the diagram shows the expenditure mounting as each new child was born, and dropping each time a child died or gained self-sufficiency. After rearing to the age of almost 16 the eldest son, Thomas, cost Josselin nearly £100 to apprentice [14. 4. 60], a sum Josselin had been saving for over a period of at least 2 years [26. 3. 58]. The next son, John, was bound apprentice for less, a mere £45 [13. 11. 68]. Boys were apprenticed, in theory, for 8 years. This expenditure is spread out in the diagram over the following 8 years although, of course, in reality the sum had been collected before the beginning of the apprenticeship.[4] But even after the apprenticeship had ended the expenses continued. When Thomas had almost served his 8 years his father gave him another £50 with which to stock a shop [March 1667]. He died some 5 years later, so that this £50 has again been evenly distributed at £10 p.a. for this period. The other son, John, continued to live at home for most of the period until his marriage at the age of 30. It has been assumed that he continued to be partially dependent on his parents until then.

[1] See table v, p. 82 below.

[2] This is the conclusion, for example, of the United Nations study *The Determinants and Consequences of Population Trends* (New York, 1953), pp. 78, 202. A useful table of the age at which males become 'economically active' is given in the same study on p. 195.

[3] For example, William Stout (*Autobiography*, p. 70) described how children helped with peat gathering and harvesting in the north of England.

[4] The diagram is also unrealistic because John did not stay in London as an apprentice but came home to Earls Colne where he enraged his father for the next fifteen years (see pp. 120–4 below). It is assumed, however, that little of the money paid for his apprenticeship would have been retrieved and that, anyhow, John would have continued to be an expense at home.

Of the 5 girls who survived long enough to leave home, we know the partial expenses of only one. To set up Anne as a servant at the age of 14 cost Josselin £50 [18. 7. 69]. This would mean that he continued to support her, if we average out this sum at £6 p.a. for another 8 years, until she reached her 22nd birthday—or would have done if she had not died before then. We do not know how much the other daughters cost, but there is no reason for believing that they were less expensive than Anne.[1] Three of them were being boarded out at school for a number of years, and such 'tabling' out cost £6 p.a. for the children from yeoman families, as we know from other diaries.[2] Josselin alluded to these expenses on one occasion when he doubted whether he would be able to pay off all his debts 'by reason of my daughters going out' [25. 4. 74]; two days previously his daughters Mary and Elizabeth had gone off to school at Bury St Edmunds. For the purposes of calculation, therefore, it has been assumed that Josselin spent some £6 p.a. on average, on each of his daughters and that they became self-sufficient at the age of 20. On the basis of these assumptions, it cost him £120 to raise a daughter from birth to the age of 20. That this is no exaggerated sum may be seen by comparing it with the calculations of two other yeoman-clerics, the Rev. Giles Moore and Adam Martindale. Moore seems to have been slightly less wealthy than Josselin, but also seems to have spoiled his adopted, and only, daughter Martha. We do not known the age at which she was adopted, but he calculated that 'the exact amount of all I layed out upon Mat[Martha], from the time of my resolving to take her, till the day of her marriage, besydes her diet and washing in my house, was £163 12s. 6d.'[3] If food had

---

[1] The custom of giving money with girl apprentices, as well as with boys, is illustrated in the late seventeenth century when £20 was given with a girl apprenticed to a milliner 'and her maintenance in her apprenticeship cost as much more' (Stout, *Autobiography*, p. 168). Parents in New England seem to have had to pay for the keep of their daughters even when they were merely acting as servants in other households (E. S. Morgan, *The Puritan Family*, Harper Torchbook edn (1966), p. 76).

[2] For example, Timothy Whittingham 'tabled out' one son at £18 p.a., and boarded out another at £6 p.a. ('The Diary of Timothy Whittingham of Holmside', extracts by J. C. Hodgson, *Arch. Ael.*, 3rd series, vol. XXI (1924), pp. 206, 209). William Stout mentions children being boarded out in Lancashire for £4 p.a. (*Autobiography*, p. 72). The Verneys, at a higher social level, would expect to pay something like £18 p.a. in diet and £12 p.a. in clothes for a child boarded out in another family, at the least (*Memoirs of the Verney Family During the Seventeenth Century*, compiled by F. P. and M. M. Verney (2 vols, New York, 1907), vol. I, pp. 433, 434).

[3] Blencoe, 'Extracts from Journal and Account Book of Moore', *Suss. Arch. Coll.*, vol. I, p. 117. It had cost him £12 p.a. for 'schooling' alone he reckoned (p. 105), and her dowry was worth £300 (p. 117).

been included, this would have been a far higher sum than Josselin spent on any one of his children. The Lancashire diarist Adam Martindale was also slightly less wealthy than Josselin. He stated that he 'would not take any man's 30 pounds to doe for his [deceased son's] child what we have alreadie done for it', when it was aged 5. He reckoned that he would have to spend at least '80 or 90 pounds' on this grandchild altogether.[1]

We may now turn once more to the diagram of expenditure on children. The main outlines are obvious. Expenditure mounted until the mid 1660s, although, of course, in reality the burden was distributed slightly earlier since lump sums for apprenticeship had to be collected at the start of the new phase. By the 1660s something between £40 and £60 p.a. of Josselin's income was going directly to maintain his 7 children. After that the total decreased, but it was not until the mid 1670s that it dropped below the £40 p.a. level. Between the age of 35 and 55 Ralph Josselin was spending between $\frac{1}{4}$ and $\frac{1}{3}$ of his total income on his children. In order of age the children cost, at the above rates, the following minimum sums (those in italics predeceased Josselin): *Mary* (£46), *Thomas* (£260), Jane (£120), *Ralph* (the second) (£5), John (£200), Anne (£114), Mary (£120), Elizabeth (£120), Rebecka (£120). The total cost was some £1,305, almost the sum Josselin spent on himself, his wife and servant. These minimum expenses do not include extra gifts and other minor expenses, for instance gifts of plate [e.g. on 22. 2. 58].

On those children who lived to survive him he had spent at least £680, on those who predeceased him, excluding the infant dead at 10 days, he had spent £425. This was quite apart from the 'cost' to the mother of the 10 pregnancies in these instances and in the minimum of 5 pregnancies leading to miscarriages.[2] Approximately $\frac{1}{3}$ of his total investment in his children had been wasted through high mortality, approximately $\frac{1}{12}$ of his total income was spent on children who did not reach their 30th birthday.[3] If Josselin had been one of the less prosperous and less long-lived villagers, the proportionate loss with such a mortality pattern would have been even greater. For those labourers upon whose expenditure figures we have calculated Josselin's spending, who were getting less than a quarter of Josselin's income but, like him, losing many of their children, the

---

[1] *The Life of Adam Martindale*, ed. R. Parkinson, Chet. Soc., vol. IV (1845), p. 221.

[2] These miscarriages are listed on p. 199 below.

[3] The loss to the individual and the society through high child and infant mortality has long been of concern to demographers, a particularly interesting discussion of some of the problems is contained in United Nations, *Determinants and Consequences*, p. 280.

waste of economic assets must have taken a considerable part of their life's earnings. Since Josselin does not seem to have profited much from his children's labour or been supported by them in his old age, the loss was indirect rather than immediately felt. Above all, it was the pattern of economic growth in the whole society that was affected.

Even when the daughters reached the age of 20, however, their demands on their parent did not cease. As another diarist quoting an old proverb, put it 'An old child sucks hard . . . children when they growe to age prove chargeable.'[1] Much the most 'chargeable' aspect of these later expenses were dowries. Josselin proceeded to give his daughters dowries worth at least £800 in cash and £400 in land.[2] Some £500 of this, Mary's dowry of £100 in cash and £400 of land, was left in Josselin's will at his death. This may be deducted from his estate but not included in this account of his expenditure while alive. If we add the other £700 of dowry to the total of £1,305 above we see that, quite apart from legacies and the expenses on children's 'leisure and ritual' which will be analysed shortly, Josselin had spent a total of about £2,000 on his children, or ⅓ of his total income.[3]

Josselin's village was 'full of poore' [12. 9. 48] who were, many of them, 'in a sad condicon' [1. 3. 51]. As a clergyman, Josselin had a special duty to distribute charity and he was, he claimed, 'desirous to doe god service & help the poore' [9. 2. 75]. We do not know, however, what proportion of his income went in charity. What is clear is that Josselin did not look on such charity as a one-way process; he regarded it as investment which would bring returns of a spiritual and social kind. 'He that gives to the poore lends to the Lord' [17. 1. 45], he remarked; it was a loan which was to be repaid. Often the payment was, he believed, immediate; for instance he noted 'I observe no kindness of mine at any time to any poore distressed ones but god quickly makes it up' [19. 11. 46]. Poor-relief was a long-term investment in the future life, and would bring immediate benefits in an improved reputation in the village and small 'blessings' showered from heaven.[4] The problem of estimating

---

[1] *The Diary of John Manningham*, 1602–3, ed. J. Bruce, Cam. Soc., vol. xcix (1868), p. 12.

[2] The dowries are described in more detail on p. 93 below.

[3] These calculations lend additional force to W. G. Hoskins's remarks about the post-Reformation clergy: 'The country parson began to find that an income which had been just sufficient for an unmarried predecessor was wholly inadequate for his new status of husband and father' (*Essays in Leicestershire History* (Liverpool, 1950), p. 18.

[4] The idea of reciprocal benefits is discussed further on p. 195 below. It was a

his expenditure on this spiritual investment is complicated by the fact that sometimes he would cut down expenditure on himself and his wife, so that he could give to the poor; he fasted and the saving on one or two meals a week he gave to the needy [25. 11. 49].

On two occasions he worked out detailed budgets so that he could see how much to spend on 'charitable uses' and on his library. In 1652 he decided to 'sett out the 10th of all receipts in mony that are paid unto [me] as rents, or profits, towards charitable uses, thus viz. in 10s. because of giving many things in kinde at the doore, every 4s. towards bookes and necessary things for my study, and the other 6s. to dispose towards such charitable uses' [24. 3. 52].[1] If by 'rents, or profits' he meant only profits from his lands, then throughout his life he should have spent something like £200 on such 'charitable uses', of which £160 would go towards helping the poor. The total, of course, would have been a great deal more if he had included his ecclesiastical living and schoolmastership. This wider interpretation of his intentions is clearly justified in a later attempted budget. Now that most of his children would soon be off his hands and his old age approached, he asked the Lord to 'pardon all my neglect or breach of any vowes' (presumably his failure to give to the poor was among the sins of omission), and continued

I sett apart the tenth of all my incomes in money as minister, the 10 of my rents in money, & the 10th of my profitt by any bargains. the 20th part of the money I take for all corn I sell. to pay my tenths & to serve in gods worship and free charitable bounty to gods peace as neare as I can, allowing out 20s. yearly for books. [4. 11. 71]

A tenth of his income at this time brought in something like £14 p.a., but it seems unlikely that he did, in fact, spend this amount on charity for the next 9 years. Probably a sum of something like £250 covered these 2 expenses over his life. If we add on to this his hospitality to his friends, neighbours and kin, the frequent meals and small gifts which are recorded throughout the pages of his Diary,[2] this brings the total sum up to an approximate £400—an average of a little under £10 p.a. spread over his life at Earls Colne.

familiar concept but nowhere better expressed than by George Herbert when describing the ideal clergyman: 'He resolves with himself never to omit any present good deed of charity, in consideration of providing a stock for his children; but assures himself that mony thus lent to God is placed surer for his children's advantage than if it were given to the Chamber of London' (*Priest to the Temple*, p. 235).

[1] It was, of course, a legal obligation (under ecclesiastical law) for priests to give at least one-tenth of their income for charitable uses.

[2] See pp. 129–31 below, for example.

Such 'hospitality' constituted, with purchases for his library, the bulk of Josselin's expenses on 'leisure'. As a clergyman, he also had to expend considerable time and labour on activities which we might term 'ritual', that is to say, activity designed to promote his own and the community's supernatural welfare. All the ecclesiastical activities discussed in the previous chapter fall within this category. We may also wonder how much money and time Josselin spent, not in his public but his private capacity, on family rituals. There is no evidence in the Diary that he spent much of his resources in preserving the memory of his ancestors[1] or on sacrifices of material goods designed to please God. Fortunately for Josselin's expense sheet, Protestant reformers had long undermined the efficacy of material sacrifices, declaring that it was spiritual sacrifices that were required. One form of conspicuous consumption, however, remained, despite attempts to prune even this; expenditure on the three *rites de passage*, birth, marriage and death.

Only once did Josselin state how much he spent on a baptism; on that occasion the entertaining of godparents and friends cost him £6 13s. 4d. [14. 4. 42]. This was the baptism of the first child; if we assume that growing wealth in later years was balanced by decreasing enthusiasm for the celebration, he would have spent approximately £65 on all his 10 children. Likewise, he only mentioned wedding expenses for his first daughter's wedding: the wedding and the clothes cost him £10 [30. 8. 70]. At this rate his 4 daughters would have cost him £40; since he did not learn of his son's marriage until after it had occurred, it seems unlikely that it cost him anything. We have no idea how much it cost to bury the 5 children who predeceased him. Probably, if we take into consideration their age, the average cost cannot have worked out at over £3 each, to judge from other contemporary accounts.[2] Thus we may add another £15 to the total. It would seem, therefore, that a sum of approximately £120 went on celebrating the major *rites de passage* of his children. His wife survived him and, as we will see later, he seems to have spent practically nothing on such rituals in the case of his kin.

The foregoing discussion has covered Josselin's annual expenditure, but we need also to consider his periodic expenses incurred when purchasing capital assets, land and housing. These are a separate

---

[1] The absence of ancestor rites is discussed on p. 101.

[2] For example, an ex-fellow of Queen's College, Oxford, when he retired to a Yorkshire village, described in detail the expenses of a large funeral in 1653, at which the guests ranged from a baronet to the local villagers; the total cost was some £6 11s. 6d. (*The Diary of Thomas Crosfield*, ed. F. S. Boas (1935), p. 100). It seems safe to deduce that Josselin would not have spent over half this sum on each of his children's funerals.

category of expenses if we are considering his yearly expenditure pattern, but they need to be considered in an assessment of his total life's costs. The points at which Josselin purchased land and houses are indicated in table III below. We know, in detail, of over £750 spent on particular acquisitions; other pieces of land and some cottages, neither of which he valued, brought the value of his purchases to just over £1,000. He then built on some of the acquired land, his recorded spending on this activity being some £170. The most important of these buildings was the house on Colne Green which was paid for between 1660 and 1664, and into which Josselin moved in 1662 [27. 10. 62]. On 31 March 1661 he had 'laid out above £80 on the house on the green', and had another £50 gathered towards further building; in the year 1663–4 he spent at least another £40 on this [March 1664]. Thereafter his building activities tailed off, but it does not seem unreasonable in view of other, occasional, references to minor building expenses [e.g. 22. 3. 68], to assess his total expenditure on building at a round £200, especially if we make allowance for the cost of the labour which Josselin himself undertook to help in the building [18. 7. 61]. If we combine the purchase of land and of building materials, the total cost over his life was about £1,250.

The totals on expenditure on various items are summarized in the following table.

TABLE II. *The items of Josselin's expenditure, 1641–83*

Items of expenditure	Total cost	%
Running costs; taxes, agricultural re-investment	£900	14.7
Maintenance of adults; self, wife, servant	£1,400	23.0
Education, rearing and dowering of children	£2,000	32.8
Charity, hospitality and library	£400	6.6
Baptism, wedding and funeral of children	£120	1.9
Miscellaneous additional expenses	£30	0.5
Purchase of land and buildings	£1,250	20.5
	£6,100	100

It is likely that both income and expenditure were several hundred pounds higher than suggested in tables I and II for obviously a number of minor items have been omitted. Yet the major outlines would appear to be clear enough. A quarter of Josselin's income went on purchasing land and housing, one third on children, over a quarter on maintaining the adult members of the household. Only a small proportion went into the 'leisure and ritual' category. Until we have similar studies of other yeomen, and of other villagers at an even lower level of living, we will not know to what degree Josselin was exceptional. It will be obvious that the calculations above are extremely rough; their main purpose is to suggest some problems for future research, no doubt they will need adjustment. Josselin's Diary does show, however, how much may be learnt about the economic life of the past from diaries.

One aspect of Josselin's economic activities has been deliberately omitted from the preceding discussion; this is the subject of his debts to and from other villagers. Such loans and debts are frequently recorded in the Diary and both these types of transaction, in so far as they are noted down, are illustrated in figure 6 below.

It will be seen that at the first entry on the subject, in 1646, Josselin was in debt to the tune of some £220 at the least. This was due to a short-term loan from Richard Harlakenden. A farm had come on the market at £220 and 'Mr Harlakenden & I went up to the widdow Bentals, to view the land' [20. 7. 46]. They decided it was worth purchasing and on the 23rd Josselin noted 'Coxe Gray surrendered the land to mee, paying them in their money, which I had all of Mr Harlakenden, to whom againe I surrendered the land for his security'. Yet this was not a long-term loan of capital to launch Josselin; the mortgage was paid off within five months, and on the last day of the year Josselin was able to record that he 'went to the Pryory to Mr Harlakenden & fully dischardged my morgage & made even with him'. Presumably he must have been saving for a number of years, but only been able to gather in these savings slowly, hence the need for a short-term loan to make the actual purchase. Josselin was still in debt to other people at this early point in his career, and though the sums were not great he seems to have been anxious to pay them off.

In 1647 he was in debt to the sum of £100; the amount dropped, then rose, and was finally paid off in 1654, as illustrated in figure 6. By 1650 Josselin was himself lending out some £50 and by the end of the following year his loans of £250 far exceeded his debts. For the rest of his life he was probably, on balance, a creditor rather than a debtor. There is no evidence from the Diary that interest was paid on these transactions; the sum repaid was often stated to be exactly the same as the amount borrowed. Such a surprising absence of a rate of interest may be explained if we look at the loans as primarily a way of storing money in the absence of banks. Any surpluses that were being saved were loaned out to friends until the occasion arose for them to be used to dower a daughter or purchase land. This provided security as well as strengthening ties with other

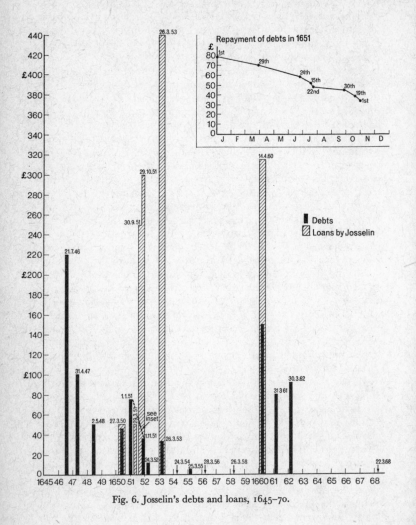

Fig. 6. Josselin's debts and loans, 1645-70.

wealthy families.[1] The symbolic and cohesive nature of these exchanges will be examined later. All we need to note here is that Josselin received, in all, something like £500 in loans from others, of which £220 was the 5-month mortgage discussed above. He himself lent out probably twice this total to other people. It is therefore obvious that borrowed capital did not play a central part in Josselin's economic 'take off'. Since loans and debts finally balanced each other out or were repaid and cannot be properly counted as income or expenditure they have not been included in the tables of Josselin's total assets and costs. Clearly Josselin disliked being in debt. He wrote in 1663, after the unusually heavy borrowing of the years 1659–60 had been largely paid off, 'Its one of the best peices of moral wisdom to our estates, to live within our bounds and so pay our debts because wee contract none' [8. 5. 63]. It is not certain, however, that he disliked making loans to others, as long as they were dependable friends.

INCREASES IN JOSSELIN'S CAPITAL ASSETS

From the preceding section it would be possible to make some rough estimates of the rate of growth of Josselin's capital assets, principally land, housing, and ready money. It would be seen that there was considerable growth in Josselin's wealth between 1650 and 1658; thereafter growth was slower and the main task was the accumulation of the money for dowries. Fortunately we can gain a more detailed picture of the way in which Josselin built up his estate from two other types of information in the Diary. Firstly, between 1651 and 1658 Josselin gave either the yearly value of his 'estate' or the increase over the previous year. Secondly, from manorial records as well as the Diary we can reconstruct his land transactions and note more or less precisely the number of acres he had at any given point in time. The former calculations include most of Josselin's capital; land, stock, money, probably debts owing to him, although he never, unfortunately, makes it very clear what *is* included. The latter reconstruction accounts only for a part of his assets, the land he owned. We may then develop this analysis to see from whom he acquired the land and in what proportions he passed it on to each of his family. Finally, we may turn to the way he ran his farm and the modifying effects of weather and prices on his daily life.

[1] Anthropologists have frequently pointed out that loans in rural communities usually have very high rates of interest, up to 100% at times, or no interest at all where they are between friends (Paul Stirling, *Turkish Village* (New York, 1965), pp. 91–2, for example, describes such a situation). Josselin's loans may have come within this second category.

Some indication of the general pattern of Josselin's accumulation of capital may be gained from figure 7 below.

The first recorded assessment he made of the total value of the estate was in 1654, when he stated 'Lands as formerly, & money as

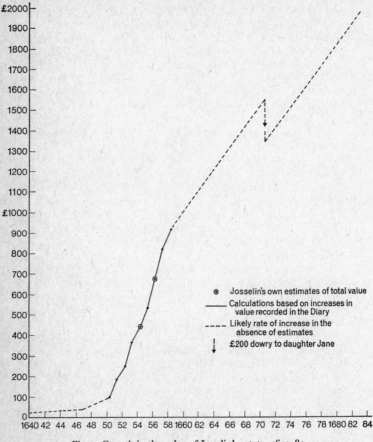

Fig. 7. Growth in the value of Josselin's estate, 1640–83.

formerly: viz... £440' [24. 3. 54]. We can work backwards from this, for in the years since 1651 he had calculated the yearly increases in the value of his total estate. The calculations are indicated in figure 7. The increases were as follows: 1653–4, £69 [24. 3. 54];

1652–3, £114 5s. 0d. [26. 3. 53]; 1651–2, £70 [24. 3. 52]; 1650–1, £88 [29. 3. 51]. In the previous section we calculated that Josselin's income at this period was about £200 p.a. It is therefore plain that he was saving between one quarter and a half of this each year. We can take the figures on from 1654 also. In 1654–5 his estate increased in value by £96 10s. 0d. [25. 3. 55], and the following year it must have increased by £133 10s. 0d. for Josselin calculated that his personal estate now amounted to £670 [28. 3. 56]. The following year he added £145 to the total value [25. 3. 57], and a year later another £100 [26. 3. 58]. By 1660 his estate was worth just over £900.

In the years after 1658 no further figures are given. A number of statements indicate that the rate of accumulation had slowed down, however. Josselin remarked 'I cannot say I either loose or gaine directly, yett my thoughts are my outward estate will this yeare appeare to better' [5. 4. 65]; 'I find no great gain, and its of mercy I doe not goe behind hand' [22. 3. 68]. For the rest of his life he mixed optimism with pessimism: 'my grounds are full stocke, and my barnes pretty full' he wrote on one occasion [12. 10. 73], but on another lamented that 'I am sensible of a blast on my corne, losse on my estate, all goeth on very heavily' [20. 1. 76]. Yet it seems likely that Josselin continued to accumulate capital after 1658, even if it was at only half the rate of the 1650s. In the absence of yearly totals, we are forced to work backwards from 1683. In that year he gave land and money worth £1,000 to his 2 daughters as dowries and bequeathed land, houses and other possessions worth at least £1,000 in his will. If we average out the growth from 1659 to 1683, taking into account the dowry of £200 paid to daughter Jane in 1670, we have the rate of growth indicated by the broken line in figure 7. Rough though it is, the whole diagram does give us some clue as to the rate at which a clergyman-farmer could save. We see what a large proportion of his income, which usually ranged between £120–£180 p.a., could be handed over to the next generation. In the 1650s he is known to have saved up to ½ his income p.a., in the following 20 years he probably saved, on average, over ⅓.

LAND ACQUISITIONS

The overall pattern of land acquisition is, not surprisingly, the same as that of capital accumulation; the period of the most rapid expansion was the 1650s. The greatest part of the relevant details concerning Josselin's property acquisitions are laid out in the table below, based on his own statements and upon the manorial records of Earls Colne and Colne Priory manors. The nature of the

TABLE III. Josselin's land acquisitions

Name of property	Number on figs. 2, 8 and 9	Date of acquisition	Previous owner	Size (acres)	Price paid	Entry fine and rent	Value (p.a.)	Inherited by
1640–9								
Vicarage—croft	40A	1641	previous vicar	c. 1½	—	rent 8d.		next vicar
—garden	40	,,		c. ¾	—	,, 4d.		
—'style'	?			(1?)	—	,, 6d.		
Mallories farm	41	1646?	Wid. Bental	c. 15	£220	£8	£14	sold, 1651
Bollinghatch	in Roxwell	1647	Uncle Ralph	?	£100	—	£7. 16s.	sold, 1673
1650–9								
Little Bridgmans	18	1650	S. Hauksby	c. 3	£36. 15s.	£2; r. 4s.	c. 50s.	John
Mordens	39?	,,	,,	c. 1½	?	?; r. 5d.	?	John
Sawyers	20	,,	,,	4	£50	£2; r. 4s.	50s.	Elizab.
Readings/10 acres	13, 14, 15		Mrs. M.? Church	c. 12	legacy	£12 r. 21s.	£18	John
Stonebridge	7	,,?	,,	c. 2	,,			Jane
Clark's + 5	21, 24, 25, 28, 29, 30, 31	1650/7*	,,	(c. 8)	,,			John
Gate's croft	23	,,	,,	(c. 2)	,,	r. 2od.		John
Spriggs Marsh	38	,,	,,	c. 1½	,,	10s.; r. 1od.	£3	Jane
Stulps	37	,,	,,	c. 1¼	,,	£1		Jane
				TOTAL 27				

Name of property	Number on figs. 2, 8 and 9	Date of acquisition	Previous owner	Size (acres)	Price paid	Entry fine and rent	Value (p.a.)	Inherited by
Brockholes	16	1657/8†	Butcher & Neville	7			?	*John*
Coes—upper	35 (27)	,,	,,	19		£3. 10s. (1683)		*Mary*
—lower	34	,,	,,	8				*Jane*
Soonihills	1, 12, 17	,,	,,	11	£320	£17		*John*
Tredgolds	22	,,	,,	c. 3				*Jane*
Hobstevens and	3, 4, 5	,,	,,	18		} r. £2. 5s. 9d.		*John*
Pitchards	19	,,	,,	20				*John*
1660–9								
Wife inherits land			Uncle Shepherd				....sold for £57, 1663	*Mary*
Colne green, waste	36B	1661	waste	⅛	grant	r. 1d.		*Elizab.*
Doddingpole Hoe	10, 11	1662	J. Allen	1½	£28	30s.; r. 1s.	30s.	*Elizab.*
Gillot's Cottage	21A	1664	T. Wade	¼	£20	30s.; r. 2s.	30s.	
Britton's (Burton)	32	1669	J. Burton	¼	£16	£1; r. 10d.	20s.	*Rebecka*
1670–9								
Inhams (Rainhams)	33	1678	J. Fletcher	} 8	?	£3	} £7	John
Stoneleys	33B	,,	,,		?	£7		John
Loveland	12	,,	,,	10	?	£7	£7	John
Stacys/Watchmans	36C?	1679	R. Carter	(c. 5)	?	?	£5	*Mary*

SOURCES (*apart from Josselin's Diary*): E.R.O., D/DPr/42, 100, 113, 619; D/DSm/P2.

NOTES

1. Lands leased by Josselin as schoolmaster are not included in the table.
2. In the last column, 'Jane' always refers to Josselin's wife, not daughter; persons with italicized names inherited at Josselin's death—otherwise, at purchase.
3. Parentheses ( ) indicate my estimate.
4. r. indicates the rental of 1671 (D/DPr/113).
5. * indicates a legacy which Josselin leased at £18 p.a. from 1650 and obtained in 1657.
6. † indicates a purchase, ⅔ of which came to Josselin in 1657; the rest in 1658.

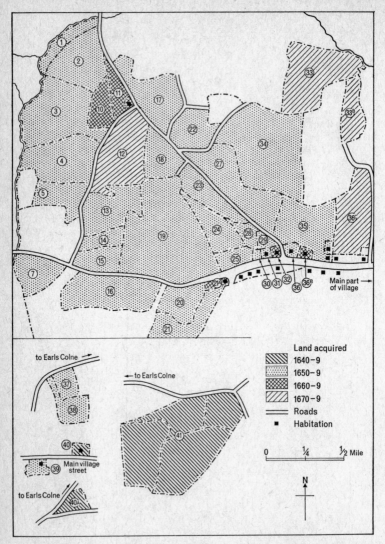

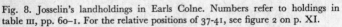

Fig. 8. Josselin's landholdings in Earls Colne. Numbers refer to holdings in table III, pp. 60–1. For the relative positions of 37–41, see figure 2 on p. XI.

acquisitions is best illustrated by a map (see fig. 8), to be used in conjunction with the table.

In the period 1640–9, apart from the vicarage lands, Josselin's acquisitions were Mallories farm, which he bought for £220, and 'Bollinghatch', a farm in the village of Roxwell, which he inherited from his father's brother on payment of £100.[1]

This modest estate was considerably augmented in the 1650s. Josselin bought three small properties in 1650 and, on the death of his friend, the unmarried Mary Church, inherited her land. Half of this came to him straightaway, the other half when Mary's mother, Rose Church, died in 1657 [25. 3. 57]. Previously he had leased the land which was due to come to him for £18 p.a. from Rose Church.[2] In 1657 he added to this property by making a purchase of various lands for £310, ⅔ of which he received in 1657, the rest in 1658. This more than compensated for his earlier sale of Mallories farm which, we can see, lay too far from his other lands. It is clear that when Josselin found that he was going to inherit land from Mary Church at Earls Colne Green, he decided to sell off his land elsewhere in the parish and to consolidate his holdings in this area. In the 1660s he bought two cottages and a little land, but, his main effort went into building himself a new house. In the 1670s the family land at Roxwell—Bollinghatch—was sold off for £123, but again this was more than recompensed by further purchases in Earls Colne.

We are now in a position to see how Josselin acquired his land. The largest proportion came from direct purchases. We have earlier calculated that Josselin spent just over £1,000 on such purchases. He had several advantages in competing for land. Not only did he have the friendship of the lord of both manors, Richard Harlakenden, but also Josselin's 'cousin' John Josselin, married to Harlakenden's niece, was steward of the two manors. We know for certain that he gave Josselin advice and aid.[3] It is not surprising that such patronage led to bitterness on the part of other families.[4] Another advantage was his position as vicar which may have enabled Josselin to befriend

[1] The chancery case concerning the legal dispute over the Bollinghatch property is printed on p. 219 below. The location of Roxwell in relation to Earls Colne (about 20 miles apart) is shown on figure 1.

[2] There is an abstract of Mary Church's will on p. 216 below. Josselin's tender feelings towards her and sadness at her death are described on p. 172 below.

[3] Josselin's relationship to 'cousin John' is discussed on p. 138 below.

[4] Josselin described how he 'was taxed for lording & domineering & doing R[obert] A[bbott] the greatest wrong that ever any did him'; this is probably, as the transcriber of the Diary (E.R.O., T/B/9/1) put it 'the first grumble about his [i.e. Josselin's] using his friendship with the Squire and the steward to get hold of Copyhold tenures that fell in'.

the rich spinster Mary Church. The total property he inherited from
her was valued at £21 p.a. If we compare this to the annual value of
Mallories and Bollinghatch farms, it would seem that this legacy
was worth at least £300 to Josselin. This was an especially important
acquisition since it occurred early in his career when he needed
capital. With the schoolmaster's fees it gave him the boost which
enlarged his capital assets so much in the 1650s. Lands inherited
through ties of kinship seem to have been of no great importance,
financially at least. Bollinghatch, which Josselin had inherited from
his uncle after such a struggle, still cost him £100 and he sold it for
only £123 20 years later. His wife brought some land to him as her
dowry it would seem, for Josselin referred to his 'wives land'
[30. 4. 47]. It is unlikely that this was worth more than £50 in all,
the sum left to his wife's sister.[1] She also inherited some land in 1661
which was sold within two years for £57 10s. [29. 3. 63]. At the very
most, Josselin had freely inherited land worth only some £150 from
his kin. His own children, profiting from his energy and planning,
were more fortunate.

THE TRANSMISSION OF JOSSELIN'S WEALTH

The survival of Josselin's Diary enables us to check the accuracy of
the impression we receive of Josselin's transmission of property from
his will and from manorial records. If we use the will alone as the
basis of calculations, we gain the following picture. As illustrated in
column 4 of table IV below, the bulk of the property was divided
between daughter Mary, son John and wife Jane. Daughter
Elizabeth was to inherit a little land after the death of her mother.
Daughter Jane was left a mere £40 out of which she had to pay £2
p.a. to her mother until her mother's death in 1693. Rebecka was
only given 10s. with which to buy a ring in remembrance of her
father. The table clearly shows the omission from the will not only
of the considerable sums of money spent on Mary, Thomas and
Anne who had predeceased their father, but also the £500 which,
only a few months before the making of the will, had gone as a dowry
to Rebecka. Nor would we have known of Jane's dowry or the lands
and cottages bought in the children's names and passed on to them
before the making of the will, as indicated in column 2 of the table.
The table indicates the distortions created by using a will as the
only source for the study of inheritance patterns. The actual transmission of wealth to the next generation was a much more gradual
process than the will makes it appear; the division between the

[1] By the will printed on p. 214 below.

TABLE IV. *The transmission of Josselin's wealth*

Name	(1) Upbringing & education	(2) land/houses settled on before will was made	(3) marriage portion	(4) legacies in will
Wife				
Jane	£245 (cost of living, very approximate)	—	—	various lands worth c. £10 p.a.; stock, plate, etc.
Children				
Mary	£46	died when a child		
Thomas	£250	died before his father		
Jane	£120	(£100 from will of Mrs Church)		
Ralph (2)	£5	died when a child		
John	£200		£200	£40 (£20 paid to mother)
Anne	£114	died before her father		
Mary	£120	Stacys/Watchmans		land worth c. £50 p.a.
Elizabeth	£120	Sawyers, Gillott's, Doddingpole Hoe	as in will: (c. £20?)	£100 & land worth £400 ring (10s.); land on mo's death
Rebecka	£120	Briton's tenement	£500	ring (10s.)

NOTE

Often land would be settled on a child who subsequently died; this would then be transmitted to another child (for example 'Sawyers' which Elizabeth inherited had passed to the first Mary, then to Thomas, then, when they had both died, to Elizabeth. In both this and table III, only the name of the person who held the land at Josselin's death is given. Likewise, in table III, 'Inhams, Stoneleys, Loveland' were purchased in wife Jane's name, though they were left, in fact, to son John.

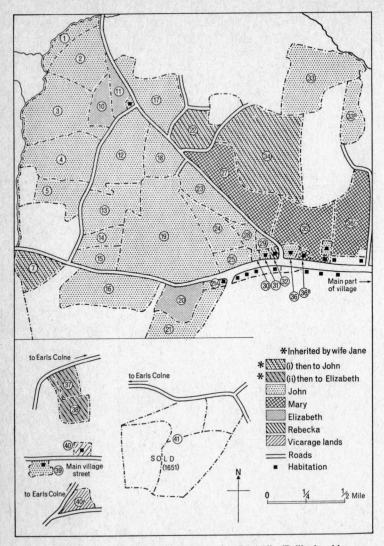

Fig. 9. The disposal of Josselin's lands. His land in Roxwell—'Bollinghatch'—was sold in 1673.

children was also much more even. The way in which the estate was actually distributed is illustrated in figure 9.

John finally acquired most of the land, but Josselin was clearly not averse to hiving off parts of the estate for the other children; particularly if, like Stulps and Spriggs Marsh (nos. 37, 38) they were at a distance from the main part of the land. He seems to have tried to leave at least one dwelling-place to each of his children, John would clearly have received a larger proportion of the total estate if he had not been such a nuisance to his father, activity which led him to be disowned at least once.[1]

[1] John's strained relations with his father are outlined on pp. 120–4 below.

4

Josselin's economic activities (ii): farming, weather and prices

Josselin leased out the larger part of his land. This was the case from the beginning. The day after he had received Mallories farm, valued at £14 p.a. at the manorial court, he let it 'for 3 yeares to Brewer old Spooners sonne in lawe, without wood to dischardge Lords rent, tith, and pay mee £12 5s. per annum: I am to get it in repayre and he is to keepe the same' [24. 7. 46]. He also let out the school lands, from which he drew the profits as schoolmaster in the 1650s [e.g. 11. 7. 50]. Josselin's descriptions of leases are not, unfortunately, complete, and we cannot be certain as to what proportion of his lands were in fact leased out. The fullest statement of the arrangements occurs in 1660. He had, in 1656, let out his farm 'for one yeare at £50' [24. 9. 56], and probably continued to do so during the following years. On 3 February 1660,

Tibbald and I had discourse about the farme for 6 or 9 yeares. He is to have Crows, Sawyers, Bridgmans, 2 sonnels, Hobstevens & the meadow: only I am to have the pightell [i.e. small meadow] by Mr Littels, & 2 acres in Hobstevens, and passage; the rent £60 per annum, about £3 lords rent, pay tithes, ditch 30 rod every yeare, allow 2 load logs, 1 of small wood.

Fortunately for us, Josselin had laid out the value of each part of his estate less than a year previously, from this and the above account we can estimate the amount he retained to farm himself.

The total annual value of his land, the year before he made the above agreement with Tibbald, was £84 14s. 0d. [5. 4. 59]. This had included land worth £47 already let to Tibbald and 'John Crows' worth £21 8s. 0d. 'Crows', we can see above, was in 1660 also let to 'Tibbald'; the total value of £68 8s. 0d. was reduced by £8 8s. 0d., presumably because Tibbald was going to pay tithe and lord's rent. This leaves land worth some £16 6s. 0d. unaccounted for. If we subtract the £7 16s. 0d. p.a. land in Roxwell which Josselin must have leased out since it was too far away for him to work himself, and add on the vicarage land worth about £4 p.a., which was omitted in the 1659 accounts, it would appear that Josselin was himself farming, at the most, land worth £12 10s. p.a., perhaps less.

This would represent between 12 and 20 acres of land. He may have extended his operations in 1665 for his tenant died and the farm was 'turned into my hands' [23. 7. 65]; there are no further references to leasing, but it seems highly probable that he did so. The deteriorating standard of Josselin's accounts at this time probably explains the omission. When we come to consider Josselin's farming activities it is probably safe to assume that he himself was working land of between 10 and 20 acres. His descriptions of the extent of land he ploughed and sowed confirm this view; for example he described sowing an area of about 11 acres in 1675: it took him 9 days [25. 9. 75].

Josselin practised a mixed economy on his land, although the emphasis was heavily on arable crops. It is possible to calculate fairly accurately the number of animals he kept over the years. In 1644 he bought two pigs for 9s.; these were 'the first beasts that ever I bought in all my dayes hitherto' he wrote [29. 10. 44]. They were presumably kept on the vicarage lands. In 1650 he bought Smith's cow for £6 10s., and the following day he began to milk it. Two days later he fetched another cow from Halstead, the neighbouring town. This cost £6 5s. and was less docile than the previous one: Josselin 'had great trouble in the cowes unquietnes' [24–7. 6. 50]. Yet the following spring he bought 2 more cows with their calves from the same man, to whom he also, incidentally, sold his farm 'Mallories' in this year. These further purchases cost £10 15s. [5. 3. 51]. A couple of weeks later one of his other cows, 'Brownebacke', calved; it was 'the first of creatures that brought us young' [18. 3. 51]. On the 29th of the month he estimated his total stock to be worth £32; this was made up of '5 cowes at £5 round [i.e. average each], my nagge, £3, my hogges and hay £4'.

From this 1651 assessment we can work out that throughout the 1650s Josselin's livestock varied in value from £32 in 1652, when he had pigs and a horse to twice that value (though we do not know what animals composed that sum) in 1658. His March assessments give the value of his 'stock' as follows: 1652—£32; 1653—£32; 1654—'as before'; 1655—£20; 1656—£10; 1657—no estimate; 1658—£68; 1659—no estimate; 1660—£25; 1661—£35. He seems to have expanded his livestock sector in the 1660s, for, although he does not give us exact estimates, he usually made a note each year that 'my stocke is fuller than it was last yeare'. It seems that he now began to fatten cattle for resale; he spoke of this in 1666 [18. 10. 66] and described, for example, how he bought 13 young 'steers' at Haverhill fair in 1668 [17. 6. 68]. These he later referred to as his 'Haverhill steers' [4. 9. 74]. In 1661 he described how he 'found a lambe in my field, our first this yeare' [31. 12. 61] so that we know that from that date, at least, he was keeping a few sheep. We do not know how many he kept. In 1674 he 'found my lost sheep with 2 lambs, 3 sheep lambd well this morning' [10. 2. 74]. But it was certainly an important enough item of income for him to include in his charity budget 'the 20th part of all my sheep and wool that I sell and lambs of my own breeding' [19. 7. 74].

Another minor source of profit was his orchard. This seems to have consisted mainly of apple and pear trees, although we know that he also grew apricots, gooseberries and mulligatawny.[1] Josselin planted '12 pears and 24 apples in the orchard' in 1659 [10. 10. 59] and grafted 'neare upon 70 heads of pears and apples' 5 years later [19. 3. 64]. Yet, as the Diary with its anxious accounts of each harvest amply displays, it was the hay and, above all, the corn crops which provided the bulk of Josselin's income. Josselin's fields were mainly used for arable farming.[2] The fact that a number of different crops were grown is well illustrated in the descriptions of ploughing and sowing. When the ploughing and sowing of winter grain was under way in September and October, Josselin himself seems to have undertaken them. For example he described how 'being Munday I plowed my selfe Sprigs marsh' [17. 9. 63], and frequently gave accounts of ploughing and sowing in the first person singular. Even when he was aged over 64 he was still trying to wield a plough: 'wett; flouds this weeke; I could not stirre a plow' [7. 5. 82]. He sowed wheat, rye, oats and 'mislain', a mixture of wheat and rye; for example, he sowed about '7 acres wheat' in 1670 [8. 10. 70] and sowed rye in 'Hobstevens' in 1675 [10. 9. 74]. Unfortunately, there is not quite enough evidence to enable us to build up a picture of the proportion of his land which he devoted to each of these grains. He seems to have bought some of the seed for sowing; for example the 3 bushels of white wheat he sowed in 1664 at 'Hobstevens gate' he 'bought of Niccols' for 10s. [12. 10. 64]. It is difficult to estimate how much labour he expended on weeding the growing crops. His one remark on the subject was 'wett, growing weather, god keepe down weeds' [26. 5. 78].

Then came the harvesting. The Diary is full of references to the weather and progress of the harvest; it was clearly one of the most important events in Josselin's year and occupies as much, if not more, space than all his religious meditations. In 1650 he harvested

---

[1] These fruits are mentioned in Josselin's descriptions of the weather, quoted below. 'Mulligatawny' is an ingredient of mulligatawny soup, 'An East Indian highly seasoned soup'—*Oxford English Dictionary*.

[2] In the tithe award of 1838 (E.R.O., D/CT/101A) the fields which had previously belonged to Josselin (Colne Green Farm) were all described as arable.

about 2¼ tons of 'very good hay' [9. 7. 50]. The yield per acre in a
good year is indicated when he gathered in a ton of hay from Sprigs
Marsh, a field of 1¼ acres, in 1659 [28. 6. 59].[1] If he managed to sell
this hay at the 2s. per quarter he had obtained from Mr. Harlakenden
some years earlier [8. 3. 52], he would have made £8 on this piece
of land. His hay harvest was usually ended by mid-July, and then
came the cereals. He gives only one estimate of his total harvest of
oats, rye, wheat and maslin; in 1678 he gathered '206 jags [i.e. 'a
small load'[2]] of one corne & other' [29. 8. 78]. Unfortunately it is
impossible from this to work out, as we can do from Robert Loder's
accounts, the return on seed planted.[3]

THE WEATHER AND CROPS

Josselin's interest in the weather is reflected on almost every page of
his Diary; there are dozens of entries describing the amount of rain,
the degree of warmth, and the excesses of wind. His interest was a
double one. As a farmer he worried about his crops, especially at
harvest-time. As a clergyman, he seems to have used the weather
as a gauge of God's attitude towards him and his countrymen. The
clouds were both symbols and portents. This latter aspect of his
weather observations will be discussed later. Here we will restrict
ourselves to the physical characteristics of an element which had
such a profound influence on his life. The weather affected Josselin's
food supply, the amount he was able to save and to spend on his
children, the amount he was forced to spend on fuel. It is difficult
for us to conceive of the huge importance of this factor in Josselin's
daily life, except when we remember that he spent much of his time
out-of-doors. Even when he was inside, poor heating and sanitation
would exacerbate the effects of damp and cold. Every frost would
mean a great deal to the diarist and we are not surprised to find that
he rejoiced when the sun shone. The two months whose weather he
most frequently described were February and September, the former

[1] The edited version of the Diary wrongly puts this as 20 tons of hay; it is clearly
20 cwt., or 1 ton. It is possible that Josselin included his adjacent field of 'Stulps'
when he spoke of 'Sprigs Marsh'; in that case the yield per acre would be
halved since Stulps was also 1¼ acres in size.

[2] The most precise definition of a 'jag' comes from west Essex in the nineteenth
century, though we cannot be sure it applies two centuries earlier: 'A jag of
wood, hay, straw, manure, &c., is intended to mean a little less than a one-
horse cartload' (quoted in Joseph Wright (ed.), *The English Dialect Dictionary*
(6 vols, Oxford, 1923), vol. III, p. 343).

[3] *Loder's Farm Accounts*, ed. Fussell, p. xvii. W. G. Hoskins, 'Harvest Fluctuations
and English Economic History, 1620–1759', *Agric. Hist. Rev.*, vol. 16, part 1
(1968), pp. 25–7, discusses this crop to seed ratio and summarizes much of the
evidence.

because it was the coldest, the latter because it was frequently wet and the harvest was threatened. The last mentioned were December, when relatively little of agricultural importance was happening, and June to July, before the harvest really began.

The three coldest winters, to judge from the Diary, were those of 1645–6; 1659–60 and 1662–3. Josselin gave the following description of conditions during them.

Decemb. 8. at night, on Monday, new moone, it began to frize, and so continued exceeding violent; the ice of wonderfull thicknes, after a months time it thawed, a little, and raynd, but continued to frize untill Jan: 28: it begun to thawe, & raynd; the frost wonderfully in the ground, and the ice of wonderfull thicknes; nigh half a yard in some places; a quarter of an ell [an ell = 45 inches] at least in my pond: by reason of thawes it was wonderfull glancy: the thawe as earnest as the frost: admirable in its kind; the frost & ice was sooner out of the ground then [sic] expected [10. 1. 46] . . . The season very vehement cold; this hard weather hath continued from Novemb: 11 till now [15. 1. 60] . . . This winter was the hardest I ever remembered: very wett And cold in Octob. Novemb. on the 24 day whereof it began to frize & so continued frost & snow very hard, until Feb. 18th. it began to thaw much, but the frost scarce full out of the earth. And this 23 Feb. a little frost again: 27 to this day frost; so 28; March 1, snow lying in my guttar; hence goodly weather. [1. 3. 63]

These bitter years were balanced by one outstandingly warm winter during Josselin's time at Earls Colne (though he could remember another in about 1638), that of 1674–5. This he described lyrically:

Warme, dry, calme Christmas, grasse springing, herbes budding, birds singing, plowes going; a little rain only in two dayes, viz. Dec. 29, 30: fogge Jan. 5, 6, no mention of frost, though some dayes cleare sun shining, moon & starrs appearing by night: most persons said never such a Christmas known in the memory of man; yet I suppose 37 years before the like & one said 46 or 47 was such an one. [3. 1. 75]

Another early spring, though this time there was frost, is recorded for 1645:

grounds so hard they could scarce be plowed. No old man could ever remember the like . . . violets were commonly blowne, rose bushes fully leaved, apricockes & my malegotoone [1] fully blossomed out. [February 1645]

Yet an early spring was not necessarily a blessing and an early experience should have taught Josselin to be cautious. In January 1648 he had described how,

[1] 'Malegotoone' = mulligatawny; see note 1, p. 70 above.

This month of January passed without any frost to mention, or much wett, but was dry, and open, and warme, and free from winde even to the admiracon of persons; roses leaved out; fruite trees beginning to shoote out and so appricockes more, hedges budding out, gooseberries had litle leaves on them. [January 1648]

But a late frost led to disaster:

Among all the severall judgments on this nacon, God this spring, in the latter end of April, when rye was earing & eared, sent such terrible frosts, that the eare was frozen & so dyed, and cometh unto nothing: young ashes also that leaved were nipt, and blackt, and those shootes died. [9. 5. 48]

Another disaster was the freak high wind in February 1662. Josselin gave an extremely lively account of this:

In the night it raind, the wind rose and was 18, violent beyond measure, overturning a windmill at Colchester, wherin a youth kild, divers barnes, stables, outhouses, trees, rending divers dwellings; few escapd, my losse much, but not like some others; God sanctifie all to us; throwing down stackes of chimneys, part of houses; the Lady Saltonstall kild in her bed, her house falling. Whitehall twice on fire that day, some orchards almost ruind. 27th, Trees blown down within priory wall. Timber trees rent up in high standing woods; the winde was generall in England & Holland sea coast, but not in Scotland. [17. 2. 62]

The place where the priory wall had to be re-built can still be seen to this day.

Although Josselin spoke of 'drought' on a few occasions, for instance in 1665, 1668, 1669, 1675,[1] and even, on one occasion, prayed for rain [20. 4. 45], it was floods that really worried him. The effect of too much rain on his farm is graphically described in the Diary. The connexion between high food prices and a wet summer and harvest-time was only too obvious to Josselin. Excessive rain also made other activities difficult, particularly transport and travel on the mud roads; thus he noted, 'After hopes of a dry Sturbridge faire it rained very much, so that the wayes were exceeding heavy and dirtie' [9. 9. 57]. The wettest years were undoubtedly those between 1646 and 1648.[2] The account of these disastrous years is especially detailed in the Diary for 1646–8:

A merveylous wett season, winter coming on very early; a great hop yeare: wheat this yeare was exceedingly smitten & dwindled & lanke,

[1] Precise dates are 14.5.65; 22.3.68; 12.9.69; 17.10.75.

[2] It is therefore not surprising to find that the years 1647–8 were among the worst for wheat harvests in the seventeenth century; other bad harvests during Josselin's residence at Earls Colne occurred in 1661, 1673, 1678 (Hoskins, 'Harvest Fluctuations', p. 16, figure 2).

especially on strong grounds; all manner of meates excessive deare [15. 9. 46] ... This weeke the weather continued very wett and sad in respect of the season, litle rye & mislen or wheat sowne [11. 10. 46] ... A wonderfull sad wett season, much corne in many places abroad, rotted & spoyled in the fields, grass exceedingly trodden under foote & spoyled by cattle through the wett which hath continued almost since the Assizes; worke very dead, woolle risen to 16d in the pound & upwards, butter and cheese, and meate very deare, and corne rising: litle corne sowne, and a very sad season still continued [24. 10. 46] ... This weeke the wettnes of the season continued with litle or no intermission & so it hath continued for above two months [2. 11. 46] ... The sad wett season still continued. [25. 11. 46]

The description for June to September 1648 is even more detailed:

The Lord goeth out against us in the season, which was wonderfull wett; flouds every weeke, hay rotted abroad, much was carried away with the flouds, much inned but very dirty, and dangerous for catle; corne layd, pulled downe with weeds; wee never had the like in my memory, and that for the greatest part of the summer; it continued to August: 14: when it rained that it made a little floud, and commonly wee had 1 or 2 flouds weekely, or indeed in the meadowes their was as it were a continuall floud [28. 6. 48] ... A very great floud with the great rains last day & night: the season sad, and threatning ... the nacons judgments are, 1: continual raine to the spoyling of much grasse, and threatning of the harvest [16. 8. 48] ... Dayly raines, but especially this morning, wee found it exceeding wett; it caused a very great floud, aboundance of hay rotten, much corne cutt and not cutt groweth, and yet men repent not [24. 8. 48] ... a wett night, and wettish day, as if God would have called men to his worship [30. 8. 48] ... A fayre day. Septemb. 1, it was very wett and hindred men in their harvesting [31. 8. 48] ... This weeke die 20.22, was very wett, the seaon very sad both in reference to corne and unto fallowes, very few lands being fitt to bee sowne upon; some say that divers catle that feed in the meadowes dye, their bowells being eaten out with gravel & durt. [20. 9. 48]

These descriptions have been given in full since it is seldom that we receive from seventeenth-century sources such a telling account of the physical conditions of life. The background of rotting crops and flooded fields was clearly of immense importance. The other references to floods and wet weather are much shorter. They suggest, if there is no particular bias in the record, that the late 1660s and 1670s were periods of reasonable harvests.[1] The Diary also contains a

[1] For those particularly interested in the weather references, instances of further wet weather will be found under the following dates in the printed version of the Diary: 22.9.50; 25.9.58; 23.4.61; 15.7.62; 12.7.63; 7.5.82.

number of other short references to the weather, varying from 'This day was very warme & comfortable' to 'sweet showers, and dewing weather through mercy'.[1] They indicate the more normal variations from season to season and year to year in between the peaks earlier illustrated.

PRICES

Only when prices were very high, up to twice their normal level, did Josselin record them in any detail. More than half of all his references occur during the year 1649 when the bad weather described in the previous section had its most disastrous effect. The full quotation of the 1649 descriptions illustrates not only the fluctuations in prices from month to month, but also the basic items in Josselin's budget at the time: beef, wheat, malt for beer, butter and cheese. It is perhaps no coincidence that from the following year onwards, as we have seen, he avoided buying nearly all these articles by acquiring several cows. His descriptions are as follows:[2]

beefe at 3½d. per p[oun]d, wheate 7s. 6d. rye 6s. 4d. cheese 4d. butter 6½d. per pound, and men expect it will bee dearer and dearer [7. 1. 49] ... Great dearth and want of all things, I gave 4d. per pound for porke [18. 2. 49] ... Cheese now at 4¾d. per pound, butter sold by some at 8d: porke 4¼d. or 4½d., beefe 3¾d. great feare of the decay of trade [18. 3. 49] ... their [sic] is a great scarcitie of all things, beefe ordinarily 4d. per lb: butter 7 or 8d. cheese 5d., wheate 7s. 6d. rye 6s. 8d. yett we wanted nothing needfull or fitting for us [15. 4. 49] ... the great scarcity of all things, rye at 6s. 8d bushel, butter at 7d pound, cheese 6d, beefe 5d, lambe 7d [20. 5. 49] ... This day I paid for beefe about 4¾d. a pound, and 5d. the pound for mutton, but beefe was commonly 5d. the pound: 9s. and 10s. the score, the best in the markets [25. 5. 49] ... I gave 8s. 2d. for a score of indifferent beefe [3. 6. 49] ... A weeke of harvest, corne abated in price a litle [19. 8. 49] ... This weeke all things very deare, wheate. 8s. 6d. rye 6s. barley 5s. a bushel, cheese 4½d. butter 7½d. the pound [7. 10. 49] ... This time all things were wonderfull deare, wheate 9s. malte 4s. 8d, rye 7s. 6d, oatemeale 8s, per bushel, and cheese 4½d; all things deare. [1–16. 12. 49]

[1] These further references to the weather are made under the following dates: 1647—23.5, 26.9; 1651—1.3, 2.3; 21.5.54; 18.2.55; 14.8.56; 20.11.59; 12.11.62; 1665—12.2, 2.7, 6.8, 22.10, 26.11, 9.12; 1666 *passim*; 26.3.71; 7.2.75; 1679— 9.2, 10.6, 14.12, 28.12; 8.2.80; 27.11.81; 25.2.83.

[2] The highest London bread prices during Josselin's incumbency were in 1647, 1649 and 1661. During 1646–50, we are told, 'food-prices rocketed by nearly 50 percent in five years' (Hoskins, 'Harvest Fluctuations', pp. 20–1). Josselin, seems to have paid less attention to the dearth of 1661 than to the 1649 shortage, although in some ways it was even more serious.

High prices had commenced in the autumn of 1646, with the heavy rains of that summer. To judge from Josselin's slackening interest in the subject, they had dropped back almost to their normal level by the end of 1650. There were again high prices in the 1660s, wheat was 8s. 6d. per bushel in 1661, for instance [17. 11. 61]. Yet there was never again a crisis as bad as that of the late 1640s and even in the worst period Josselin and his family do not seem to have gone hungry, unlike the poor who crowded the streets of Earls Colne. Thus in the worst year, 1649, he could write 'This weeke the Lord good and mercifull to me and mine in our health, peace, in providing for us, notwithstanding the great dearnes of every thing' [7. 1. 49]; later in the year he made the same statement, word for word [20. 5. 49], and in April wrote that 'we wanted nothing needfull or fitting for us' [15. 4. 49]. Although changes in prices would have a particularly marked effect on Josselin's farming activities, he did not consider them worth mentioning, except very occasionally, in years other than 1648 and 1649.

JOSSELIN COMPARED TO OTHER CLERGY AND YEOMEN

We may now compare Josselin's economic position with that of other clergy and yeomen, and with the other inhabitants of Earls Colne. Comparison with other clerics is the most difficult largely because, as we have seen so clearly in Josselin's case, a clergyman's actual income might be very much greater than that given in contemporary ecclesiastical surveys. The parliamentary surveyors assessed Earls Colne as worth £28 p.a., including glebe, in 1650. On this rating it was one of the poorest livings in Essex. Only 28 out of a total of 350 Essex livings assessed at that date were valued at less than £29. Nearly 70% of the rectories were worth £70 and over.[1] But we know that Josselin was, in fact, promised some £80 p.a. and drew that sum after 1659, having received some £60 p.a. until that year. Since we did not know to what extent other livings in fact exceeded the official assessment, or whether many other Essex clergy were active farmers,[2] it is impossible to be sure of Josselin's relative wealth. Nor do we yet know how many other clergy supplemented their income by becoming village schoolmasters; as Josselin's short tenure of the post showed, this could be an extremely lucrative office.

[1] The 1650 survey of Essex is analysed in Christopher Hill, *Economic Problems of the Church* (Oxford, 1963), p. 113.

[2] Hoskins, 'The Leicestershire Country Parson in the Sixteenth Century', in *Essays in Leicestershire History*, has shown the widespread farming activities of Leicestershire clergy and it seems likely that their Essex counterparts would have behaved similarly; he concludes that 'most parsons were farmers in their spare time' (p. 6).

Combined with the profits of his farming it meant that, as he him-self stated, only about half of his total income had come from his ecclesiastical living.

Another possible method of discovering Josselin's economic position compared with that of his clerical neighbours is to use the hearth tax assessments. In the assessment for 1662 Josselin was assessed at eleven hearths: this was a much larger number than other ministers nearby, who usually possessed between three and eight apiece. Yet there are clearly difficulties in using such an estimate as an index of actual wealth since we do not know how many of the clergy were living in the vicarage or rectory, how many in their own private houses. Although the latter would appear poorer, they might well be better off than a minister who had in-herited with his job a house far too big for himself and his family. That Josselin was in this position seems implied when he moved from the eleven-hearth house to a house of his own construction with six hearths [20. 10. 62]. If we judged solely from the number of hearths in his house, he seemed to have got poorer; in fact he was able to live more comfortably, more cheaply and in his own property. After his move he was more or less at an equal level with the neighbouring clerics at Wivenhoe, Colne Engaine and Stanway.[1]

Even if we include his non-farming income, Josselin was by no means an exceptionally wealthy yeoman, at least by the standards of the counties near London. He was less prosperous, for example, than Robert Loder, a Berkshire yeoman whose account book for the years 1610–20 show that his total income and expenditure, even at the age of 23, was higher than Josselin's. Loder's total income in 1612 was £382 10s. 0d., his expenses £120 14s. 4d. A detailed com-parison of the accounts of Josselin and Loder suggests some interest-ing differences; for instance, we note that there were, as yet, no children in Loder's case and hence a large item in Josselin's expenses was missing.[2] One writer in 1669 stated that £40 or £50 p.a. was a 'very ordinary' income for a yeoman, and £100 and £200 'not rare', while in Kent there were some worth £1,000 or £1,500 p.a.[3] By these standards Josselin, at his peak, with his total income at about £200 p.a., would be a very prosperous, but by no means exceptional, yeoman.

[1] The Hearth Taxes are at the E.R.O. Q/RTh/1 (1662) and 5 (1671).
[2] *Loder's Farm Accounts* ed. Fussell, p. xxvi, summarizes details of the yearly income and expenditure.
[3] This was Robert Chamberlayne's estimate, quoted in M. Campbell, *The English Yeoman* (New Haven, 1942), p. 217. Other remarks about the wealth of yeomen are discussed on the same page of Campbell.

In his own village of Earls Colne he seems to have come just below the leaders in wealth. Taking the later hearth tax assessment of 6 hearths as representative of his position, we find that he was among the top dozen families in a village which, according to the 1671 Hearth Tax, contained some 239 houses. At the Priory, Richard Harlakenden was the richest man in the village with 20 hearths, and his son had 8 according to the 1662 assessment. Then came George Cressner, gentleman, with 11 hearths. Next came Henry Abbott, senior, with 7 hearths in the 1671 list, followed by Josselin and half a dozen other families with 6 each. Most of the houses in the village—for instance, that in which Josselin's future son-in-law Jonathan Woodthorpe lived with 3—had between 1 and 3 hearths. On his clerical fees alone, Josselin would have found it hard to keep up with the leaders; with his additional income he was among the most prosperous, and counted the heads of most wealthy families in the village as his especial friends—the Harlakendens, Cressners and Ellistons.[1]

The final chapters of this study will deal with the way in which his attitudes shaped and were shaped by Josselin's economic activities. We will then see how he dreamt about his farm work and the way in which he connected his attitude to his crops and towards God and his neighbours. His basic economic philosophy is seldom stated as clearly as on the occasion when he was entrusted to pay the estate debts of his neighbour Mr Edward Elliston. He meditated that

Its one of the best peices of moral wisdom to our estates, to live within our bounds and so pay our debts because wee contract none; he that once overshoots on hope of a good crop, to repay and cleare, in my mind runs into the dirt to better his shoes by thougts of wiping them. If god raise my expense at one time beyond my income, I will shorten it, if I can, to come even. [8. 5. 63]

We have seen that Josselin generally lived within his means, seldom got into debt, and budgeted carefully. A large proportion of his profits he ploughed back into land or into raising his children. His whole Diary is an example of the hard-working, endlessly accumulating and re-investing type whose features have been so widely analysed in recent discussions of the 'protestant ethic'.[2] How such a man conducted his domestic and social life it will be the task of the following chapters to analyse.

[1] Josselin's friendships with these and other families are discussed on p. 151 below.
[2] For instance, in the works by Christopher Hill, Riesman, Tawney and Walzer listed in the bibliography.

PART II

The Life-cycle

5

Birth and childhood

Recognizing that domestic life centres around the three basic facts of birth, marriage, and death, social anthropologists have often used this three-fold division of the 'life-cycle' as one method of presenting their material.[1] Although historians appear to have been limited by their interests, as much as by their material, from following this lead,[2] it would appear to be a presentation ideally suited to the biographical-type analysis of Ralph Josselin's domestic life. Commencing with his own marriage and the general size and spacing of his subsequent family, we will then proceed to examine childbirth and child-rearing until the children left home in their early teens. In the following chapter we will examine the preparations for marriage, the marriage ceremony, and the decline towards old age and death. All this will be seen through one pair of eyes and will, therefore, be necessarily patchy and often superficial. But it is hoped that it will suggest a number of problems which may find fuller answers in other sources for the period.

Ralph Josselin married on 28 October 1640. He was 20 years and 9 months old, his bride Jane Constable was 19 years and 11 months. Their union produced 10 live-born children in 21 years, 5 of whom predeceased their parents, although only 1 died under a year old.[3] The essential features of the parents' and children's lives are indicated in table v below.

The first sentence of the Diary shows that children were eagerly welcomed by their parents. 'I was borne to the great joy of Father & mother being much desired as being their third child and, as it pleased God, their only sonne' [1616]. Josselin wrote with a confidence that included the assumption that his sex perhaps gave as much satisfaction as his mere arrival. He himself was delighted when his wife became pregnant some ten months after the wedding, and blessed the name of the Lord when 'some hopes of my wives breeding' proved to be well founded 'to our great joy and comfort' [July

[1] For example, G. Gorer, *Himalayan Village* (1938), chs. 11–13 and Redfield, *Little Community*, ch. 4.

[2] A partial exception is Laslett, *Lost World*, ch. 4—'Births, Marriages and Deaths'.

[3] Ten children were more than average; the mean completed family size for the village of Colyton in Devon was 7.3 for the period 1560–1629 and 5.0 for 1646–1719 (E. A. Wrigley, 'Family Limitation in Pre-Industrial England', *Econ. Hist. Rev.*, 2nd series, vol. XIX, no. 1 (1966), p. 97.

1641]. It is clear that he valued children highly, 'above gold and jewels' as he put it [26. 5. 50], both for the pleasure they afforded, and the comfort they would later provide. When one of his children pined, Josselin pleaded to God to preserve her 'a comfort to me' [23. 5. 47] and on another occasion when he thought his wife might be pregnant he prayed that the child would be a 'comfort' to 'our grey haires' [16. 11. 50]. His views on the duties of children to parents are set out in a sermon preached in 1669.[1] He stressed that children had received much from their parents and should 'returne

TABLE V. *The vital statistics of Ralph Josselin's family*

Ralph Josselin: born 26.1.17: buried 30.8.83
married, on 28.10.40, to
Jane Constable: christened 26.11.21, buried 1693

Children							
No.	Name	Date of birth	Interval between (months)	Date of marriage	Age at marriage years/ months	Date of death	Age at death years/ months
1	Mary	12.4.42	17½	—	—	27.5.50	8.1
2	Thomas	30.12.43	20½	—	—	15.6.73	29.6
3	Jane	25.11.45	23	30.8.70	24.9	—	—
4	Ralph	11.2.48	25½	—	—	21.2.48	10 days
5	Ralph	5.5.49	15	—	—	2.6.50	13 months
6	John	19.9.51	29½	-.10.81	30	—	—
7	Anne	20.6.54	33	—	—	31.7.73	19.1
8	Mary	14.1.58	43	10.4.83	25.3	—	—
9	Elizab.	20.6.60	29	5.6.77	16.11	—	—
10	Rebecka	26.11.63	41	6.5.83	19.6	—	—

NOTES
1. All dates are from the Diary and most of them are confirmed by parish register entries: they are contracted, and expanded would read 16—.
2. The intervals are those between births, except in the first case, where it is between marriage and the first birth.

that love and tenderness'. He ended with the plea 'Oh then children, requite your parents for the cost they have laid out about you, follow their counsells, & chear up their sperits in their gray haires'.

Josselin was convinced of God's interest in this aspect of his life, as in every other: 'God hath added a child to my number' he noted on 26 March 1658; but there is no direct assertion that children were produced to glorify or please God. Nor is there much indication that he was interested in perpetuating the family line for its own sake, or in propitiating his ancestors; his remoter descendants interested him not at all. 'Lord marre not my inheritance' [20. 7. 73], he cried out when his children started dying, but this seems to have

[1] The location of this sermon, and other extracts from it, are given on p. 222 below.

referred merely to his immediate successors. On another occasion he prayed, 'oh bee my God and of my Spouse, & our seeds after us' [1. 9. 44], but how far he saw his seed as stretching is not clear. His image of his family was obviously that of a tree or vine; he and his wife were the trunk and his children were branches. Thus he dreamt of his children as '3 shoots in my parlo[u]r' [25. 1. 58] and spoke of 'our Wives like Vines, and our Children like Plants and Branches'.[1]

The Diary contains three types of information which enable us to analyze in great detail the fertility of Ralph Josselin's wife. Josselin recorded the day and often the hour of birth of all his children; he also noted when his wife thought she was pregnant and the date on which she started to wean her children; finally, he made a list of his wife's live births and miscarriages. We may deduce from this information the relationship between breast-feeding and conception and make some guesses at the possible presence or absence of birth control. The detailed analysis of this unique information is contained in appendix A at the end of the book.

The appendix shows that Josselin's wife usually recognized her pregnancy within 2 months of conception. Josselin noted such 'breeding' in all the pregnancies terminated by live births except the last 2. The increasing gaps between the births of children is partly explained by 5 recorded miscarriages between the births of the 7th and 10th children. It is not yet possible to be certain whether these miscarriages were merely the result of increased age, or whether they were consciously induced as a form of birth control. What is more certain is that by breast-feeding all her own children Mrs Josselin helped to space their births. Her children were all weaned at between 12 and 19 months of age and it appears that no child was conceived during the breast-feeding of the previous infant. On one occasion, however, Mrs Josselin thought herself '7 weekes with a boy' some 2 months before she weaned the previous child. Unless there was an unrecorded miscarriage, she seems to have been wrong in thinking herself pregnant. Nevertheless, the belief that she *could* be pregnant indicates that sexual intercourse had been resumed before the end of the suckling period.

Children were greatly desired, and welcomed, until they became an economic burden to their parents; then there are indications that a brake was put on the enlarging family, though not a very effective one. Of sexual relations between husband and wife nothing is said, at least explicitly; how often it occurred, the attitude of the partners, when it ceased. On one occasion Josselin reprimanded himself for 'a wantoness' in his 'private converse with my wife'

[1] Funeral sermon for Mrs S. Harlakenden, sig.A6ᵛ. Full reference on p. 221 below.

83

[18. 11. 55] which may indicate that his control was not as tight as the moralists enjoined.[1] His wife's menstrual habits are not considered suitable material for his Diary either, beyond one note on 20 August 1655 that 'my deare wife very ill at night it ariseth from her nature'.[2] Whether there were any taboos connected with the menstrual cycle,[3] or whether Josselin's attitude was one of distaste or disinterest we cannot tell.

There is much fuller information on the sickness and pain accompanying child-bearing, and pregnancy was constantly interrupted by morning sickness and other unpleasant symptoms. Considering how little of her married life was free from 'breeding', Mrs Josselin's lot was hardly enviable. The Diary is full of such references as: 'My wife faint and paind with her child in her back' [14. 1. 49] (child born five months later), 'my wife exercised with qualms and weakness incident to her condicon' [29. 8. 47], 'my deare wife ill of this child' [5. 9. 47], 'my poore wife very ill, she breeds with difficulty' [30. 10. 53]. Measures were probably taken to ease her, though nothing is said of them. On several occasions Josselin brought her special delicacies she craved, such as fresh cherries on 3 June 1647. Once, when the child quickened at about two months, 'the women met with her [i.e. Jane his wife] in prayer' [23. 6. 57]. It would be interesting to know whether this was a normal part of the ritual surrounding pregnancy.[4]

The actual delivery was a time of fear, amounting to dread, on Mrs Josselin's part. The night before the birth of her third child her husband prayed for her as she was 'oppressed with feares that she should not doe well on this child' [24. 11. 45]. Each time her labour began the same sense of panic set in: she was 'under great feares' on 11 February 1648, although it was 'the easiest and speediest labour that ever she had', as compared to the 'sad long labour' on 20 June 1660. Her last delivery at the age of forty-three was described as follows: 'My deare wife after many sad pains, and

---

[1] The prohibition of excessive intercourse, or intercourse at various times, for instance during menstruation or after childbirth, is discussed in A. Macfarlane, 'The Regulation of Marital and Sexual Relationships in Seventeenth Century England' (London Univ. M.Phil. thesis, 1968), ch. 7.

[2] An excellent example of contemporary opinions about menstruation is contained in *A Rational Account of the Naturall Weaknesses of Women*, by a 'Physician' (2nd edn, 1716; B.M. 1177 c.1).

[3] Menstruation was described as the 'natural infirmitie' of woman at this time (Thomas Phaire, *The Boke of Chyldren* (1545; reprinted 1965), p. 57), and it therefore seems likely that it was to menstruation that Josselin referred.

[4] Christopher Hill, *Economic Problems of the Church*, p. 168, notes that priests received fees for blessing pregnant women.

sadder feares, in respect of the unkindlines of her labour, was yett through Gods mercy, delivered of her 10th child' [26. 11. 63]. Despite the ceaseless procession of children, alive and dead, and the qualms attending their arrivals, Mrs Josselin outlived her husband.

The most detailed and interesting description of a delivery is that of 14 January 1658. Labour pains started on the 12th and Jane judged from the early labour that it would be a girl. On the 14th the pains 'so increased on her by two of the clocke in this morning that I called up the midwife and nurse' Josselin wrote. He continued: 'gott fires and all redie, and then her labour came on so strongly and speedily that the child was borne, only 2 or 3 women more gott in to her but god supplied all . . . my wives labour was different from all former, exceeding sharpe'.[1] The impression from this account is that he himself was present and assisted. There were also a number of others in the room; midwife, nurse and some women.

It seems that a midwife was not absolutely necessary; she was absent from the confinements of 11 February 1648 and 5 May 1649. Even when she was present, as on the occasion described above, she was criticized for adding to the pain because she 'did not doe her part'. Neighbours, on the other hand, were necessary as helpers. At the third delivery Josselin recorded: 'about midnight on Monday I rose, called up some neighbours . . . towards day I called in the women by daylight, almost all came' [24. 11. 45]. How many attended the delivery it is hard to say; at the fifth confinement 'some few women were with her' [5. 5. 49], and at the fourth there were 'only' five women present [11. 2. 48]. It is clear that birth was a public, and in view of the size of the rooms, a crowded occasion. The neighbours probably fulfilled the double role of helpers and witnesses.[2]

Relatives, especially the mother of the labouring woman, were often at hand; for instance on 30 April 1676 Josselin's wife was summoned to her daughter's confinement and again on 23 October 1678 she rode to London to be with her daughter at the delivery. Sometimes the daughter returned to the family home for her child's birth, as the Josselin's eldest daughter did [21. 10. 73]. After the delivery the helpers were feasted for their assistance. Josselin

[1] A contemporary account of the shrieks and cries which were believed to accompany childbirth is given in William Gouge, *Of Domesticall Duties* (1622), p. 400. A description of labour and delivery in another pre-industrial society is given in I. Schapera, *Married Life in an African Tribe* (reprinted, 1966), pp. 232–3.

[2] The rituals surrounding childbirth in various societies are usefully summarized in A. van Gennep, *The Rites of Passage* (translated, 1965), ch. 5. A description of those who might attend in another pre-industrial society is given by S. F. Nadel, *Nupe Religion* (1954), p. 116.

described how 'wee had made a good pastry for this houre, and that also was kept well' [24. 11. 45].

After the birth there was a general preoccupation with the health of mother and child. Between one and two months seem to have elapsed before the mother was able to go out of the house, although she might leave her bed within three weeks of the delivery. Jane gave birth on 20 June 1660; on 12 July she was 'about in the house' and on 22 July Josselin noted 'my wife abroad this day'. Jane went to both Sunday sermons on 20 June 1649, six weeks after her delivery, and Josselin was thanking the lord for 'the revivall of the spirits of my deare wife from under sad feares of ilnes and death' [9. 4. 48] two months after the birth of her fourth child.

Josselin watched his wife's health carefully in the few days after birth. Having been delivered on 14 January 1658, Jane was 'very well' the following two days and 'upwards' on the 20th, 21st and 24th. God was thought to be concerned with her breast-feeding: on one occasion 'it pleased God my wives breasts were sore' soon after the birth of the first child in 1642, 'which was a greivance and sad cutt to her, but with the use of means in some distance of time they healed up'. We know that 'God blessed my wife to bee a nurse' to at least four of her children, the second [14. 1. 44], third [30. 11. 45], and sixth [21. 9. 51] are explicitly described as being breast-fed, as well as the first.[1] The death of the fourth child at ten days caused serious problems. Three days after the death, 'my wife weake and faint with the turning of her milke; yett blessed bee god finely upward in the day, and at night shee thought her milke was even gone away' [24. 2. 48].[2]

[1] Most writers on family life during the sixteenth and seventeenth centuries stressed that a mother should, if possible, nurse her own children, for example Gouge, *Domesticall Duties*, pp. 513, 515, and William Perkins, *Christian Oeconomie* (1609), pp. 135–6. Yet Gouge noted that 'many poore women maintaine their house by nursing other folkes children' (*Domesticall Duties*, p. 516) and Mrs Jane Sharp in her *Midwives Book* (1671), p. 353, stated that it was 'The usual way for rich people to put forth their children to nurse'. Ariès, *Centuries of Childhood*, pp. 105, 374, suggests that there was an increased interest in breast-feeding in fifteenth-century France, and an increase in wet-nursing in the later seventeenth century. How England compared we do not yet know.

[2] This must have been a frequent source of illness given the high infant mortality rates of the period. For example, the seventeenth-century Yorkshire diarist Alice Thornton noted that her own milk turned sour after her child died and that she had developed gangrene in her breast (*The Autobiography of Mrs Alice Thornton of East Newton, co. York*, ed. C. Jackson, Sur. Soc., vol. LXII (1873), p. 166). There seem to have been numerous remedies circulating to deal with sore and inflamed teats, for 'women's milk that faileth' and for milk that had hardened in the breast. See, for example, W. R. Dawson, *A Leechbook or Collection*

The fact that Mrs Josselin probably nursed all her own children did not prevent her husband hiring a 'dry' nurse to help at the birth and during the few weeks following; Josselin recorded her departure some 17 days after the birth, and 5 days after the death, of his son Ralph [28. 2. 48]. She left between 3 and 4 weeks after the 3rd child was born [21. 12. 45] and was called away to another client when the 8th baby was some 2 weeks old [1. 2. 58]. Josselin did not bother to mention her name, whereas he recorded those of his servants, and it seems likely that she was only there to help whilst his wife was still in bed. A different kind of nurse was employed on 11 November 1674 to look after a grandchild of over a year old who had temporarily been left with the Josselins. Her name was Mrs Andrews and she was paid 5s. per week.

The possible correlation between dates of weaning and dates of conception is discussed fully in appendix A. The age at which the children were weaned varied from 1 year to 19 months: the first at about a year [spring 1643], the second at 13 months [3. 1. 45], the third at 18 months [9. 5. 47], the sixth at 19 months [3. 4. 53], the seventh at 16 months [14. 10. 55], and the ninth at a year [9. 6. 61]. The fourth child died at 10 days old and the fifth at 13 months, a death possibly connected with weaning. Josselin's grandchild 'went homewards well weaned' [5. 11. 74] at 1 year and 2 weeks old, and his other grandchild, left with her grandparents at the age of 9 months, was presumably weaned by then [1. 8. 79].[1]

---

of *Medical Recipes of the Fifteenth Century* (1934), pp. 31, 197, 279, and R.C., *The Compleat Midwife's Practice Enlarged* (1659), pp. 173 ff.

[1] Although it has been suggested on very slender evidence that weaning was late in the sixteenth century (Ariès, *Centuries of Childhood*, p. 34), it seems likely that between 12 and 18 months was the normal length of breast-feeding, at least among the yeoman class and above. Thus John Evelyn was weaned at $14\frac{1}{2}$ months (*The Diary and Correspondence of John Evelyn, F.R.S.*, ed. William Bray (no date), p. 3) and Lady Jane Grey was weaned at 18 months, amidst considerable ceremonial (described without a reference in L. E. Pearson, *Elizabethans at Home* (Stanford, 1957), p. 87). The great variations between different classes and even within the same family, as well as over time, are obvious. Three of John Dee's daughters were weaned at $8\frac{1}{2}$, 13, $14\frac{1}{2}$ months (*The Private Diary of Dr John Dee*, ed. J. O. Halliwell, Cam. Soc., vol. XIX (1842), pp. 16–7, 43, 55). One of John Greene's children was weaned by the wet-nurse at 9 months ('The Diary of John Greene', ed. E. M. Symonds, *Eng. Hist. Rev.*, vol. XLIV (1929), p. 107), while, at the other extreme, two daughters of the merchant Johnson's family were not weaned from their wet-nurse until they were nearly 3 years old (B. Winchester, *Tudor Family Portrait* (1955), p. 106). Most contemporary authorities argued that breast-feeding should end when the child was between 1 and 2 years old, for example, Mrs Sharp, *Midwives Book*, p. 375. A description of weaning methods and their probable consequences is given in Margaret Mead, *Sex and Temperament in Three Primitive Societies* (1935), pp. 38,

Josselin's constant interest in weaning suggests that it was of considerable importance in family life, a period of anxiety and uncertainty; puberty, in contrast, goes unrecorded. On 9 May 1647 he noted 'this weeke my wife weaned her daughter Jane: shee tooke it very contentedly'. Two years earlier, on 30 January, his wife 'began to weane her sonne Thomas' and eleven days later, on 9 February 'my wife weaned her sonne with much ease to her selfe and the child also quiett and content'. On 14 October 1655 Josselin wrote 'my wife somewhat ill, wee resolved to wean An', as if this was a matter of joint consultation. A week later 'my little An tooke her weaning very well' and a week after that, on the 28th, 'my wife gets strength, and An does well in her weaning'. He also noted of a later child that 'Betty weaneth well' [9. 6. 61]. The process was obviously a fairly gradual one, extended over several weeks. It was also a worrying time and there was little anyone could do if things went wrong.

Alongside the physical development of the child went the social events which marked his or her entry into village life. The first, and most important, of these was baptism. Josselin prayed over his first child, 'God wash it from it[s] corruption and sanctify it and make it his owne' [14. 4. 42], implying that one function of this rite was to cleanse the baby from the pollution of original sin and birth. There is no mention of Mrs Josselin undergoing the 'churching' ceremony designed to cleanse her from the pollution of birth. This omission is not surprising since many Puritans regarded such a rite as a legacy of popery.

Another purpose of baptism was to give the children names. To a certain extent this was merely a confirmation of their already existing names. Indeed it almost seems as if the names were present before the children, who were afterwards fitted into them. Thus, when the first Mary and the first Ralph died, subsequent babies took over their names. When a child was born on 25 November 1645 it was 'intended for a Jane' and similarly the father noted of another child 'I intend to name him John' [19. 9. 51]. Clearly children were given names already prepared for them; the child that died at ten days was already referred to as Ralph.

The period between birth and baptism varied between one day and a month; variations cannot be accounted for by either the sex of the child or the order of birth. The intervals, in birth order, were 2 days, 2 weeks, 2 weeks, 7 days, 8 days, 10 days, 1 month, same day,

---

198, 249, and in Schapera, *Married Life*, pp. 241–2. Unfortunately, Josselin's Diary gives no hint at the methods his wife employed.

4 days, 2½ weeks.[1] Some people delayed much longer; Josselin, for instance, baptized two boys of 3 years old [19. 5. 57]. Although a clergyman might be expected to conduct the service in church, on only one of the occasions where the Diary specifies the place of baptism was it held before the 'public congregation' [24. 6. 60]. On 19 July 1654 the service occurred in the 'hall chamber' and on 25 October 1655 the son of Mr Harlakenden was baptized 'at home'.

Nevertheless it was a public event. Neighbours and friends and, to a certain extent, relatives, gathered to witness the naming of the child and to recognize its entry into the social world. Both god-parents and other neighbours were feasted after the religious ritual. Josselin noted how the first baptismal feast cost him £6 13s. 4d. 'at least' [1642]; this would have paid for a considerable amount of food and drink. He attended another such 'cheerly banquett' with his friends at the baptism of his last child on 13 December 1663, and was often invited to similar entertainments with others, as, for instance, the feast given by his friends the Harlakendens on 25 October 1655.[2]

The Diary is tantalizingly brief about the rearing of the children between birth and the time of departure to school or apprenticeship. Josselin, like most fathers, found 'his little ones a great greife' in their 'sudden cryings out in the forepart of the night' [20. 10. 50], and noted that his daughter Elizabeth was 'more quiet in nights than formerly' [24. 3. 61]. The children's constant illnesses gave their parents many extra sleepless nights, for instance, 'In the night, my wife awaked by the child, found her sonne had a most sad cold' [13. 11. 44]. From an early age children seem to have spent a good deal of time in the homes of friends and relatives. Grandchildren under a year old were left with Josselin for several weeks at a time [28. 9. 79]. Josselin's daughter Mary, aged just over four years, 'would [have] staine behind' when her father visited his friends the Ellistons, but 'at night nothing would content her but home' [18. 6. 46]. Aged seven and a half, 'Mary was out at Mrs Ellistons where shee learned to sew'; presumably her own mother was unable or unwilling to teach her this skill.

Training and discipline were probably left to the mother in the early years, though this is not specifically stated. Nor is there any

[1] The gap between birth and baptism is crucial in the work of 'family reconstitu-tion' and these dates are therefore of considerable importance (E. A. Wrigley (ed.), *An Introduction to English Historical Demography* (1966), pp. 107–8).

[2] Herbert, *Priest to the Temple*, p. 256, argued that 'all' should attend a baptism, but we do not know who, in fact, did attend. A vivid description of a naming ritual, with many parallels to English baptism, is given by Nadel, *Nupe Religion*, pp. 116–17.

reference to toilet training.[1] Referring to his own childhood Josselin spoke of 'the strange prodigious uncleane lusts when I was yett a child'. These lusts were partly inflamed by reading, but firmly suppressed for God 'kept me from all outward uncleannesse'. If he was recalling sexual feelings, it is likely that any symptoms of such 'lusts' in his children would have been heavily censured, for his own memories made him want to 'loath and abhorre my selfe' [1618]. When his family were grown up, but still under his authority, he attempted godly exhortation for their improvement, treating them to a long sermon full of biblical precedents [19. 12. 76]. Whether his corrections were always verbal, or how frequently he administered them, remains a mystery.[2]

The babies seem to have developed at much the same rate as they do today. Their teeth usually came through within a year; Anne at 4 months was the youngest to cut a tooth [8. 10. 54], John had two cut 'when just halfe a yeare old' [21. 3. 52], and two of the other children were also teething at 6 months [25. 5. 46 and 25. 11. 49]. Jane was 'ill two or 3 dayes' with teeth trouble at 13 months old [20. 12. 46]. Clearly the children were breast-fed for up to a year after their teeth began to appear.[3]

They seem to have started to walk at about a year, for her father wrote 'my little daughter Jane began to goe alone' at just under a year old [15. 11. 46], and it seems likely that he meant she was walking, for the timing compares with a note he made on 6 December 1644 that 'My sonne Tho: now would walke up and downe the house of his owne accord; he wants above 3 weekes of a yeare old'. The same Thomas could close the parlour door at 13 months [7. 2. 45]. Changes in clothing provide a hint of social recognition for the movement from stage to stage; absolute infancy may have been deemed to end when the baby was first 'coated' or taken from swaddling bands, as Rebecka was at 7 weeks [14. 2. 64]. Similarly, when John was 'put in breeches' at 6 years old [3. 10. 57] it was

[1] In fact, the Diary never mentions anything connected with the natural functions: the attitudes to urination and defecation as well as the location and condition of toilets are never discussed. It is therefore impossible to deduce anything about sanitation and difficult to make an analysis of 'personality types' along Freudian lines. We do not know whether omission reveals disgust, shame, or mere indifference.

[2] This gap means that the many fascinating topics treated in books such as M. Mead, *Coming of Age in Samoa* (Pelican edn, 1963) and Erik H. Erikson, *Childhood and Society* (Pelican edn 1965), cannot be discussed here, although Ariès, *Centuries of Childhood*, indicates how much material can be collected on childhood habits.

[3] One authority (Phaire, *Boke of Chyldren*, p. 38), stated that teeth usually appeared 'about the seventh moneth'. Josselin's children were thus about normal for their time.

probably a sign that this was the age when the sexes were different-iated and treated accordingly.[1]

Josselin was himself the schoolmaster at Earls Colne until the summer of 1658 [12. 7. 58]. He was therefore able to supervise the early stages of his children's teaching. The first part of their education was a period at Earls Colne school when they were aged between about 4 and 10 years, then they were sent away to a more distant school or to apprenticeship. At Earls Colne they were taught the principles of reading, though they do not seem to have learnt to write until they had been away to school. The first letter Josselin received from one of his daughters was when she was 14 years and 4 months old and had been away at a Colchester school for 4 years [11. 3. 60].

We are not told when the children began to speak, but by the time she was 2½ years old Josselin thought that Jane would remember particular outstanding events, such as the fierce storm they had experienced [9. 4. 48]. Anne went 'to learne her book' when she was 3 years and 10 months old [19. 4. 58], and we know that Mary, just over 4 years old, had a 'towardlyness to learn' [14. 6. 46] and by November of the same year had developed 'an aptness to her booke' [15. 11. 46]. By the time he was 5 years and 10 months Thomas was described as 'of a good memory, a good speller, apt to learne, and attaine the hardest words in his bible or accidence in which he reads' [1. 11. 49]. On the following 1 March he 'began to learn his accidence, by heart as wee say, memoriter; he is now 6 yeares old and about two months'. Josselin was proud of his children's achievements, but did not appear to press them unduly. The only clue to the mentality of the children lies in the two dreams of Mary, then aged 5, and Thomas, then aged 11. They indicate that the children had already imbued their father's religious beliefs, but had embellished them with their own personal fantasies in which Jesus Christ became a play-mate and heavenly mansions were seen 'shining like the inside of oister shells'.[2]

---

[1] There were a number of views on age-boundaries in the sixteenth and seventeenth centuries. Galen, as expounded in Thomas Cogan, *The Haven of Health* (1589), pp. 191–2, divided a person's life into five stages: childhood to 15, adolescence to 25, youth to 35, middle age to 49, old age from 49 onwards. Sir Thomas Browne recognized only four divisions, having blended Galen's 'Youth' and 'Middle Age' into 'Manhood' ('Christian Morals', reprinted with *Religio Medici* (Everyman edn, 1962), p. 269). But there also seems to have been a boundary at 7; for instance, William Harrington, *The Commendacions of Matrymony* (1528), sig. Eii[v], stated that at that age members of the opposite sex in the nuclear family should no longer sleep together. This fitted into the seven ages of man, which began with the periods 1-7, 7-14 and were outlined in many sixteenth-century texts (Ariès, *Centuries of Childhood*, pp. 21, 66).

[2] The dreams are recounted in full on p. 185 below.

6

Adolescence, marriage and death

Among the many problems to be faced in rearing a family is the transition from childhood to adolescence, involving changes in the relationships in the nuclear family with the sexual development of the children. Of Josselin's ten offspring, only one died before it reached a year old, and two others before the age of ten. He was left with seven to steer through puberty and its attendant problems, and though he believed that God 'would helpe in portioning, placing, providing for and sanctifying' them in a general way [9. 1. 70], he was still faced with day-to-day decisions about a group of children competing with their parents for both economic and sexual resources.

Seventeenth-century Englishmen did not provide formal rituals to deal with the changes in relative status within the family, as some societies do. Rather, some Englishmen at least, relied on physical space to separate the generations at a time when they might threaten one another.[1] None of Josselin's children remained permanently in the home. In effect, all the girls had left home for good by the age of $14\frac{1}{2}$, though they frequently visited their parents after that age. Josselin never discussed the sexual development of his children, but it seems likely that the girls reached puberty at between 13 and 15 years of age, the boys at between 15 and 17.[2] It is surely more than a coincidence that it was exactly at this age that they all left home to be subjected to outside discipline and freed from the incestuous dangers of crowded living.

Although it is possible that some of the children left home earlier than shown in table VI and that Josselin did not mention this, it is certain that they had all left home by the age of puberty. Whether

[1] There is a general discussion of adolescence and putting out children in appendix B below, which expands these remarks. A useful preliminary description of age-grade systems is given by R. Firth, *Human Types* (revised edn, 1956), p. 102. Age rituals are summarized in Van Gennep, *Rites of Passage*, p. 59 and *passim*.

[2] The mean age of menarche (sexual maturity) in 169 groups of women examined by Pearl varied from 13 to 16 years, the mean of the means was 15.7 (M. Nag, *Factors Affecting Human Fertility in Nonindustrial Societies* (New Haven, 1962), p. 105). It was assumed by contemporaries that no male under 8 years of age could procreate (Richard Burn, *Ecclesiastical Law* (4th edn, 1781), vol. 1, p. 110) and some women were unable to conceive until they were 'Nineteen, Twenty or Twenty two or three Years of Age, or more' (*Rational Account*, p. 57). The 'Physician' author of the *Rational Account* (p. 1) stated that menstruation usually began at 'about fourteen years old, & in some sooner'.

the girls who left at 10 years were physically more mature than those who set off at 13 we do not know, nor can we be certain whom the children stayed with after their departure. There is no evidence that they resided with kin, for no mention is made of an uncle or aunt by the visiting parents. Furthermore, if we compare the destinations of the children with the map of the known distribution of Josselin's relatives the only known overlap was at Colchester.[1] However, it is unlikely that Jane stayed with her father's cousin John for we are explicitly told that she went to 'Mr Piggots at Colchester' [21. 4. 56]. The names of the masters to whom the boys were bound apprentices do not suggest any family relationship, so it appears that the children were not entrusted to the care of godly kinsfolk when they were farmed out.[2]

TABLE VI. *Movement of children away from home*

Name	Date of leaving	Age years/months	Place/occupation to which bound
Thomas	25.5.59	15.5	London, bound apprentice
Jane	21.4.56	10.6	Colchester, education
John	9.1.67	15.4	London, bound apprentice
Anne	24.6.68	14.0	London, bound as servant
Mary	2.2.68	10.0	White Colne, education
Elizab.	23.4.74	13.9	Bury St Edmunds, education
Rebecka	17.5.77	13.5	London, bound as servant

The expense of rearing the children and the loss through heavy mortality have already been discussed.[3] The most costly part of bringing up the family was the provision of marriage portions for the daughters. The first daughter to marry, Jane, was given a portion of £200, and also had 'plate and work' worth £40 and £20 in cash [30. 8. 70]. The next marriage, Elizabeth's, was exceptional in two ways. Firstly she was much younger at her wedding than any of the others, only 16 years and 11 months as compared to 19.6 (Rebecka), 24.9 (Jane), and 23.3 (Mary). Secondly, Josselin apparently contributed very little; apart from the mention of some 'household' sent to London a week after the wedding [16. 6. 77] nothing is said of a dowry. Her father admitted that the 'ground and bottom of the match among us was not estate, but good qualities' [5. 6. 77], implying that both sides to the agreement should be matched, and that if he offered little he could expect little in return.

[1] See figure 10, p. 142 below.
[2] See appendix B for a discussion of where the children went.
[3] See pp. 50–1 above.

Probably a girl could only marry young if she was prepared to accept a man of modest means who would, in his turn, take her equally modest dowry. Probably, too, Josselin was quite relieved to see one of his daughters go at little expense, for he still had another two to settle.

The two final daughters were given handsome portions; in fact their elder sister, who had been married with a more moderate sum, grumbled that their dowries were 'too great' [2. 5. 83]. It seems that Josselin was giving them their inheritance early, in anticipation of his death which occurred within a year; he was already very sick. To Mary he gave part of his property, house and land worth £400, plus £100 in cash [10. 4. 83], to Rebecka the same amount of £500, but all in cash [6. 5. 83]. The cash had already been handed over when the will was made in June 1683, but the land and £100 to Mary were included in the legacies.

Marriage was a time of crucial economic adjustment, especially in the lives of the girls. They had already been away from their parental home for a number of years, but marriage made them financially independent. The system of farming out the children, which permitted them a moderate freedom without forcing them to resort to marriage, allowed them to marry late. This may help to explain why English men and women were able to marry much later than members of agricultural societies in other parts of the world.[1] In fact there seems to have been no particular urge to marry. Thomas died single at twenty-nine although, with his business and as the eldest living son, he could undoubtedly have afforded a wife.

When Mary was courted at the age of twenty-two by a suitor from London of whom her parents approved she nevertheless refused him. The grounds of her refusal suggest a number of factors which might affect the choice of a spouse. He was too old, she said, some fourteen years older than herself, and so 'shee might be left a wid[ow] with children'. He was not rich enough, 'his estate being not suitable to her porcon', and, perhaps most important of all, he 'seemed to her not loving' [4. 6. 81]. She was apparently looking for someone who would fit into a general category of the right age and wealth, but who would also be specifically attractive and attracted.

It was an advantage if the estates of the two marriage partners were equal, since a new household was set up at some distance from either sets of parents and there do not seem to have been important

[1] The classic discussion of the unique 'European marriage pattern', which combined high age of marriage with a large number of never-married adults, is J. Hajnal, 'European Marriage Patterns in Perspective', in *Population in History*, (eds.) D. V. Glass and D. E. C. Eversley (1965), pp. 101 ff.

rights and duties from which one founding family rather than the other would benefit; they each contributed an equal amount to setting up the new household. Nothing equivalent to the 'bride price' or 'groom price', paid in certain societies by one family who have gained the services of an in-coming son or daughter-in-law to recompense the other family who have sustained a loss, seems to be apparent in Josselin's arrangements. He provided a dowry, while the groom's family provided their son with wealth and, if he died, a 'jointure' for his widow. In the case of Jane this was a 'prettie thing' [30. 8. 70], though the sum is not specified. There is little evidence in the Diary of where the dowry went, except that on one occasion Josselin recorded paying it to his daughter's new husband five months after the wedding [17. 11. 71].[1]

Despite the importance of financial arrangements, the choice of a marriage partner, the selection of one among a number of possible suitors, still depended on non-economic considerations, and still lay in the hands of the children rather than the parents. Ralph Josselin's own courtship is enough to lay the myth that the 'romantic love complex' is a post-industrial phenomenon and that seventeenth-century marriages were arranged, and entirely devoid of affective overtones in the first few months or years. When Josselin described how, 'the first Lords day being Oct:6 my eye fixed with love upon a Mayd, & hers upon mee, who afterwards proved my wife' [1639], he was describing the phenomenon even then called 'falling in love'.[2] Josselin upheld the theoretical right of parents to control their children's marriages, even giving his daughter Elizabeth a long

[1] Different societies find various uses for dowries; in Ireland, for example, parents once found them useful for financing other weddings (K. H. Connell, 'Peasant Marriage in Ireland: its Structure and Development since the Famine', *Econ. Hist. Rev.*, 2nd series, vol. XIV, no. 3 (1962), p. 508). The size and regulation of aristocratic dowries is discussed in Lawrence Stone, 'Marriage among the English Nobility in the 16th and 17th Centuries', *Comp. Stud. Soc. & Hist.*, vol. III, no. 2 (1961), pp. 187–93.

[2] For example, two servants in Essex were described as 'falling in love togethers' (E.R.O., D/AED/1 fol. 13) and a woman refused to marry a suitor because 'she could not find [it] in her to love him' (E.R.O., D/AED/1, fol. 18)—both cases come from sixteenth-century ecclesiastical records. Walzer, *Revolution of the Saints*, p. 194, has suggested that Puritanism fostered 'romantic love' and helped to break down the tight control of marriage choice by parents and kin. It is clear, however, that the choice of marriage partners may be based on spontaneous physical attraction in very primitive, far from industrialized, societies (e.g., C. von Fürer-Haimendorf, *Morals and Merit* (1967), p. 19). W. J. Goode, *The Family* (New Jersey, 1964), p. 41, has argued that 'the romantic love complex' was 'widespread among the peasantry of Europe prior to industrialization' and has suggested some reasons why this should have been so (p. 39).

sermon when she seemed reluctant to marry a man of whom her father approved. He told her of Isaac's wise action in taking the wife picked by Abraham, and of the 'instance of a headie marriage in Samson; it turnd to his death; against his parents advice he would marry' [19. 12. 76]. Yet, in practice, his children clearly initiated the process themselves. The exception may have been Thomas, for when he was twenty-three his father 'made mocons [i.e. motions] in a match' for him, prompted by his son or not, we cannot tell [2. 6. 67]. John carried freedom of choice to the extreme of marrying without his father's knowledge.

With daughters the courting pattern was for the suitors who lived at a distance to come and stay in the town, or possibly in the Josselin's house itself, to be looked over by the parents. Jane found her husband in her own village, but the other daughters found theirs in London; the geographical range of their marriage choice would have made it especially difficult for parental control to be very strong. The element of control entered the situation when the parents' consent was sought. Jane's suitor, a local man, came to Josselin and 'askt my consent to come to my daughter'; he was welcomed as a 'sober, hopefull man, his estate about £500' [21. 7. 70]. Two wooers from London came down to stay for five days at Christmas 1682 [24. 12. 82]. On another occasion opinions on a suitor had split the family, for Josselin approved of the Mr Shirley who was courting his daughter Mary, whilst his wife did not [3. 10. 76]. Mary herself gave the reason that the man who was courting her was 'not loving' as sufficient grounds for rejecting him; her father showed his respect for her feelings and concern for her future when he declared that he 'could not desire it, when shee said it would make both their lives miserable' [4. 6. 81].

The period of courtship generally lasted between six months and a year after the suitor's introduction to the parents; probably the daughters in London had known their young men for some time before this. The period between the first visit of the suitor to the household and the marriage was as follows: Jane—7 months, Elizabeth—6 months, Mary—4 months, and Rebecka—5 months; the last two possibly cut short by the realization of Josselin's impending death. The period might be lengthened by the need to accumulate sufficient money, as in Josselin's own case, who 'being Mr of Arts & minister' and already contracted, yet 'could not see any convenience how to live' since his father could not help him [spring 1640]. It was not until he was finally given a living in 1640 that he was able to accomplish the last stage of the contract.

That marriage was in fact a series of stages is plain from an examination of Jane's wooing and wedding in 1670. Her suitor asked permission to woo her on 21 January and on 18 March they 'testified their agreement to marry'. After this an interval was considered appropriate, for the young couple to get to know each other better,[1] and for Josselin to collect the girl's portion, which he began to do on 29 April. They finally married on 30 August. An even more detailed account of the timing of the stages is given by Josselin when describing his own wedding. He first saw his future bride on 6 October 1639 and by 13 December was sufficiently interested to reject, on her account, his uncle's offer of a living in Norfolk. On 1 January they proposed the match 'one to another' and three weeks later, on the 23rd, undertook their 'mutuall promise'. This was their private contract, and to make it completely binding a public contract followed on 28 September. A month later, a year from their first meeting, they were married. The wedding was on a Wednesday and on the following Monday they set out for their new home at Cranham in Essex.[2] We do not know the degree of intimacy or privacy allowed the couple at the various stages of their courtship.

The celebrations themselves were on a modest scale compared to those at gentry weddings. For instance, Josselin spent £10 on clothes and food at his first daughter's wedding [30. 8. 70], whilst Mrs Harlakenden of the nearby priory paid £120 for her clothes alone [17. 11. 57]. Nor is it likely that the celebrations lasted for several days, as they did at a wedding Josselin attended [15. 12. 57]. Presents such as ribbons and gloves were probably distributed to the guests, however, as at another wedding feast he described [11. 12. 44]. Whether guests in their turn gave the newly-wedded couple presents is not stated, nor do we know which relatives actually attended. Josselin sometimes mentioned the weddings of his relatives but seemed to feel no desire or duty to attend them, so probably they felt the same. It must have been an advantage to have a good crowd present because large sums could be gathered towards the expenses

[1] J. Dod and R. Clever, *A Godlie Forme of Household Government* (1612), p. 109, stressed that the pair should gain an intimate knowledge of their future partner's eating, walking, working and other habits, though they would doubtless have been horrified at the suggestion, attributed to Sir Thomas More by John Aubrey, *Brief Lives* (Peregrine edn., 1962), p. 283, that they should see each other naked in bed.

[2] Courting habits are briefly discussed in Laslett, *Lost World*, pp. 142–3 and Campbell, *English Yeoman*, pp. 302–3. Much of interest to the historian is contained in A. Percival Moore, *Marriage Contracts or Espousals in the Reign of Queen Elizabeth*, Ass. Arch. Soc., vol. xxx, pt 1 (1909), *passim*—e.g. p. 290. E. Westermarck, *History of Human Marriage* (5th edn, 3 vols, 1921), in its various editions provides the best summary of all aspects of the anthropological literature on marriage.

of setting up a new home; according to a note Josselin made about a
friend's wedding, the company 'offerd freely; he tooke about 56
pounds' [8. 7. 47]. His only mention of a wedding present at his
own wedding was £10 promised by his wife's aunt but not forthcoming for some thirteen years [23. 8. 53].

After the ceremony the couple went to their new home, in
Josselin's case five days later. Josselin's son John had to wait at least
seven months before he could settle into his own house. Perhaps this
was because he had married without his parent's knowledge and thus
deprived his father of the six or seven months' courtship time in
which things were normally arranged. From the slender evidence
in the Diary it appears that residence after marriage was 'neolocal'
in Josselin's family, the young couple setting up their household away
from both their sets of parents. Josselin himself had settled at Earls
Colne after a short stay near an uncle at Cranham, and his daughters
all went to live with their husbands, Jane at Lexden, and the other
three in London.[1] Despite the distance, however, the married
children maintained close links with their parents, as we shall see
in a later chapter.

By the time all the children were married, Josselin was only a few
months from his death at the age of sixty-eight. His retirement can,
in one sense, be dated from the wedding of his first child, Jane, in
1670 when he was fifty-five. At that time he began to break up his
estate amongst his children. Never again did he fill his Diary with
the meticulous and anxious accounts which had characterized the
period when he was building it up. Retirement, nevertheless, was a
gradual process and the bulk of the property was not handed over
until a few months before his death. There was no sudden with-
drawal, nor immediate loss of power and occupation.[2] He was never
left dependent on the support of his children or others.[3] In fact, he
was still doing manual work on his farm at the age of sixty-five
[7. 5. 82].

[1] It is probable that they lived in independent nuclear households. That this was
the predominant pattern in various parts of England is shown by P. Laslett and
J. Harrison, 'Clayworth and Cogenhoe' in *Historical Essays Presented to David
Ogg*, (eds.) H. E. Bell and R. L. Ollard (1963), pp. 166–8, and also by Philip
Styles, 'A Census of a Warwickshire Village in 1698', *Univ. Birm. Hist. Jour.*,
vol. III (1951–2), p. 37.
[2] The problem of the degree of abruptness of retirement has been raised by
Keith Thomas, 'Work and Leisure in Pre-industrial Society', *P. & P.*, vol. 29
(1964), p. 62. The many problems concerning the transmission of authority and
wealth, as well as the attitude towards the old and the methods of supporting
them, urgently require investigation.
[3] Unlike a neighbour of Josselin's, whose son, 'the stay of his old dayes, was
strangely drowned' [2. 3. 61].

There are a few hints about Josselin's attitude to ageing. An attack of cramp when he was forty was interpreted as 'a warning of old age' [4. 3. 57], and in the notes at the beginning of the Diary he wrote: 'If mans age bee 70; then I now being in my 58 am almost at my Friday midnight, lord fitt mee for a blessed sabbath at hand'. An entry for 26 January 1676 remarked, 'entred my 60 yeare; I grow an old man' and at the end of the next year he prayed 'Lord, I am now old and I have no worke like serving thee and assuring my salvacon through Christ' [1. 12. 77]. He was evidently aware of the current belief that 'the great Climacterical which few escape is seven times nine, which makes sixty three',[1] for he noted 'not troubled in 63 as a critical & dangerous year though I often thought of it' [26. 1. 80]. His wife's attitudes to ageing are passed over in silence, as are the physical symptoms she suffered, particularly the menopause.[2] Any of the many illnesses she endured between 1664 and 1669 may have been a symptom of sexual changes and the pains and strains connected with them, for instance when she was 'ill of her backe' at the age of forty-seven [27. 10. 67].

Josselin's assumptions about death and suffering must await later discussion, but the actual rituals and social re-adjustments at death merit treatment here as the last crisis through which the family passed. The brief comments he supplies us with need to be compared with other descriptions.[3] The funeral usually took place within two or three days or, at the most, a week after death. In the funerals Josselin described, the gaps between death and burial were as follows:

19–20.6.56	one day
17.7.73	two days
20–22.2.78	two days
28.3.57	three days
19–26.10.81	one week

The funeral service, especially the sermon, was an opportunity for a

[1] Mrs Sharp, *Midwives Book*, p. 174.

[2] Recent research suggests that the menopause usually occurs in women at between 44 and 50 years of age (Nag, *Factors Affecting Human Fertility*, p. 113). The 'physician' author of *Rational Account*, p. 2, stated that menstruation continued 'till Forty Forty-five, and sometimes till Fifty Years of Age or longer' and that disorders resulting from the menopause usually occurred between the ages of forty and fifty' (p. 31).

[3] The function of funeral rites for the living is outlined in Firth, *Human Types*, p. 183, and by Sir Thomas Browne, 'Urn Burial' (with *Religio Medici*), p. 123. Among the many anthropological descriptions of the elaborate rituals at death two may serve as models; Nadel, *Nupe Religion*, pp. 121 ff., and C. von Fürer-Haimendorf, *The Sherpas of Nepal* (1964), pp. 224 ff.

release of emotion; when Josselin preached 'until sundown' at a funeral he confessed to having lost his 'greife and trouble much in the pulpitt' [4. 4. 57].

We catch glimpses of some of the other rituals surrounding burial. When Josselin's infant of ten days was buried 'the gravest matrons in our towne layde his tombe into the earth' and two other friends 'closed up each of them one of his eyes when it dyed' [22. 2. 48]. The child was buried with 'the teares and sorrows' of parents and neighbours. His little daughter was carried to the grave by friends and a sister; 'I kist her lips last, & carefully laid up that body, the soule being with Jesus' [28. 5. 50]. Mrs Mabel Harlakenden, as befitted the gentry, was splendidly buried: 'her father bestowed a beautiful funeral on her. Many of her friends carried her to the ground. Mr. R. H. and I laid her into grave at the head and 2 uncles at the feet. the sermon continued till sundown, a great number of freinds.' [4. 4. 57]

It is clear that funerals were dignified occasions, filled with processions, tears, solemn gestures and lengthy sermons, but they were also occasions for feasting and the exchange of gifts. Nothing is said about expense, but we can infer from the fact that Josselin sent six dozen cakes to a funeral [8. 4. 57] that the neighbours were feasted. It was obviously considered odd that when Lady Honeywood was buried 'not a glove, ribband, scutcheon, wine, beare, bisquett given at her burial but a little mourning to servants' [26. 10. 81], and one must presume that gloves and ribbons were usually distributed.

At the same Lady Honeywood's funeral 'the servants carried her, six persons with scarfs & gloves bare up the pall'. Mrs Mabel Harlakenden on the other hand was carried to the grave by friends, and laid in it by a clergyman and three kinsmen, again symbols of her exalted status [4. 4. 57]. At Josselin's level it was the neighbours who were mobilized into helping, and the quality of their commiseration was seen as a test of his relationship with them, a 'testimonie of their love to me' as he put it and of their 'respect to my babe' [22. 2. 48].

At Josselin's daughter Mary's funeral she was accompanied to the grave by 'most of the Towne' and laid in it by Mrs Margaret Harlakenden and Mrs Mabel Elliston, 'those two and Mrs. Jane Church, & my sister carryed her in their hands to the grave' [28. 5. 50]. There were thus three friends and one sister at the final commitment, all members of the same sex as the deceased, a possible attempt to mirror her status and condition.[1] At his son's funeral

[1] Aubrey, *Brief Lives*, p. 367, for example, described how the number present at

things were different, however: 'Mrs King and Mrs Church—2 doctor of divinities widows—the gravest matrons in our towne, layde his tombe into the earth . . . Mrs. King and Mr. Harlakenden of the priory closed up each of them one of his eyes when it dyed.' [22. 2. 48] Here the sexes were mixed, and there was no mention of kin.

There is further, negative, evidence that kin did not assemble at funerals in Josselin's failure to attend that of 'deare Uncle Ralph Josselin' which was carried out by his children [28. 3. 57]. Distance was a big difficulty here, and in fact by the time Josselin heard of his uncle's funeral in London he had been four days in his grave. It was primarily the nuclear family's responsibility to be present; thus it was proper that Uncle Ralph should be buried by his children, and improper that at the funeral of a neighbour 'his sonne and grand-children of our towne would not be present' [5. 4. 45].

From the much more detailed descriptions given of them, funerals interested and impressed Josselin more than baptisms or marriages, but once buried his relatives exerted little influence on his life. There is no mention of the anniversaries of their deaths,[1] and there is nothing to suggest that he attempted to please, appease, or worship his ancestors, or that he conceived of them as a group who still existed. Several months after the death of a child he felt the loss 'bitter as death' [14. 7. 50], but there is no sense of the dead being present in the same terrestrial sphere as the living.[2]

On the exceptional occasion when Josselin did mention members of his nuclear family long dead, the entry shows that it was his own loss and sorrow that moved him, not awe or curiosity about their possible survival. A visit to Stortford on 18 June 1649 affected him deeply 'with the thoughts of my deare mother and 2 sisters who were there buried' but the memories of his mother must in fact have been very dim as she had died within his first seven years, thirty years before [1618], and both his sisters died in 1624, also when he was seven. It would seem that the dead and the living were held apart

---

the funeral equalled the age of the deceased, and *The Life of Adam Martindale*, ed. Parkinson, Chet. Soc., vol. IV, p. 206, describes how the young women of the parish insisted on carrying a girl to her grave.

[1] This is a striking contrast to the visits to the dead mother's grave, and family anniversaries of the dead mother, in a modern urban setting (Peter Wilmott and Michael Young, *Family and Kinship in East London* (Pelican edn, 1962), p. 78).

[2] The abolition of masses for the dead and of Purgatory at the Reformation may have undermined any existing ancestor-worship since it was no longer possible, officially at least, to contribute to the progress of the dead. A study of tomb-stones, graves and funeral customs may well yet reveal that the dead played an important part in seventeenth-century life.

and that elaborate burials catered for the immediate release of pain and grief by the survivors, and provided an occasion for neighbours and friends to show their solidarity. There is little hint of honouring the dead, or any sense of speeding them on their way to heaven.

This description of Josselin's domestic life has been necessarily superficial and full of gaps. It has pivoted on the three central crises of birth, marriage and death. Large areas of thought and experience have been unexplored; his wider relationships with kin and neighbours and his own involvement with his physical and social surroundings. The same facts, examined from a different viewpoint, can be made to yield more information and fill some of the gaps.

PART III

The social world:
family, kin and neighbours

7

Husband–wife, parents–children

As several historians have certainly pointed out, we know very little about family life and kinship in pre-industrial England.[1] This section is an attempt to show that the vacuum could well be filled. It supplements the few existing studies and suggests some of the problems which might be investigated,[2] bearing in mind that the evidence from the Diary of Ralph Josselin is obviously inadequate to provide the basis for satisfactory generalizations. The importance of the whole subject of the family and kinship is self-evident to anthropologists, one of whom writes, for instance, 'An understanding of the kinship system in any society is essential as a clue to the working of some of the most fundamental relationships—sexual, marital, economic, in that society'.[3] Historians seem to have been slower to recognize the need for its study.

Before starting to assess the evidence there is always the major problem of creating indices. To estimate the quality of a relationship, say between first cousins, a number of measures must be introduced. Sociologists and anthropologists often choose the following: the frequency of visits; the frequency of gifts, messages, and other communications; the choice of names and the choice of godparents; the degree of interest shown in each other's affairs, for example in the death of a relative; the inheritance of property; the recruitment to ceremonies marking birth, death and marriage; aid offered in crises (illness for instance) or in finding work; kinship

[1] For example, Joan Thirsk, 'The Family', *P. & P.*, vol. 27 (1964), p. 116, and Thomas, 'History and Anthropology', p. 15. The latter points out, quite rightly, that 'the study of the family in English history has simply not begun'.

[2] Among the few recent contributions on pre-twentieth-century kinship are Lawrence Stone, *Crisis of the Aristocracy, 1558–1641* (Oxford, 1965), ch. 11; L. Lancaster, 'Kinship in Anglo-Saxon Society', 2 parts, *Brit. Jour. Soc.*, vol. IX, nos. 3 and 4 (1958); D. Crozier, 'Kinship and Occupational Succession', *Soc. Rev.*, new series, vol. 13, no. 1 (1965); G. C. Homans, *English Villagers of the Thirteenth Century* (New York, 1960), pt 2. A. R. Radcliffe-Brown, 'Introduction' in *African Systems of Kinship and Marriage*, ed. A. R. Radcliffe-Brown and D. Forde (Oxford, 1950), pp. 14–17, 160–3, gives a very general account of the English system. For the nineteenth century there is W. M. Williams, *A West Country Village: Ashworthy* (1963). The work by the 'Cambridge Group for the Study of Population and Social Structure' cited in the following notes provides a major contribution in this field.

[3] Raymond Firth (ed.), *Two Studies of Kinship in London* (1956), p. 11.

terminology.[1] Obviously many of these indices overlap, and areas exist in which the investigator can only guess at the significance of the presented facts. Any yardstick he carries into a world 300 years behind him is naturally an imperfect instrument.

In the previous part we saw, through Josselin's eyes, the domestic cycle as it revolved around the three *rites de passage*, birth, marriage and death. Rituals tell us little, however, without an understanding of the relationships of the nuclear family participating in them, particularly the relationship of man and wife, parents and children as a united family, and then parents with married offspring separated from them. Immediately there emerges one of the main difficulties in using a diary as a source for social history, the problem of assessing the unsaid.

Often a physical separation brings words for an emotional involvement for the first time; for instance we know far more about Josselin's relations with his children *after* they left home than about such ties when their presence was taken for granted. A slight optical illusion is created; far more interest and concern seems to be shown by Josselin for relatives at a distance than for his wife. The historian is left contemplating meaningful silences, groups of years when Josselin's wife and children are not mentioned at all. These may be interpreted in completely contrary ways, as evidence of a tie too deep to need expression, or as a lack of warmth and interest. With this danger in mind we may turn to look at Josselin and his wife.

It will be remembered that Josselin married Jane Constable on 28 October 1640 when he was twenty-three and a half years old, and she was one month off twenty. Three facts immediately suggest that their relationship was likely to develop into a deep one. Firstly, as we have seen, the match was based on physical attraction as well as economic consideration. Secondly the young couple set up their own household at once, they did not merely become an adjunct of a wider kinship group for whom they worked.[2] Thirdly they spent the next forty-three years living together and raising a large family; they only seem to have been separated for a few months during the whole period, and the separation, as we shall see, was hurtful.

The general impression from the Diary is that the husband–wife bond was the most important in Josselin's life. In this he followed the

[1] A number of these indices, for example, are employed and discussed in Firth, *Two Studies*, pp. 51 ff.

[2] When there is no change of residence the young married man may be expected to spend most of his time with his father rather than with his new wife; such a situation is described, for example, in Fürer-Haimendorf, *Morals and Merit*, p. 172.

injunction of moralists: 'For the first, a man must love his wife above all the creatures in the world besides . . . no neighbour, no kinsman, no friend, no parent, no child should be so neare and deare.'[1] It is impossible to tell whether husband and wife grew closer over the years, drawn together by the birth of children;[2] whether, as Bullinger suggested, sexual compatibility increased with time.[3] Separation drew their own attention, and draws ours, to the warmth of their feelings for one another; after four and a half years of marriage when, during the Civil War, Josselin was serving as a chaplain in the army he recorded that 'Abundance of love made my wife greive' [12. 5. 45] When he returned to her on 4 September of the same year he found her 'indifferently cheerful only. In my absence shee was wondrous sad and discontented'. On another occasion, when he was about to set off for a long journey, Josselin noted, 'my wife sad at the thoughts of my journey' [11. 3. 60]. Her absences from home on visits to London to see their children made him equally restless and distressed. 'My wife not with me, and my mind very foolish' [29. 3. 63], he complained on one occasion, and on another 'my mind very full of roving thoughts, in my wives absence' [23. 5. 69]. Tenderness showed itself during the many illnesses they both suffered; 'my dearest very ill' [4. 12. 45], and 'my deare wife [was] exceeding tender and careful of me' [22. 11. 46] are typical entries. It also revealed itself in the presents he brought for Jane, such as the fruit on 3 June 1647, to comfort her pregnant whims. It is also probable that he was drawing on his own, albeit idealized, experience, when he described the joys of connubial love in a funeral sermon's preface: 'you can consider, here I was wont to see my dear Wife; here to enjoy her delightsome imbraces; her counsel, spiritual Discourses, furtherance, encouragement in the wayes of God, I was wont to finde her an help to ease me of the burthen and trouble of household-affaires, whose countenance welcomed me home with joy'.[4]

Deep emotional bonds could, however, generate bitterness and in this affectionate marriage there were considerable tensions. We do not know the origin of the marital disputes, but they seem largely to have been limited to the last ten years of Josselin's life, though there is discord in 1650, after twelve years together, when the Diary records:

[1] William Whately, *A Bride-Bush: or A Direction for Married Persons* (1619), p. 38.
[2] There is an excellent description of the change in the nature of family relationships after marriage in J. K. Campbell, *Honour, Family and Patronage* (Oxford, 1964), p. 70.
[3] Myles Coverdale (trans.), *The Christian State of Matrimony* (1543), sig. 63ᵛ.
[4] The exact reference and other abstracts from this sermon are given on p. 221 below.

I find my heart apt to unquietnes in my relation [i.e. wife] and it troubles mee, and yett it returneth on mee, I thinke I have cause, but I am sure I should bee more patient, and counsellable than I am, oh that I could looke at my wife not as under weaknes but as an heire of the same grace of life and live with her as such. [7. 11. 52]

A few days later, on the 28th, Josselin prayed for 'strength of spirit' to bear 'vanity and vexation' from his fellow creatures, and for twenty years there is no record of further trouble.

Then in 1673 during a painful illness in his leg Josselin entered into his Diary with a note of petulance: 'I beare my infirmities about mee, but my wife taxes mee for great impatience, when I feare there is a carelesnes in her &c. & impatience too much, that beares nothing, but expects I must beare all.' [27. 2. 73] Possibly the festering leg made him especially querulous and turned his wife's preoccupation into studied neglect. Possibly he was using the leg as a weapon against her, and she sensed this, for on 16 November 1676 he complained again 'my wife on some discontent which I know not, would not assist mee in dressing my poore leg'. As we never hear Jane's side of any story it is difficult to decide the depth of the rift between them. His daughter Mary dressed her father's leg and he scribbled his grievances down for us to ponder over, with the light of psycho-analysis to guide us but with the special circumstances elusive; how painful the leg was, how childish Josselin himself in his demands for attention from a woman whose many labours and losses must have made her sceptical of his suffering.

The really difficult period came when there were no children left to balance against his wife. On 4 January 1680, at the age of sixty-two, Josselin wrote 'not a child at home', but added with real appreciation, 'sensible of the comfort of my wife, my love, seeing every thing more pleasant because I have her'. It seemed that they were to share a serene old age, and yet in the four and a half years preceding his death there were many fretful entries: 'my wife afflicts mee and her self' [1. 5. 81], 'my family troubles continue, esp. a froward wife' [7. 5. 82], 'my life very unquiet: esp. from my wife' [23. 4. 82], 'a bitter morning from my wife' [28. 1. 83]. Friction continued to the end, but they stayed together and he left her land and furniture in his will, as well as three or four rooms in the mansion house in which to live.

We may wonder to what extent husband and wife had a 'joint role relationship', that is to say, entertained together, had the same friends, shared the care of the children, took joint decisions over matters previously discussed together, and participated generally in one another's activities.[1] Illumination on these points only occurs incidentally, though it is likely that more intensive research would produce a more complete picture. For example, we discover that husband and wife helped one another in the farm work; as an illustration of God's mercy Josselin described how 'when my wife and I pulling down a tree with a rope with our pulling all fell together, but no hurt God bee praised' [26. 8. 44]. In a situation where kinsfolk lived at a distance, and children left home at puberty, husband and wife were the effective economic producers and depended on one another's labour.

We do not know to what extent the husband controlled the household finances: it is quite possible that, as in some modern farming communities, the wife was in charge of part of them.[2] There are hints that all important decisions were jointly taken; in the matter of daughters' marriages, for example, Josselin recorded his wife's opinions. When a suitor called on their daughter Mary this 'seemed a speaking providence' to him, but 'to the contrary, my wife ill pleased with it' [3. 10. 76]. For whatever reason, Mary did not marry this suitor. Husband and wife seem to have shared, to a considerable extent, the task of rearing the children; their father's interest in them and in their progress is evident all through the Diary. Much of his work both as farmer and clergyman kept him near to his growing family, and it is likely that his contacts with them were close and sustained. There is no evidence of any conflict with his wife in this, the major preoccupation of their lives. When he delivered a long sermon to his children in the attempt to reform his tiresome son and advise his daughter who was being courted, he noted at the end 'their mother gave them the same advice' [19. 12. 76].

Activities they obviously shared in many spheres, attitudes it is harder to pronounce on. The dreams of his wife, recorded by Josselin, do suggest that she involved herself in his political and apocalyptic interests. On 22 November 1654 he dreamt that he 'was familiar with the pope. wife dreamed we were so with the protector', and early in the following year she dreamt of 'a curious building in the heavens towards North, out of it came men and presently an innumerable company of horsemen marching' [3. 2. 55]. There is no suggestion in the Diary that he and his wife had separate friends, or spent their leisure hours apart.

[1] E. Bott, *Family and Social Network* (Tavistock Publications Ltd., 1957), pp. 59–60, discusses such joint-role relationships and their possible correlates in the general kinship network.

[2] As in Cumberland farms (W. M. Williams, *The Sociology of an English Village: Gosforth* (1964), p. 42).

Adding up the allusions and accepting that Josselin's wife remains a shadowy figure, the impression is that this marriage could be classified sociologically as a 'joint-role relationship' and described as an emotional success. Ralph Josselin and his wife lived in a world both generally and personally insecure, shared illness and economic worries, and generated tensions that spilled over in irritated outbursts into his Diary. Nevertheless, in spite of, or perhaps because of, their disagreements and disappointments, their relationship seems to have remained important and close.

The second important relationship, that between parents and children, has an especial interest in the Josselin family, for it has been asserted that the Puritans (of whom Josselin was one) were changing the structure and function of the family. Arguments have been produced for the view that Calvinism emphasized the role and responsibilities of the father,[1] that the father in fact replaced the priest at the Reformation,[2] and that there was a slow but significant humanization of relations between parents and children which took place in the sixteenth and seventeenth centuries'.[3] The general features of parent–child relationships have already been described for Puritan[4] and Elizabethan families;[5] the accepted picture is one of a fairly rigid patriarchalism.[6] Contemporary works on the family are quoted to show that 'children have not power over themselves' and that 'the son in respect of his body, is part of the fathers goods',[7] that children should kneel to their parents[8] and uncover their heads in their presence.[9] Children should not speak until spoken to[10] and should revere and respect their parents.[11] The parental curse was powerful and dreaded[12] and if cursing was not a strong enough sanction, the child might be physically punished.[13]

[1] *Walzer, Revolution of the Saints*, p. 49.
[2] Hill, *Society and Puritanism*, p. 466, suggests this.   [3] *Ibid.*, p. 453
[4] Morgan, *Puritan Family*, ch. 3.
[5] Pearson, *Elizabethans at Home*, pp. 99 ff.
[6] As described in Laslett, *Lost World, passim*.
[7] Perkins, *Christian Oeconomie*, p. 76.
[8] Donne, quoted in Stone, 'Marriage among the Nobility', p. 183.
[9] Dod and Clever, *Godlie Forme*, p. 279.
[10] Gouge, *Domesticall Duties*, p. 431. Cobbett, quoted in Morgan, *Puritan Family*, p. 106, was of the same opinion.
[11] Thomas Becon, *Workes* (1560), sig. DCXXXII[v].
[12] On the fact that parental cursing might lead to the death of the child there is John Gaule, *Select Cases of Conscience Touching Witches and Witchcrafts* (1646), p. 185. The importance of night parental blessings is stressed in Richard Whitforde, *A Werke for Housholders* (1533), sig. Div[v].
[13] Pepys, *Diary*, p. 357, shows that a man would have whipped a child if it had been his.

This was the ideal of deference and humility on the part of the children, strictness amounting to absolute authority on the parents' side, but we know surprisingly little about how the actual situation corresponded to it. Did the patriarchal, the almost god-like power pursue the children into the world outside the home, when they became apprentices or married? Did the conflict implicit in the relationship between two generations, and sometimes expressed in seventeenth-century literature,[1] lead to competition in the nuclear family? The actual territory of parent–child relations remains largely unexplored; it was, no doubt, a varied landscape, the degree to which there was 'more love than terrour' decided by the father's character.[2]

For convenience's sake, the territory may be divided in half, with time as the boundary mark: on one side the years when parents and children formed a nuclear family, even if the children were away from home, on the other the years after the marriage of the children when the relationship was one between two nuclear families. The division was crucial only where marriage coincided with economic independence, as it seems to have done in the case of Ralph Josselin. The change from the 'family of origin' to that of 'marriage'[3] meant that 'a man and a woman that before were members of another family, doe therefore joyne together in marriage, that they become the rootes of a new family, and begetting children and training them up.'[4] In the earlier period money was still being invested in the children by the parents, and wealth and authority transferred from one generation to another. In the second stage the relationship was more balanced; it was between two nuclear families.

Some of the general features of the Josselins' relations with their children have already been described: their treatment of them as infants and children until they left home to become educated as servants or apprentices between the ages of ten and fifteen; the degree to which they controlled and financed their children's marriages; the way in which wealth was transmitted in a series of gifts at apprenticeship, marriage and the parents' death. We may therefore turn to more specific ties, those between father–daughter, mother–daughter, father–son, mother–son. The evidence is more complete for daughters, five of whom survived beyond childhood as

[1] For example, Henry Percy, ninth earl of Northumberland, *Advice To His Son* ed. G. B. Harrison (1930), p. 56.

[2] Herbert, *Priest to the Temple*, p. 236.

[3] I agree with Campbell, *Honour and Patronage*, p. 42, that these terms are preferable to 'orientation' and 'procreation'.

[4] Whately, *Bride-Bush*, pp. 87–8.

against two sons. The fact that historians have tended to be more interested in father–son relationships, since wealth and authority is thought to flow down this line, makes a case for exploring daughter relationships first.

The eldest surviving daughter, Jane, left home at the age of ten and a half to be educated at Colchester. She left on 21 April 1656, taken by her father, and within three weeks he visited her and 'found Jane well' [10. 5. 56]. Three months later she returned home after a bout of measles [3. 8. 56]. In the subsequent four years Josselin noted her visits to, and returns from, Colchester: she was 'well' at school in 1657, after a year away from home [27. 3. 57], and was again at school the following April [13. 4. 58]; then after a gap of only four months she was visiting her parents again [4. 8. 58]. Josselin recorded taking her back to 'Mrs Piggotts' [10. 3. 60] for the last time in March 1660, though it seems from the previous pattern of visits that she had been home in the spring of 1659.

During the next ten years, between her fourteenth and twenty-fourth years, Josselin mentioned Jane four times. She was at communion with him [26. 3. 65]; he rode off to try and seek work for her, unsuccessfully [5. 9. 67]; he noted that she went off to wait on his old friend Mrs Harlakenden [5. 10. 67]; she came back to look after her sick mother [8. 11. 68]. Finally she married at the age of nearly twenty-five with a 'portion' of £200 [30. 8. 70].

The next daughter, Anne, went to London when she was fourteen [24. 6. 68] and was bound as a servant there for eight years [20. 8. 68]. Within three weeks of her arrival in London Josselin heard that she was very well [12. 7. 68], but two and a half months later news reached him that she was ill [26. 9. 68]. Ten days after this he heard that she was 'hopefully upwards of the small Pox' [4. 10. 68] and a month later, on a visit to London on business about his son, he 'saw An. after the small Pox' [11. 11. 68]. He received cheerful news of her the following June [27. 6. 69], but a month afterwards, less happily, of a quarrel with her mistress [18. 7. 69]. Also she appeared to have been ill for in August came the report that her eyes were better [22. 8. 69].

The Diary does not mention her for five months, and then notes two sad letters from her about her 'condition' [22. 1. 70, 20. 2. 70]. She visited home later in the year to recuperate from whatever mental or physical disturbance this implied [5. 8. 70]. A month later she was back in London and well [4. 9. 70]; there is no further recorded news of her for three years. Then she became ill again, and her father was worried enough to bring sister Jane over to visit her [20–23. 6. 73]. Indeed her condition was very serious, and she died at home on 31 July 1673: 'This morning after 2 of the clocke my deare Ann in her twentieth year died with mee at Colne; a good child.' In the parish register Josselin wrote: 'M[ist]r[es]s Anne Josselin citizen of London and daughter of Ralph Josselin vicar of this parish was buried August 1st 1673'.

The final three girls may be treated more briefly, since we have already received an impression of the considerable degree of contact between parents and children, even after the children left home. Mary and Elizabeth spent some time at various places away from home before they went to London together in June 1675, joined there two years later by their youngest sister Rebecka straight from home [17. 5. 77]. A month after this Elizabeth married, aged just under seventeen years [5. 6. 77], and in July and September Josselin heard 'with joy' from the three sisters [15. 7. 77, 2. 9. 77]. It seems likely that the 'news from London' which flowed for the next six years was from and about all of them.

Josselin heard of the children's health and affairs every few months at least in the following years. Rebecka was going through a difficult period two years after leaving home; she was ill in August of 1679, though 'abroad' again a month later [28. 9. 79], and then in May of the following year went down with the apparently inevitable smallpox [27. 5. 80]. It was four months before she was 'hopeful' from this illness [19. 9. 80] and she may have come home for a spell, as Mary did for eleven months [18. 4. 80]. Their mother visited the children later that year [27. 3. 81, 28. 8. 81], causing Josselin some anxiety as he did not hear from her for two weeks [18. 9. 81]. In 1682 it was his turn to go to London [16. 5. 82], his wife's again in July of 1683 [1. 7. 83]. There were messages about the girls twice between the visits [8. 10. 82, 4. 5. 83].

As well as the contacts mentioned in the Diary, there were probably periodic gatherings of all the nuclear family, for instance in July 1679 [6. 7. 79], and at Christmas [25. 12. 67]. The close concern of the children for their father is best illustrated when they feared that he was dying. Very ill in March 1683, Josselin noted 'my children alarmd at London' [3. 3. 83], and three days later 'my children came down'; they stayed with him for a week [12. 3. 83]. As we have already seen, the various daughters brought their suitors to visit their parents at Earls Colne before they married, and their father clearly fretted about them a good deal, for instance during Anne's tribulations when he wrote 'my children I hope well at London, prayer hath gon for them' [3. 3. 70].

If anything, contact between parents and children seems to have increased after the daughters' marriages. Only two of Josselin's

family married early enough to leave us a record of how the relationship progressed from the wedding: Jane, who married John Woodthorpe in 1670, and Elizabeth, married in 1677 to Gilbert Smith.
Jane, the elder, may be treated first. After the marriage she was no
longer usually referred to as 'Jane' but rather 'my daughter Woodthorpe', as Elizabeth was referred to as 'good daughter Smith'
[11. 6. 81]. This change in terminology was a recognition that her
primary allegiance was to her husband, with whom she went off to
live at Lexden, a village some seven miles to the east of Earls Colne.
In the year following the wedding Josselin was relieved that 'God
[was] good in dispatch of son Woodthorpe's affaire' [31. 7. 71],
having earlier noted the death of 'My son Woodthorps mother'
[18. 12. 70].

Five months later Josselin stayed with his 'son Woodthorpe'
[15. 12. 71]; possibly on a visit to collect Jane, who was some five
months pregnant by this time. Jane clearly returned home to have
this first child[1] as on 29 April 1672 Josselin wrote, 'Monday neare 3 a
clocke after noon my daughter Woodthorpe delivered of a son, the
first grandchild; God blesse him with his Christ.' God did not see
fit to preserve this child, however, for it was buried five weeks later,
on 4 June. Jane remained at Earls Colne for a further five months;
she was described as 'ill' on 11 August but by the 16th of the same
month Josselin had 'some hopes in Jane'. She 'went away well',
presumably to her home, on 8 September.

Two months later [27. 11. 72] we learn by chance that Josselin was
staying with his daughter and her husband; 'being at my daughter
Janes at Lexden I was taken in my bed, or coming out of it with the
sciatica pain'. Eight months after this he went to fetch Jane to her
dying sister Anne [23. 7. 73], and though she returned home she
was back at Earls Colne within a few weeks to have her second
child [21. 9. 73]. On 12 October Josselin wrote; 'my daughter Woodthorpe holds up, god send her a good delivery', and on the 21st,
'About 5 of the clocke, my daughter Jane deliv[ere]d of a daughter,
which wee baptized that day ... her name is Jane' [21. 10. 73].
Mother and baby stayed at Earls Colne for six weeks, and then
returned home accompanied by Mrs Josselin and another daughter
Mary [2. 12. 73].

Josselin went to see Jane the following spring, and two months
later she and her 'little one' returned the visit, both 'in health'
[17. 5. 74]. In the same year she was back [5. 7. 74], this time leaving

[1] Such a custom of returning home to have children, if widespread, will obviously
affect all attempts to use 'family reconstitution' methods (such methods are
outlined in Wrigley (ed.), *Historical Demography*, ch. 4).

the child with its grandparents, for on 5 November there is Josselin's record that 'my grandchild went homewards well weaned'. Twenty-three days later came the news 'our only grandchild . . . burnt so as they feared the life thereof', but his wife rode over to Lexden the following day and was able to bring Josselin back the information that the child was 'not dangerously hurt' [29. 11. 74]. There is no further reference to Jane for over a year, and then she had apparently suffered some misfortune for they heard she was 'hopefully upward' [28. 3. 75]. Six months later her father was again riding to Lexden to see her [28. 9. 75].

The next contact was at the birth of Jane's third child, when Mrs Josselin went to Lexden to help at the delivery [30. 4. 76]. The grandchild, another daughter, was reported not well five weeks later [4. 6. 76], but Josselin found his daughter 'better than she was' when he saw her in August [24. 8. 76]; she was still 'ill', however, in November [20. 11. 76]. Jane visited home the following July [7. 7. 77], and in January of the next year she was reported at home and 'full of her discontents' [1. 1. 78]. As we will shortly see, this may have been connected with trouble over the inheritance, but it did not stop the frequent visits and Josselin returned from one of these later in the year because of illness [3. 7. 78]. Three days after he got home he heard that his daughter was 'in bed of a daughter'; baptism of the infant was noted in the Lexden parish register for the 6th.

On 4 August Josselin heard that the grandchildren were ill, and his wife 'rid to see them'. When Jane herself was ill two months later, her sister Mary was sent 'to be with her' [6. 10. 78]; Mrs Josselin could not go for she was planning to attend the delivery of the first child of her other married daughter, Elizabeth. Jane obviously came back to Earls Colne with Mary, for she left there on 25 October 'with all her children indifferent well'. Nineteen months later she 'buried her youngest daughter' [16. 5. 80], a child of twenty-two months. On 2 October of the following year Josselin recorded that 'it is with regret Mary rid to Lexden with the child', which implies that his grandchildren came on short visits alone. A year later daughter Jane 'had a dangerous fit' [26. 3. 82] and she may have come home to be nursed for it is recorded that 'Jane went home' in July [9. 7. 82].

This very detailed account of relations between Josselin and his married daughter illustrates how close the bonds between the two nuclear families continued to be, and also how much material on such relations may be obtained from a good diary. An equally detailed description could be elicited for the other daughter

Elizabeth, but only a few items will be selected. The general impression is that despite the greater distance between the two families—Elizabeth settled with her husband in London—the contacts remained as close as in Jane's case. In the period between her marriage in June 1677 and the end of 1682 there are at least twenty-two occasions when Elizabeth's affairs are mentioned: during the same period Jane was only mentioned twelve times. Josselin greeted her visits with 'great joy' [21. 2. 78] and described the time she spent with them as full of 'sweetness and content' [15. 8. 82]. In the six years after the wedding the parents visited the Smiths at least six times; four times it was Mrs Josselin who went, twice Josselin himself. The Smiths returned these visits on the same number of occasions, so that on average there seems to have been personal contact at least every six months.

As with Jane, Mrs Josselin was in particular demand when her daughter was pregnant. She arrived too late for the first delivery [27. 10. 78] but at the second birth stayed almost seven weeks to help [1. 10. 81]. When she heard that her daughter was dying, Mrs Josselin rushed straight up to London by coach [5. 3. 82]: fortunately it was a false alarm. The grandparents were used as baby-minders by this daughter too; when Elizabeth left for London on 1 August 1679 Josselin noted that 'the babe staid with us', though it was only nine months old at the time, and remained for nearly two months. On one occasion Mr Smith brought a child to visit the Josselins without his wife [12. 2. 82].

In some societies the tie between father and daughter is one of avoidance after puberty,[1] or of no great emotional importance.[2] In Ralph Josselin's family the interest and affection shown for daughters is as strong and sustained as that for sons, and the money invested in them almost as much. There was no taboo to prevent them from bandaging his leg [16. 11. 76]; their deaths in childhood were the occasion for as much, if not more, grief than was shown over sons. The impression, supported by the evidence from other contemporary diaries,[3] is of a father–daughter relationship of great warmth and intimacy.

It seems probable that the emotional tie between mother and daughter, found to be so important in many societies,[4] was even

[1] For example, Campbell, *Honour and Patronage*, p. 159.
[2] A few general points concerning the father–daughter relationship are made in Stirling, *Turkish Village*, p. 116.
[3] There is a very moving and affectionate description of a father's grief at his daughter's death in Evelyn, *Diary*, pp. 425–8.
[4] For instance, Stirling, *Turkish Village*, p. 108; and, especially, Wilmott and Young, *Family and Kinship*, ch. 3.

stronger. We have seen Mrs Josselin rushing off whenever she heard of the imminent delivery or serious illness of her daughters, and there are other signs of a close bond on both sides. Mrs Josselin attributed a seven-year-old daughter's illness to the pain she was herself suffering from a swelling on her finger, the child sick 'with feare and griefe to see her mother so tormented' [26. 2. 53]. When the same child left home finally at the age of twenty-two to be a servant 'her mother wept for it' [5. 10. 67].

Parents and daughters seem to have kept close and loving contact throughout their lives, in spite of the harsh social necessity for early separation. The situation brings to mind the twentieth-century West Country village of Ashworthy; here there is constant visiting, children are christened in the parents' village, and in the difficult months just before and after childbirth parents play an important part.[1] Such continued affection is not necessarily implicit in family life; in Greece, for example, visits of the wife to her original home are rare.[2]

The father–son relationship in the seventeenth century has been examined in some detail by historians, who have generally pronounced the father's role to be authoritarian and patriarchal.[3] As in many societies, the father and son could be defined as rivals, likely to compete for limited resources.[4] This could lead to strict avoidance[5] and to an excessively domineering and rigid rule by the father.[6] This state of affairs was epitomized in a contemporary translation of Ovid, which spoke of 'when the sonne too soone dooth aske how long his father is to live'.[7] Josselin himself admitted that, in some families, 'parents [were] neglected by children, their deaths gapd for to enjoy that they have' [16. 12. 77]. This tense, rebellious, relationship is symbolized by a story told by John Aubrey of Sir Walter Raleigh's son who, boxed on the ear by his father, dared not strike back directly but 'strikes over the face of the Gentleman that sate next to him, and sayed, "Box about, 'twill come to my father anon"'.[8]

[1] Williams, Ashworthy, p. 171.
[2] Campbell, Honour and Patronage, p. 53.
[3] For example, Stone, Crisis of the Aristocracy, p. 592, which reads very like the description in Stirling, Turkish Village, p. 101.
[4] An instance is described in Mead, Sex and Temperament, p. 180.
[5] As among the Tallensi (M. Fortes, 'Kinship, Incest and Exogamy of the Northern Territories of the Gold Coast', in Custom is King, ed. L. H. D. Buxton (1949), p. 247).
[6] Among the Ruanda the father even had access to a son's wife (J. Maquet, The Premise of Inequality in Ruanda (Oxford, 1961), p. 42).
[7] This is quoted in Reginald Scot, The Discoverie of Witchcraft (1584; reprinted Arundel, 1964), p. 114.
[8] Aubrey, Brief Lives, p. 319.

Nevertheless, there is evidence that fathers were prepared to dote upon their sons, to cherish hopes and devote much time and work to raising them higher in the social order than themselves, and that in return sons were often very fond of their fathers. A seventeenth-century writer, describing yeomen, wrote 'the bringing up and marriage of his eldest son is an ambition which afflicts him so soon as the boy is born, and the hope to see his son superior, or placed above him, drives him to dote upon the boy in his cradle.'[1] Josselin himself, though his father died when he was only nineteen, laid him in his grave 'with greife of heart' [28. 10. 36] which must presumably have been genuine since he felt it 'a continuall comfort to mee to thinke of my tender love to him' [1632]. With these opposing views in mind, we may turn to his relations with his two surviving sons, Thomas and John, remembering the general problem of the degree of tension, authority and intimacy present in the father–son bond, and asking of the evidence certain questions. Did the considerable amount of geographical mobility already noted lessen possible conflicts?[2] How did the mother enter the picture: was her position closer to the Turkish situation where, we are told, 'the mother–son relationship is probably more important to a woman than any other personal relationship',[3] or to that in a Devon village where mother–son ties are described as weakly developed?[4]

The bare facts of the life of Josselin's eldest son Thomas can be stated quite briefly; it was indeed a short life, and references to his ill-health appear so frequently as to give the impression that during the last few years it was chronic. The colds and fevers suggest consumption, and Thomas's death came as no surprise to his father, although at twenty-nine it was still a bitter blow. The fact that his eldest son was delicate, probably doomed, must have affected their relationship, even more so the feelings of Mrs Josselin. It must also have reacted on to the other surviving son John, whose behaviour suggests a violent attempt to attract to himself the love and concern that were likely to have been centred on his ailing elder brother.

Thomas left home at the age of fifteen and a half to be an apprentice in London [25. 5. 59]; it had cost his father £100 to set him up in this apprenticeship [14. 4. 60] and there is nothing to show that he tried to persuade the boy to follow in his own profession

[1] John Stephens, quoted in J. Dover Wilson, *Life in Shakespeare's England* (Pelican edn, 1962), p. 31.

[2] As suggested for an Indian society by Fürer-Haimendorf, *Morals and Merit*, p. 149.

[3] Stirling, *Turkish Village*, p. 115.

[4] Williams, *Ashworthy*, p. 162.

or to go to university. The boy returned home after two weeks with smallpox [11. 6. 59] and remained there until 8 November, when he rode back to London. In the following seven years of apprenticeship Thomas is mentioned at least eleven times. He spent holidays at home at least twice, on the second occasion a period of over six months during the Great Plague in London [4. 6. 65–31. 1. 66]. At the end of his apprenticeship in 1667 his father gave him a further £50 to set him up in business [March 1667], and a month after the apprenticeship officially ended Josselin 'made mocions in a match for Tho. and a farme buying . . . both came to nothing' [2. 6. 67].

It seems that a shop was purchased instead, somewhere near Earls Colne, for, two and a half years later, Josselin described how 'my sons shop broke open, and nigh £50 of good[s] stolen' [11. 12. 69]. He himself helped in the chase and most of the goods were regained [12. 12. 69].[1] In the following year, however, Thomas decided to return to London while the other son John 'would trade in the country' [2. 10. 70]. Thomas set out on 6 October, but soon became sick of a fever [25. 12. 70], from which he had recovered five days later [1. 1. 71]. Yet, when he visited London in the following April, Josselin found his son 'ill and dismayed' [15. 4. 71]. It was in the last year of his apprenticeship that Thomas started the recurring bouts of ill health that dogged him through his twenties; 'his illnes a cold' Josselin noted then [18. 1. 62], and ominously a few months later, 'heard of my son Toms harsh conditcion' [9. 3. 62]. Damp living conditions could have been the cause of a chest weakness turning to consumption.

In 1672 Thomas was reported well for the last time [2. 6. 72]; he obviously came down to Earls Colne for a few weeks for on 22 September both sons were 'at dinner' and Thomas left for London on 27 October. By the following spring his illness was bad enough to bring him home where he returned in March [22. 3. 73], twenty-nine years old, unmarried in spite of his father's hopes, a dying man dependent on his parents. Three months later, 'June 15th, about one a clocke in the morning my eldest sonne Thomas and my most deare child ascended early hence to keep his everlasting Sabbath with his heavenly Father . . . He was my hope, but some yeares I have feared his life'. In the Earls Colne parish register the burial is noted on the 17th thus: 'Mr Thomas Josselin of London, Grocer, sonne of Ralph Josselin, vicar, was buried'. It must have been among the hardest crosses that God ordained for Josselin to carry, particularly

[1] The thieves were found guilty and sentenced to death on 14 March 1670 at the assizes. The indictment, which gives a very detailed inventory of the haberdashery goods stolen, is printed on p. 219 below.

poignant in the Diary, where he adds drearily 'a wett morning, the heavens for some time have mourned over us'. A month later he was burying his daughter Anne.

Summarizing the impression left by this account of Thomas's life, tension between father and eldest son appears to have been absent, nor is there any mention of a harsh authoritarian attitude or of the need for physical punishment. There is nothing on either side of deference or avoidance; Josselin never expresses emotion until his son dies, but implies affection in his constant interest in Thomas's affairs. There is nothing to show that he thought of his son as a threat, indeed the cry 'he was my hope' implies the opposite; nor does he put too much pressure on his son either to follow a particular calling or to get married. Thomas ended up unmarried and followed several different jobs without a word of condemnation from his father. There is no evidence of a particularly warm relationship between mother and son; all these are negative conclusions which will need testing against other historical material. One immediate test we can make in Josselin's case is to compare his attitude to his two sons.

Josselin's second surviving son, John, was nearly seven years younger than Thomas. Like Thomas he was sent to London. He went on his first visit in 1667 [9. 1. 67] and Josselin soon heard 'uncomfortably' of his fifteen-year-old child [27. 1. 67], who returned home a few weeks later [15. 2. 67]. He was a burden at home, although Josselin felt 'the lord gives me some hopes in John' [3. 3. 67], and he was therefore bound apprentice once more in London for £45 [13. 11. 68]. He succumbed to smallpox the following spring [18–25. 4. 69] and Josselin continued to receive news of his activities during that year [16. 5. 69]. He was obviously misbehaving and his 'business' was 'grievous to me' [5. 6. 70]. It is probable that John gave up in London fairly soon for, as we have seen, it was decided in October 1670 [2. 10. 70] that he would 'trade in the country'. He obviously based himself on his father's home, though he roamed away for short periods.

Remarks passed about him in the year 1671 will illustrate the strained relationship. 'John's debauchery in swearing sad, Lord helpe mee; so bad 6,7, that I resolve to put him to his shifts, for the Lord's sake lett it tend to his good' [4. 2. 71]; 'my soule yearned over John, oh lord overcome his heart' [12. 2. 71], 'his carriage intolerable' and 'high and proud' [19. 2. 71]; 'John rid away, carried some things with him. without taking his leave of mee' [12. 3. 71]; 'my wife afflicted to see John again' [2. 4. 71]; 'John robd his mother and sister of neare 30s. and away. god in mercy breake his heart for good' [5. 7. 71]; 'John was in [a] service having spent all his mony' [9. 7. 71]; 'a letter delivered from John as I came from church. lord direct mee what to doe' [29. 10. 71]. It seems that after this disastrous year, during which John was making efforts to escape from home, he returned to settle, for he was ill in the following August [11. 8. 72]. Jane was also ill but she soon recovered: Josselin as early as 16 August noted 'some hopes in Jane. but John is John'. It almost sounds as if he considered John's illness a symptom of his waywardness: it persisted for over a month.

After his elder brother's death in June 1673 there was a slight easing of tension. Josselin had 'glimmering hopes' of his son [18. 1. 74] and prayed 'oh that John might live to thee' [i.e. God] [23. 1. 74] and reported 'a good week with John' [15. 2. 74]. But tension began to mount again, despite the fact that John was now the only remaining son. In March, Josselin was 'sad with John' [22. 3. 74], and in April he implored God to 'reclaime mine to thy feare . . . esp. disobedient John' [11. 4. 74]. In June providence was 'afflictive in John's carriage' [7. 6. 74], and by September John was described as setting himself 'on evil' [30. 9. 74]. Clearly Josselin was very distressed for he wrote five days later 'oh let not an only son bee an outcast' [4. 10. 74].

The conflict came to a head just before Christmas of the same year, in an incident which reveals plainly the type of controls which Josselin could exert, and his reluctance to disown his son. John was twenty-three years old, and in a family discussion held 'before his mother and foure sisters' the following proposition was put before him:

John set your selfe to feare God, & bee industrious in my busines, refrain your evill courses, and I will passe by all past offences, setle all my estate on you after your mothers death, and leave you some stocke on the ground and within doores to the value of an £100 and desire of you, out of your marriage portion but £400 to provide for my daughters or otherwise to charge my land with so much for their porcions; but if you continue your ill courses I shall dispose my land otherwise, and make only a provision for your life to put bread in your hand.

It was a nicely-balanced combination of threats and bribes, and John was moved to accept the offer, and 'ownd his debauchery' [15. 12. 74].

This chastened state did not last, however, and only a month later there was a relapse, causing an exasperated outburst in the Diary: 'John [was] declared for his disobedience no son; I should allow him nothing except he tooke himself to bee a servant; yet if he would depart and live in service orderly I would allow him £10 yearly; if he so walkt as to become God's son, I would yett own him for mine' [24. 1. 75]. These threats were not carried out, for John remained at home. In spite of the wistful hopes of improvement, his father's comments reflect continued trouble; John 'abounds in his evil' [6. 6. 75]; 'is in some disorder' [5. 8. 76] and drunken [15. 10. 76]; he was out all night [16. 11. 76], and out all week 'in his filthy courses' [3. 12. 76]. Josselin then tried to instruct his twenty-five-year-old son with a long sermon and prayer session, again held in the presence of the whole family. In this he instructed not only his son, but also a daughter who was being courted, to obey their father who was a mediator of God's commands [19. 12. 76].

Set apart this day with my familie to humble my soule before God, for our sins, to seeke his direction for and blessing on us & ours: the special occasion, Johns ill housbandry & Eliz. offer of a young man from London . . . I first proposed a duty to looke up to direction from God, Ezra: 8.21, who hath the cast in our lott, Is.34.17; then I commended all to God in prayer: if God cast your lot, rest in it, & to know it observe Pro.3.6; own God & he will direct you; Psal.32.8. was Gods direction, is by our parents for children . . . rest in a housbands house, Ruth.1.9.; thats done when both bring Gods feare, mutual love, & industrious prudence; the way is by parents provision, & children following their counsell, as Abraham tooke a wife for Isaac, whom he tooke & loved, Gen.24, & thus God comforts in losses in one another . . . God casts your lot in parents choice, Exod.2.19.21. Numb.30; vows to God allowd or disallowd by parents, otherwise free; therefore my children receive this counsel as Gods not mine; tis mine because Gods & so its Gods being mine, a father that is to counsel, which wilbee your crown as theirs, 1 Thes.2.13; it will effectually worke obedience, & therefore hear him, Pro. 23, 22, Pro.8.8.,9. I am perswaded a blessing will follow this counsel embraced . . . I praid thrice with them; their mother gave them the same advice, God in mercy give them his blessing.

Through the next five years the situation remained unhappy and uncomfortable, with little sign of improvement. John was still following 'an ill course of life' [15. 7. 77], and was in 'his old sottish humour' [30. 1. 78]. At twenty-eight he was 'sett in his disorder' [18. 5. 79], and two years later he was 'a severe trouble' [7. 8. 81]. By his thirtieth birthday he was still unmarried, nor is there evidence that his father had ever tried to arrange a match for him. Then on 16 October comes the announcement 'John married unknown to mee; God pardon his errors'. Perhaps because the marriage was unexpected and no provision could be made immediately for a separate home, John seems to have continued to live with his parents, with or without his wife we do not know; Josselin continued to complain that 'at home an undutifull son troubles us' [11. 12. 81]. Five months later, however, the families split and, in spite of everything, Jossselin gave his fatherly blessing: 'John went to his house. god blesse him' [14. 5. 82]. The last entry in the Diary concerning John indicates that even then the sense of strain remained and that Josselin disliked his new daughter-in-law for he noted 'John's wife likely to bee a trouble to us' [24. 9. 82]. There is no reference in the Diary to the birth of John's son, although, as vicar, Josselin noted the baptism, under the date 3 May 1683 in the parish register, of 'Ralph son of Mr John Josselin & Martha his wife'.

In the light of this very stormy history it is interesting to see how far Josselin's will reflected his feelings for his son. There are indications that there was a considerable influence. Instead of merely deducting some £400 from the estate for the marriage portions of the daughters, as he had offered in the attempted agreement in 1674, he in fact gave the last two daughters cash or estate worth £1,000, as well as a small amount to their previously married sister Elizabeth. Possible hostility is reflected, too, in the provisions that protected Josselin's widow, giving her four rooms to live in and 'free ingress egress and regress out of the same into the yards' where she could gather firewood and also the safeguarded use of a barn for a year.[1]

On the other hand, as the whole account of the troubled relationship indicates, although Josselin was exasperated and depressed by his wayward son, he was very reluctant to disinherit him, always eager to look for signs of repentance. As a result, despite all his threats, the bulk of the estate passed to John, his residuary legatee. This estate was large enough for John to have become a 'gent' by 1691, some eight years later.[2] John's side of the matter is never revealed; it is tempting to speculate on his rebelliousness as an attempt to claim for himself some of the attention that his apparently placid elder brother received. With the seven-year age gap, John would have been leaving home to start as an apprentice just at the time that Thomas's health began to cause concern. After his

[1] Similar conditions were made in other contemporary wills and it would be valuable to know whether they always indicated tension. It would seem likely, for example, that the following condition in the will of William Rolle of the Essex village of Hatfield Peverel, in 1570, indicates some conflict: 'Richard my sonne shall dwell with his mother uppon condicon that he be lovinge and gentell unto her as his dewtie is and if he be forward and does not gentlie agree with her then the said Jone my wife maye lawfullie expulse him'. (E.R.O., D/ACR/6/90).

[2] John's will is printed on p. 213 below; the legacies he received are indicated on figure 9, p. 66 above.

brother's death he may have been taunted by comparisons, and Thomas invested with a saintliness he hardly deserved.

Yet John obviously never lost all feeling for his family, and even seems to have felt warmly for the elder brother with whom he may have been competing during his early years. He asked for his body to be buried 'as neer my brother Thomas as can be'.[1] A comparison of this tense relationship with the untroubled one between Josselin and Thomas shows how differently the 'patriarchal' role could be interpreted, even within one family. As we see it in this family, the father's part was to be kind, encouraging and helpful, with the co-operation of a sober, industrious and obedient son. The harmony of the household, indeed the stability of the family, was threatened by ideas of a new kind: notions of gaiety, irresponsibility, tipsiness. Then the father brought the pressures of his position to bear on his capricious offspring with as much force as he could control: if John had not been the last surviving son he would probably have been disinherited without more ado. His mother's attitude to him remains obscure, and as in the case of Thomas it is not possible to judge from this Diary the strength of the mother–son bond. Geographical mobility seems not to have played an important part in the struggle with John: at home or in London he remained a headache.

Josselin's general views on the parent–child relationship have been implicit, and sometimes openly stated, in the preceding pages. One other place where we gain an insight into his attitudes are his sermons. During the years when he was trying to discipline John and putting pressure on Elizabeth to marry as he wished, his sermons seem to have often touched on the topic of parental authority. On one occasion he noted that he had preached a sermon in which he had 'endeavoured to stir up young persons to bee good' [12. 1. 71]; on another, of which, fortunately, we have a description, he made the following plea.[2]

If any widdow have children or nephews, let them learne first to shew piety at home, & to requite their parents; for that is good and acceptable before god; this is pleasing to god ... Now to requite, is when that we do, carries a proportion to what we have received. Now what have we received from our parents? We received from them our life under god, & our bringing up, & education, with a great deal of care & labor, & with all love & tenderness, Now to returne that love & tenderness to your parents

---

[1] As my wife pointed out, there is a remarkable similarity to the film of Steinbeck's *East of Eden*, with John playing the role of the jealous and rebellious 'Cal' (James Dean), Thomas his 'worthy' elder brother.

[2] This sermon was preached in 1669. The full reference and further extracts are printed on p. 223 below.

with all willingness, this is to . . . requite your parents for the cost they have laid out about you; follow their counsells, & cheer their sperits in their gray haires.

Josselin's plea was based on the idea of reciprocity, rather than a natural superiority and authoritiy of parents. Any idea of patriarchal aloofness that still remains is dispelled by another remark in a sermon; 'oh, when I returne home, Oh my childe that met me, hugged me, is dead'.[1] If Josselin is typical, Puritan fathers were less austere and less able to exert control of their children than some historians would have us believe.

[1] Extracts from this sermon and its location are given on p. 222 below.

8

Other kinship ties

Of two other relationships which may be included under the broad category of the nuclear family, those with step or grandparents, the Diary unfortunately tells us little. It has been pointed out by demographers that the low expectation of life in pre-industrial societies, particularly for child-bearing women, would mean that at least half the population would spend part of their lives with a step-parent. It has further been suggested that the wicked step-mother of the fairy tale must represent a popular aversion to such a relationship.[1] When Josselin's mother died he was just under the age of nine, and he 'feared a mother in law and undoing by her and truly so it proved in respect of estate as will appeare' [1618]: it is worth noting that the term used was 'mother in law' which now, of course, refers to a wife's or husband's mother.

In Josselin's case, his father remarried after a gap of six years, his second wife a widow who already had a child by another husband. Josselin, now aged fourteen or fifteen and about to leave home, commented 'though my father loved me exceedingly and my mother in law, though I hope an honest woman, yett was of a somewhat sowre spirit, yett I remember not that I ever caused any debate or division betwixt them for anything, though I was sensible of her disrespect in somethings towards mee' [March 1632]. Soon after the remarriage a child, Rebecka, was born.[2] Josselin was away at Cambridge much of the time and he was still at the university when his father died intestate some five years later. There was a quarrel over the inheritance and 'my mother in law tooke not as I conceived a course to do us justice; wee could not agree'; so he went back to Cambridge with the £20 she gave him [30. 10. 36].[3] Apart from a reference to money he received 'of my mother' in 1637, there is no further allusion to his step-mother until a note on 16 February 1668, 'My father's second wife died surviving him 31 years shee was nigh 80 old'.

The omissions in this account are as significant as the expressed

---

[1] Laslett, *Lost World*, p. 95.

[2] The dates of the death of the mother [29. 11. 24] and of the birth of the child Rebecka [20. 11. 31] are from the Bishop's Stortford parish register at the H.R.O.

[3] Josselin's step-mother was left with quite a reasonable amount of property, for she paid Ship Money on 100 acres in Steeple Bumpstead in 1636. Her assessment for 10s. was the twelfth highest in the village (E.R.O., T/A 42).

dislike. We never learn his step-mother's Christian name (although we never learn his father's for that matter) and only discover from the Bishop's Stortford register that it was Helen. He obviously kept some contact, however, for some fourteen years after his father's death he heard of the death in childbed of 'Mary Peacock, my father's second wives daughter by a former housband' [23. 8. 50]. This was the only reference to Mary, just as there was only one mention of the child of his father's second marriage. When she was forty years old 'sister Rebekah' and her husband visited Josselin [10. 9. 71]. It seems clear that step-sisters were not of great importance compared to full siblings.

Just as the demographic background made the step-parent tie a frequent if uncomfortable one, it seems unlikely that the grand-parent–grandchild tie was often significant. In other pre-industrial societies where a low expectation of life is combined with low age of marriage, it is possible that a child often has living grandparents. But with a combined high age of marriage and high mortality the chances are that grandparents could not have been a common experience in the life of growing children. It might well be argued, therefore, that grandparents, rather than playing a diminishing part in family life as some sociologists have maintained,[1] only came into their own long after the seventeenth century.

When they were alive, they may have provided that identification of 'alternate generations' of which anthropologists have written.[2] Certainly they were often indulgent to their grandchildren in a way impossible for the parents.[3] The experience of Ralph Josselin shows both extremes; the absence of grandparents, and the important link that could be created between alternate generations. He himself never mentioned his own grandparents, either on his father's or his mother's side; we happen to know that his father's parents were called Ralph and Dorothy and that they died in 1632 and 1634.[4] There is no reference to their names or impressions of their characters. On the other hand, Josselin himself probably left some impression on his grandchildren for, as we have seen, they often visited him with his two married daughters, or even spent some weeks by themselves with their grandparents. There are no recorded presents to these grandchildren, either in the Diary or in his will;

[1] For example, Riesman, *Lonely Crowd*, pp. 56–7; Wilmott and Young, *Family and Kinship*, p. 53.

[2] One such analysis is given by Radcliffe-Brown, *African Kinship and Marriage*, p. 28.

[3] As in the case of Evelyn, *Diary*, pp. 4–5.

[4] Grandfather Ralph's will is printed on p. 215 below.

his wife's father, however, left in his will 'one ewe and a lamb' to his granddaughter Mary.[1]

Josselin's eldest grandchild Mary was nearly ten years old when Josselin died, and two other grandchildren were probably old enough to remember him at seven and five years, but three of his five married children had not started to produce grandchildren. If we are to generalize from Josselin's experience, it seems very different from the modern Western pattern where three adult generations are quite commonly alive simultaneously. Josselin was fortunate to witness the overlap between three generations; his own early experience had shown that even two might not overlap long enough to be adults together. His attitude towards his grandchildren appears to have been one of kindly concern, without any signs of meddling or moralizing.

The final intimate relationship was that between siblings, that is between brothers and sisters. In a number of societies there is very close solidarity among siblings,[2] but the degree of actual emotional involvement varies. There may be a considerable taboo on brother–sister contact;[3] relations may be far from intimate even when they are very important.[4] On the other hand the tie between siblings may be the closest affective link felt by individuals in some English villages.[5] The relationship between brothers is often one of great conflict;[6] as anthropologists have pointed out, the degree of tension and avoidance is probably directly related to the inheritance system.[7] Often brothers compete for limited resources; the problem of the younger brother, felt by seventeenth-century writers, is a widespread one.[8]

We know little about the quality of this particular blood tie in Tudor and Stuart England, though there is probably much evidence to be gleaned;[9] for example some of the aristocracy argued that the

[1] Abstracts from his will are printed on p. 214 below.

[2] E.g. Campbell, *Honour and Patronage*, p. 172. There is some statistical analysis of such contacts in Wilmott and Young, *Family and Kinship*, p. 77.

[3] B. Malinowski, *Sex and Repression in Savage Society* (Paperback edn, 1960), pp. 70–1, is one of the classic instances.

[4] For example, Stirling, *Turkish Village*, p. 117.

[5] Williams, *Ashworthy*, p. 172.

[6] For instance, Mead, *Sex and Temperament*, p. 174 or E. R. Leach, *Pul Eliya, A village in Ceylon* (Cambridge, 1961), p. 107.

[7] Argued, for example, in G. Obeyesekere, *Land Tenure in Ceylon* (Cambridge, 1967), p. 259.

[8] Herbert, *Priest to the Temple*, p. 278, warned the clergy that younger sons would be a problem.

[9] There is a short account of sibling ties in Pearson, *Elizabethans at Home*, pp. 258 ff. and 268.

link with a brother was stronger than that with a child.[1] Josselin
certainly counted the sibling relationship as very strong; when he
attempted to describe a friend's kindness it was to sisterly love that
he compared it, 'Mrs Church who in all things hath beene as kinde
to, and tender of me and wife, as if shee were our sister' [7. 3. 48].
On another occasion he described with evident disapproval how
there was 'a sad sight of a brother S.B. whose sister fell to the towne
chardge; he said all in his hande was spent. £50 & all her clothes
etc; he said he would turne out the 4 children ... he seemed to mee
void of brotherly and naturall affection; the lord make some of us
strangers sensible of her condicion' [19. 10. 54]. This indeed was a
subject on which Josselin was qualified to speak, for he was the
brother of three sisters, all of whom depended on his help from time
to time. He was the only son, so in the context of his life it is only
possible to learn about the brother–sister bond.

As we can see from the kinship chart (facing p. 234), Josselin had
three full sisters who lived to maturity. All of them married, although
Mary did not do so until she was aged fifty. Born in 1611, Mary was
five and a half years older than Ralph.[2] He helped her and the other
sisters during the difficult years after their father's death, for he
wrote: 'when my father was dead, in my poverty, I blesse God I did
not forgett to doe for them' [1632]. When she was thirty-three he
noted 'my sister Mary is come under my roofe as a servant' but he
promised that 'my respect is & shall be towards her as a sister'
[5. 8. 44]. She only stayed eight months and then went to work for
Josselin's patrons and friends, the Harlakendens: 'the lord make her
fitt for her place and give her favour in the sight of them she
serveth' was his comment [22. 4. 45].

When she was sick two years later Josselin sent her 'somewhat'
[17. 1. 47] and noted her continued attack of ague during the
following weeks [31. 1. 47]. Later in the same year he seems to have
lent her £5 [9. 10. 47], possibly part of a legacy like the £7 10s.
which he started to pay her six years later [15. 8. 53]. In the last
twenty years of his life Josselin only mentioned Mary by name twice;
at the age of forty-six she was apparently still working for the
Harlakendens at the priory: Josselin described a visit thus: 'my
poore sister Mary, whose heart is broken with greife and trouble,
with mee from the priory before I was up. I advised her to submitt
to god in his providence to her' [8. 3. 57]. The final mention of Mary
shows his annoyance when she failed to see him often enough: 'all

[1] F. Osborne, *Advice to a Son* (5th edn, Oxford, 1656), p. 71, was one of those who
argued this.
[2] Roxwell parish register [30. 6. 1611].

my sisters by my father and mother here at Colne with mee supping
this night togither and not togither again, though my sister Ann went
not till October 16 about noon, my sister Mary in town never
coming up to see us in all that time' [13. 10. 61]. The brother and
sisters had probably gathered to celebrate Mary's wedding for on
25 July 1661, aged almost exactly fifty, she married Robert Finch,
widdower.[1] There is only one reference to 'brother in law Finch';
at his death Josselin was satisfied that he had shown his sister's
husband 'much love' and he preached Robert Finch's funeral
sermon [20, 22. 2. 78]. Josselin did not mention that Mary had died,
nor did he leave her any property in his will.

The first mention of Josselin's married sister Dorothy occurs when
he sent her 3s. for a 'token' in 1645 [13. 1. 45]; possibly this was a
New Year's gift. Her marriage is not recorded, but probably she had
a husband by 1646 when she suffered a 'great losse by cattle'
[28. 2. 46]. In spite of her married status he lent and gàve her small
amounts of money and property; at the end of 1646 he 'received a
letter from my sister Dorothy to borrow 30s. of me; though now in
great straites for mony, yett I intend either to give or lend'
[23. 12. 46]. It seems that the obligations towards siblings were
strong, and in spite of his many commitments towards his own
rapidly expanding family Josselin felt that they must be honoured.
He expressed gratitude that he was able to fulfil his role in this
direction, when, after a visit of Dorothy and her husband in 1647,
he wrote 'My sister Dorothy and her houseband with me; wee gave
them such old things as wee any wayes could spare. I paid her 20s.
for her legacy and lent her 20s. more. The lord be blessed that
enables mee to be a friend to any of my kindred' [20. 10. 47].
Obligations could be met in other ways, for instance by looking
after children, as when Josselin noted two years later 'My sister
Dorothy's boy went home, I gave him 2s. 6d. blessed be god who
enables mee to give' [5. 1. 50]. Another year Dorothy came to visit
him for four days and left with 'good old things, and 20s' [19. 10. 56].
There were a number of other meetings between brother and sister
in ensuing years [e.g. 1. 11. 60 and 3. 10. 76], but, as with Mary,
there is no mention of Dorothy's death, nor is any money left to
her in Josselin's will.

The third sister Anne was treated in much the same way. When
she visited the Josselins she was 'entertained with joy' [14. 9. 73]

[1] We learn of this marriage from the Earls Colne parish register; Josselin, curiously,
does not mention the wedding in his Diary. Robert Finch had paid tax on one
hearth in 1662 and paid it on six hearths in 1671, by the latter date, therefore,
he seems to have been a wealthy man (E.R.O. Q/RTh/1, 5.).

and left 'with presents' [25. 9. 73]. Alone of the sisters her death is recorded, perhaps because it took place while on a visit to Josselin. She was probably back to celebrate Christmas with them for on Christmas day 1673 Josselin wrote 'the lord hath his hand on my sister Anna, who was taken suddenly ill, dropsicall when with us . . . a good woman and now happy. she died Friday 26. god hath broken the brood there are now but three of us. shee was next above mee in age'. The tone is one of fondness, if not of deep emotion.

Throughout the Diary there are references to visits and gifts to sisters unspecified, which fill in some of the longer gaps in the individual case histories. For instance Josselin gave 3s. to one of his sisters, again probably as a New Year's present. He paid one of them 40s. [17. 1. 45] perhaps part of the pound or so a year which he had promised his sister Anne after the death of her first husband [13. 10. 49]. It was probably this same sister he was referring to when he said 'my sister's children I schooled for their disobedience' [7. 8. 54]. As the mother's brother he was taking on the father's role in the absence of a living father [8. 8. 55]. Finally, all the sisters are referred to in 1672 when he described how he 'saw my sisters with delight' in Newport [28. 7. 72]. We have already seen Josselin, returning to Bishop's Stortford, 'much affected with the thoughts of my deare mother and 2 sisters who were there buried' [18. 6. 49], but the image of these sisters must have been very imperfect since he was only seven years old when they died and they were two years and a few weeks old respectively.

There was obviously affection between Josselin's own children, who, as we have seen, often visited each other in sickness or on other occasions. When Thomas and Anne died within a few days of each other their father said of them that they were 'loving in their lives and in their death they were not divided, lying in the same grave' [31. 7. 73]. Obviously the bond between this brother and sister was very strong; this remark also shows that parents recognized such deep affection and approved of it. Between brother and brother competition for wealth and affection from their parents may have disturbed relationships all round, though John's wish to be buried near his brother reveals that warmth was not entirely smothered by resentment. Insecurity about inheritance seems to have been the chief source of tension; this is evident in the generation above Ralph Josselin's, as we shall see when we analyse ties with uncles.

It is worth noting that this sense of strain and injury which intruded on relations between brothers could also lead to trouble between sisters. All Josselin's surviving children, including the daughters, inherited large portions of money or land and they also received advance payments to set themselves up as servants. Clearly the division of property caused disagreements. The person who felt most aggrieved was Jane, the eldest surviving daughter, who felt that the later daughters were getting too generous a treatment. Shortly after he had set up Mary and Rebecka in London [17. 5. 77], Josselin was visited by Jane whom he described as 'affected with the providence' [or providing] [7. 7. 77]. It may have been the same resentment that made her 'full of her discontentents' the following January [1. 1. 78]. Dowries were another source of discontent; Jane had only received £200 as her portion, but Mary and Rebecka received £500 each and 'their sister Jane tooke on at mee and them for their great porcons' [2. 5. 83]. Josselin was unsympathetic, and Jane's isolated position left her powerless. There is nothing to show that there were favourites in the family, and it is more likely that husband and wife worked out the position and prospects of their respective daughters and arranged accordingly.

Moving beyond his nuclear family, the next most significant kinship tie, to judge from Josselin's Diary, was with uncles. G. C. Homans in his work on medieval village life stressed the significance of the uncle–nephew relationship, especially important being the unmarried uncle.[1] He also showed that the maternal uncle, the mother's brother, was given a special term, *eme*, and figured largely in wardship cases.[2] High mortality rates made it very likely that either husband or wife would die before the children were grown up, and thus we might expect that the closeness of siblings, described in the previous section, would lead to help being offered to nephews and nieces. Once again the inheritance system will be the crucial factor, for the tension it caused between siblings might well be echoed in their relations with the next generation.

The situation in Josselin's case could be compared to that described by Campbell: 'Uncles who are fathers' brothers are known better than brothers of the mother but they are not always loved better ... The favourite uncle is generally a mother's brother who was excessively indulgent to his nephews and nieces when they came on periodical visits'.[3] Concerning aunts, Campbell writes, 'Aunts who are father's sisters are generally well known, but mother's sisters may be seen very seldom'.[4] The best way to test the strength of the relationship is to see what happens when a parent dies. Does the uncle then step in and assume a greater importance, as previously implied by the wardship cases, or does the tie, never very strong,

[1] Homans, *English Villagers*, p. 139.
[2] *Ibid.* p. 192.
[3] Campbell, *Honour and Patronage*, p. 105.
[4] *Ibid.*

simply snap?[1] Josselin's Diary illustrates the state of affairs as it existed at a certain social level in seventeenth-century Essex.

We saw Josselin 'schooling' his nephews and nieces as a mother's brother, when their father died, and helping to support them; his close concern for his sisters after their marriage meant that he was partly responsible for their welfare. Yet there is not enough evidence to be able to pronounce that he played a major role. He may have given his nephews and nieces presents unrecorded in his Diary: certainly we know that his own children's uncle on the mother's side, Jeremy Constable, sent his nephew a hat [26. 11. 46]. But there is no mention of visits from sisters' children to Earls Colne, nor talk of finding them occupations. The one exception was when Josselin gave sister Dorothy's boy 2s. 6d. after he had apparently been staying with his uncle [5. 1. 50]. What is perhaps more significant is that he does not bother to name 'Sister Dorothy's boy'. He never gave the Christian names of any of his nephews and nieces, nor did he record their births, marriages or deaths. His interest in them appears negligible.

He shows no greater interest in his aunts, both his father's sisters and his father's brother's wives, and the same relatives on his mother's side. The kinship chart makes it plain that Josselin almost certainly had nine aunts on his father's side alone. Of these we learn virtually nothing. There is no record of their names, births, sickness or deaths, or the exchange of presents or visits. There are only two minor exceptions to this general lack of interest. From some friends he heard 'of my deare Aunt Josselins of Cranhams death, my uncle Ralph's wife' [1. 7. 46]; as we shall see, Uncle Ralph was his favourite uncle and he had spent some time living at Cranham with his uncle and aunt, hence the sorrow. The other reference is more casual; when Uncle Thomas Miles died the news was brought by 'my aunts man' [18. 4. 45]. In neither case is a Christian name given. The general impression, substantiated later by the lack of contact between Josselin's children and their mother's sisters, is that aunts lived too far away to be important relatives. Josselin's sister Mary who worked for eight months as a servant to him, and then with neighbours, was a possible exception and her nephews and nieces may have known her well; but it is more typical that we only learn indirectly of the existence of three of Josselin's father's sisters. They are never mentioned by name in the Diary.

Aunts may have been more important to nieces than to nephews and, conversely, uncles to nephews than to nieces. Certainly Josselin's uncles seem to have been the most important kinship category

[1] Wilmott and Young, *Family and Kinship*, p. 84.

outside his nuclear family. Of the nine uncles we know he had, he mentions eight in the Diary; Thomas, referred to as one of his father's brothers in a will of 1645,[1] is never named. Of these nine 'Uncle Thomas Miles' was probably the only named uncle on his mother's side. Almost penniless after his father's death, Josselin borrowed £1 13s. 4d. upon 'my uncle Miles his creditt' [1636]. Uncle Thomas was not mentioned again until shortly before his death. On 7 April 1645 Josselin 'Heard of the sicknesse of my Uncle Miles by his sonne Edward' and prayed 'the Lord raise him up againe'. The next day he rode over to see Uncle Thomas and found him 'weake' but was cheered by a dream a week later that 'my uncle Thomas Miles was prettily well recovered' [15. 4. 45]. Nevertheless three days later he heard by messenger of 'the death of my deare Uncle Miles of Hadham Berry. He dyed, die 17, a little before sunsett. He had not very lingering sicknes so arose almost to his Death'.

The other eight uncles were relatives of Josselin's father, all but two of them father's brothers. Four of these eight appear only once in the Diary. 'My uncle Benton entertayned mee with love and pity and offered mee to stay a while with him' [1636], Josselin recorded, at a period when he was a penniless youth, but there is no further reference to this uncle.[2] Joseph, whose will survives,[3] died in 1646 and his death occasioned the entry: 'Heard of my Uncle Joseph Josselin's death; made no reckoning that his land woul fall to mee' [5. 8. 46]. It was a dispute over the inheritance of this land that led to references to two other uncles, Richard, and Josselin's father's sister's husband, Daniel Hudson. In 1644 Uncle Richard is described as supplying five days of 'loving' company [8–13. 12. 44], but he later took Josselin and Uncle Ralph to court, engaging the assistance of Daniel Hudson in the dispute. There are several references to this quarrel in the Diary,[4] but after it was settled neither Richard nor Daniel appear again.[5] Nor is there much information about another father's brother, Simon, who was also involved in the inheritance

---

[1] The will of Joseph Josselin, printed on p. 214 below.

[2] As indicated in the kinship chart (facing p. 234), John Benton was the second husband of Josselin's Aunt Mary. We learn this from a case concerning the custody of certain deeds in which 'Ralfe Joslin the elder of Roxwell in the county of Essex & John Benton, husband of Mary, late widow of Thomas Searle ... daughter of me the said Ralfe' were all involved in 1622 (B. M., Harleian, M.S. 97, fol. 129).

[3] It is partially printed on p. 214 below.

[4] The cause of the dispute is outlined in the chancery plea printed on p. 219 below.

[5] For instance, Josselin did not mention his Uncle Richard's death which, according to the Roxwell parish register, occurred in 1668. An inventory of Richard Josselin's possessions is printed in Francis Steer, *Farm and Cottage Inventories of Mid-Essex, 1635–1749* (Colchester, 1950), pp. 107–9.

squabble and with whom Josselin negotiated at Earls Colne [23. 9. 46]. The court case did not damage their relationship permanently, for Simon promised to help Josselin with his rent [22. 2. 50]. For years later he was heard to be dying [25. 3. 54]; the fact that Josselin saw [26. 5. 56] and heard of [3. 1. 58] the desolate condition of his children strongly suggests that he did, in fact, die.

We are left with two father's brothers who, alone, appear to have taken a prolonged interest in Josselin, and he in them. Uncle Nathaniel, born in August 1602 at Roxwell, was only fourteen and a half years older than his nephew Ralph. He lived at Hardingham in Norfolk and there were many visits between the two, though apparently no gifts or other help was exchanged.[1] In 1649 Josselin noted that 'my loving uncle Mr. Nathaniel Josselin came to mee' [31. 5. 49] and stayed a night, and three months later the visit was returned [22. 8. 49]. They obviously wrote as Josselin mentions a letter from Nathaniel [3. 2. 53] urging him to continue with his 'apocaliptiq studies' and over a period of nineteen years met at least seven times; Nathaniel came to see his nephew in 1654 [26. 10. 54], 1658 [21. 9. 58], and 1663 [25. 7. 63]. An account of this last visit describes how Josselin 'joyd in the comfortable sight of my deare uncle Mr. Nath. Josselin, by him I heard from Tom, that he is well'. Relatives obviously carried news of each other about, and this 'dear uncle' was back for another stay in 1667 [2. 6. 67], but the following year Josselin 'mett the news of my uncle Nathaniel Josselins death, the last of that family line' [24. 9. 68].

Finally there was his Uncle Ralph, the next-but-one brother in age to his father, and one of the prominent inhabitants of the village of Cranham.[2] This uncle seems to have looked on himself as Josselin's protector when the diarist's father died; he was the only relative who offered help in the form of a substantial loan or in finding a job, and stood beside him in the inheritance dispute of 1646. It is not surprising that when Uncle Ralph's married children came to visit Josselin they were 'very heartily welcome unto mee, rejoycing to see them in health' [23. 6. 56]. He also repaid something of his uncle's kindness by writing his will for him, a task that must have been made more pleasant by finding himself a legatee: 'I had comfort in my uncle

[1] Venn, *Alumni Cantabrigiensis*, states that Nathaniel Josselin matriculated pensioner from Magdalen College, Cambridge, at Easter 1622; was rector of Wrampling-ham, Norfolk, from 1638–60; was rector of Hardingham in the same county from 1656; he was ejected for nonconformity in 1662/3.

[2] Uncle Ralph 'farmed the Cranham Hall land rented from Mr Francis Petre at £150 yearly; he was nominated in the "Classis" and was one of the jurors at the Parochial Inquisition of 1650' according to H. Smith, 'The Diary of Ralph Josselin', *Ess. Rev.*, vol. XXXIV (1925), p. 127.

R. Josselin's company, I writt his will for him, he was kind therein to mee' [16. 11. 56].[1]

Baptized in 1590,[2] Uncle Ralph was first mentioned in the Diary in 1640. At that time a curate at Olney, Josselin preached at Cranham and 'my uncle and all the towne desird mee to live with them'. Uncle Ralph seems to have shared his nephew's religious zeal and offered him £10 a year out of his own pocket if he would become a curate at Cranham, which he did immediately after his wedding. However, Josselin was continually ill there and when offered the position at Earls Colne was encouraged by his uncle to accept it. When he visited Earls Colne for the first time and when he moved there early in 1641 'my loving uncle Ralph Josselin' accompanied him [March 1641], and the contacts were maintained it seems, though the Diary at this period is not detailed enough to know how frequent they were. In the court case about the inheritance of Joseph's land, Ralph the elder and younger stood together, and shared the sorrow, early in the year, caused by the death of 'dear Aunt Josselin'. At the end of that year and in 1647 there were at least four meetings[3] and Uncle Ralph came to see his nephew twice early in 1648 [1. 1. 48, 29. 3. 48]; it may have been on one of these occasions that he lent him the £40 of which £35 was paid back in 1649 [19. 4. 49]. Shortly after writing his uncle's will Josselin 'heard of the death of my deare Uncle Ralph Josselin, who died at London die 21: & was buried die. 24: by his children' [28. 3. 57]. It is interesting that even after the long, close and affectionate contacts they had maintained, Josselin did not attend the funeral, perhaps because it took at least a week to hear of the death.

The children of Josselin's uncles, his first cousins, might be expected to form another important kinship category, as they do in another bilateral kinship society where 'Cousins are the most significant of a person's collateral kinsmen both for purposes of practical co-operation and for simple companionship'. There, it appears, cousins are 'genuinely concerned about each other's successes or misfortunes, hopes and fears. When a man meets a cousin after a long interval of time there is obvious pleasure on both sides'.[4] In the English village of Ashworthy, too, cousinly concern is an obvious fact; though first cousins are not normally

---

[1] A summary of his will is printed on p. 215 below. The 'kindness' consisted of a legacy of £6, 'left as a testimony of my love to him'.

[2] According to the Roxwell parish register.

[3] On 31.8.46; 28.12.46; 3.2.47; 11.3.47. Uncle Ralph's plea in the court case is printed on p. 219 below.

[4] Campbell, *Honour and Patronage*, pp. 99–100.

invited to weddings or christenings as guests, they often come to the church ceremony, and a 'considerable amount of detail is known' even about the lives and activities of second cousins.[1] 'Cousins' appear frequently in the letters of New England Puritans also; some forty-eight are mentioned by name in the letter books of Samuel Sewall, for example.[2]

Assuming that Josselin's nine known uncles had an average of just over three surviving children each (and we know that several had more than four each), then he would have had thirty first cousins. The kinship chart shows eighteen such first cousins, one of whom died before the Diary commenced. From table VII below we can see that Josselin referred by name to only some fourteen 'cousins', a few of whom may have been second cousins, since it has proved impossible to trace most of them. Even if they had all been first cousins, Josselin would have mentioned under half of the 'cousins' he probably had. The proportion noted becomes even smaller when we take into account the fact that Josselin termed the spouses of cousins as 'cousins'; thus he spoke of 'cousin Johnson' and 'cousin Benton' in contexts which show plainly that he was writing about a person married to one of his cousins. Examples of cousins being omitted from the Diary altogether may easily be found. We know from a will that Josselin's Uncle Daniel Hudson had at least five children, Daniel, Simon, William, Elizabeth and John.[3] Yet (see table VII) only one of these is mentioned in the Diary, John. It will clarify the picture to present Josselin's mentions of cousins in tabular form.

From table VII we see that Josselin noted the death of three of his cousins, and details concerning childbirth of one of them. In only three cases was aid offered. Josselin's comment on his loan to Tom Hudson shows both the obligations felt to exist between cousins, and their irritating nature. 'Tom Hudson, came to borrow of mee £20, I wonderd at my Cosin's boldnes, who had for his mother and selfe borrowed £5. and never yet paid it. It greiveth mee that relations are so unworthy not to bee trusted' [7. 10. 57]. There is nothing to show that cousins helped each other in emergencies, or attended each other's christenings, weddings, or funerals; the only exception in Josselin's case was in his relationship with John Josselin.

It is apparent from the table that only two of the 'cousins', judging from the number of times they were mentioned, played an important part in Josselin's life, namely John Josselin and Jeremy

[1] Williams, *Ashworthy*, pp. 157, 173.
[2] According to Morgan, *Puritan Family*, p. 150.
[3] The will is Uncle Joseph's, summarized on p. 214 below. Tom Hudson, referred to as borrowing from Josselin, is probably a younger brother of this family.

Benton. Josselin was in frequent touch with John Josselin, though it is not clear on what grounds he called him 'cousin' and he consequently does not appear on the kinship chart; possibly they were second cousins. John Josselin's position made it desirable, however, that Josselin should stress the closeness of their tie. 'Cousin John' was

TABLE VII. *Josselin's contacts with his cousins*

Name	Number of times mentioned	Aid, gifts, exchanged	Number of visits	Interest shown in
John Josselin	7		5	notes death
Jeremy Benton	7		4	notes death
Abraham Josselin	2		2	—
Henry Josselin	1		—	notes death
Roger Josselin	1		—	—
'Hurrill'	5	Josselin lends her £4 and helps her to London	2	hears of delivery & illness
'Johnson'	3		2	—
'Rogers'	2		2	—
'Betty'	2	Josselin helps enlarge her portion	—	—
'Bird'	1		—	—
'Gatton'	1		1	—
'Blundell'	1		—	—
John Hudson	1		—	—
Tom Hudson	1	Josselin lends him £20, unwillingly	1	—

NOTES

1. According to a transcriber's note on the E.R.O. transcript of the Diary, Samuel Blundell of Steeple Bumpstead was the husband of either Dorothy or Anne, daughters of Uncle Ralph, and was a farmer of about 200 acres of land.
2. There are two other references, to 'my kinsman' John Outing, who was given a coat and money on 15.6.74, and to the funeral of 'Minister Josselin' on 28.4.71; it is not certain that either of these were cousins.

a steward of the manors of Earls Colne and Colne Priory,[1] of which Josselin held all his land, and Josselin consequently frequently sought his advice about land matters [e.g. 14. 7. 56 and 22. 7. 46]. Cousin John's value was further enhanced by the fact that he had eloped with Richard Harlakenden's niece and hence Josselin could claim a remote kinship link with his patron.[2] The bond was made closer because John Josselin was probably in sympathy with the diarist's religious views, for it seems likely that John was an elder of

[1] For example, the Court Baron on 5 January 1658 was held before 'John Joscelyne, Esq;, Steward there' (E.R.O., D/DPr/79).
[2] The wedding is noted in Josselin's Diary on 31.8.47.

the St James, Colchester, classis.[1] Furthermore, Ralph was able to reciprocate his 'cousin's' help by preaching at the baptism of his two sons [1. 6. 47 and 6. 6. 49]. During the period between 1647 and 1672, when news came of 'John Josselin's burial of Kelvedon' [21. 1. 72],[2] the cousins visited each other at least five times, according to the Diary.

During roughly the same period Josselin exchanged four recorded visits with his cousin Jeremy Benton, minister of Little Yeldham in Essex.[3] Apart from these visits he noted three pieces of information about his cousin; that his wife had miscarried [1. 9. 44], that both his children had been buried [6. 11. 46], and that he had 'heard of my Cosin Benton's death' [8. 6. 79].

Cousins, it seems, were not of great emotional or economic importance to Josselin. Their children played little part in his life; none of them, as far as we know, are named in the Diary. It becomes apparent, and will become more so, that the range of his kin relationships was extremely narrow compared to that in most societies.

If his concern for his own kin was limited, it is of interest to see how much contact was preserved with his affinal kin; to what extent he involved himself in their affairs and they in his. In some modern village studies the relationship between affines has been described as far less significant than that between blood relatives.[4] Actual behaviour is constrained[5] and there may be shame and embarrassment felt, for instance, by brothers-in-law.[6] The mother-in-law daughter-in-law relationship can be particularly tense[7] and may lead to avoidance behaviour;[8] that such tension may have been present in some seventeenth-century families is evident, and further research may illustrate whether the crucial factor was co-residence with a parent-in-law.[9] If it was, it seems unlikely that such tension

[1] Shaw, *History of the English Church*, vol. II, p. 391.
[2] The Kelvedon parish register (E.R.O., T/R 12) notes the burial of John Joscelyn of Feering, gent. on 2 January 1672.
[3] According to a note in the transcript of the Diary at the E.R.O. under 6.11.46 date. Previously he had been a minister at Finchingfield in Essex (Smith, *Ecclesiastical History*, p. 108).
[4] As in Gosforth; Williams, *Gosforth*, pp. 74, 81.
[5] As described in Campbell, *Honour and Patronage*, p. 139.
[6] A case is given in Mead, *Sex and Temperament*, p. 184.
[7] As it is said to have been in Ireland (Connell, 'Peasant Marriage', pp. 516–17). For contrastingly smooth relations, see Stirling, *Turkish Village*, p. 109.
[8] For example, R. Burling, *Rengsanggri; Family and Kinship in a Garo Village* (Philadelphia, 1963), p. 122.
[9] A historical example is given in Hill, *Society and Puritanism*, p. 356.

was general, for parents-in-law seldom lived with their married children.[1]

There are a number of problems here that could profitably be explored. Clearly, affinal connexions were strategically important in some cases; thus Richard Rogers, afraid that his wife might die in childbirth, counted amongst the 'uncomfortablenesses' which would follow 'looseing freendship among her kindred'.[2] We know, however, that such a severing of ties did not necessarily result from the death of one of the partners, at least in New England, for there is evidence that some men thought they still owed obedience to the parents of a deceased wife.[3] The degree of continued contact in the large proportion of marriages broken by an early death in our period deserves further study, as does the nature of such a relationship before death. Greek daughters 'manage to visit their homes about twice a year';[4] how did seventeenth-century villagers treat their in-laws, and how often did they allow wives to return home? We know that some Essex villagers at that period often dined with affinal relatives,[5] and a return to Josselin's Diary provides further evidence on this subject.

Josselin met his wife Jane Constable at Olney in Buckinghamshire. Immediately after the marriage the couple went to Essex, first to Cranham and then to Earls Colne, thus separating Jane from her family.[6] A general picture of Josselin's contacts with his in-laws may be obtained from table VIII below; it will readily be seen that they played little part in his daily life. Only four of them are mentioned more than twice. Josselin's recognition of his own blood relatives was limited, but of his wife's practically non-existent. He mentioned some twenty-four of his own more distant blood relatives by name; eight uncles, fourteen 'cousins' and two others. Only three of his wife's family, apart from parents and siblings, are so named; Aunt and Uncle Shepherd and Aunt Berrill. Apart from Aunt Shepherd, who was godmother to the Josselin's second child, there is no record of any relatives outside her nuclear family visiting Jane at Earls Colne. Nor is there indication of much travelling in the opposite direction, even before the death of Jane's mother in 1655. Josselin and his wife

[1] Statistics showing the infrequency of co-residence are given in Laslett, *Lost World*, p. 91.
[2] M. M. Knappen (ed.), *Two Elizabethan Puritan Diaries* (1933), p. 74.
[3] E.g., Morgan, *Puritan Family*, p. 151.
[4] Campbell, *Honour and Patronage*, p. 139.
[5] There is a description of dining and meeting, for example in E.R.O., D/AED/1 p. 78, an archdeaconry deposition.
[6] From Earls Colne to Olney was approximately 70 miles by road. Although Josselin once rode there in a day [28. 6. 41], the distance must have inhibited frequent visits.

received an invitation to stay at Olney in 1646 which they may or may not have accepted; the only recorded and definite visits were in June 1641 and May 1651.

Ties were tenuous, but were not immediately snapped. For a short while after the wedding Josselin took his wife to Olney, and brought her father back with her who 'delighted to bee with us until his death' [28. 6. 41].[1] It was a year after this that his mother-in-law (termed by Josselin 'mother') came to Earls Colne to help at the

TABLE VIII. *Josselin's contacts with his affinal kin*

Name	Relation-ship (to wife)	Last mention of	No. of visits	No. of mentions	Aid/ gifts	Other interests
Jeremy	brother	1657	5	7	lent 20s. by R.J.	—
Anne	mother	1655	2	5	helps at 1st birth	hears of death
Thomas	father	1643	2	2	lives with R.J.	hears of death
Elizabeth (Worrall)	sister	1670	1	4	—	hears of marriage & birth of son
'Worrall'	sis. Eliz's husband	1676	2	3	sent away 'not empty'	letter
'Shepherd'	'aunt'	1653	—	4	Gifts of cloth & £10 at wedding	hears of death
Lawrence Shepherd	uncle	1660	—	2	—	hears of death
'Berrill'	'aunt'	1648	—	—	—	hears of death
Hannah	'sister'	1644	1	1	R.J. hopes help over house	—
Thomas	'brother'	1654	1	1	R.J. 'gives' to him	—

delivery of her first grandchild [12. 4. 42], and also acted as one of the godparents. Strangely, she seems to have left her husband behind at Earls Colne, and he died on 10 June 1643. In the following year Josselin heard of his mother-in-law's health [5. 8. 44], and he visited her and her children in 1651 and found them well [27. 5. 51]. Four years later comes the last reference to her, when she died [14. 10. 55]. There was nothing of tension evident in the relationship, nor of deliberate avoidance. Distance made a bond, that was never particularly strong, hard to maintain.

[1] In fact, it seems likely that he returned to Olney shortly before his death, for his will (see p. 214 below) of June 1643 seems to have been written there.

However this was not always the case between in-laws, for one of Josselin's closest and friendliest contacts was with his wife's brother, Jeremy Constable, some four years his junior.[1] He visited Josselin for ten days from the army in 1644 [4–15. 9. 44] and again at the end of the same year when Ralph lent him 20s. [20. 12. 44] The Diary

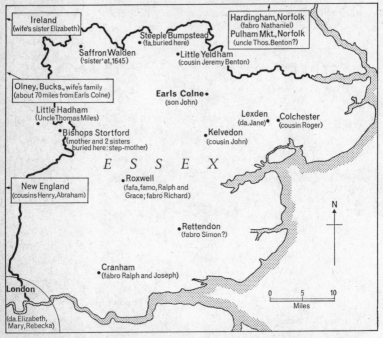

Fig. 10. The distribution of those of Josselin's kin whose residence is known. If the exact kinship is not known the general term 'cousin' or 'uncle' is employed: otherwise, fabro denotes father's brother; fafa—father's father; famo—father's mother. A question mark indicates some uncertainty as to residence. Only those children who married are included.

records another meeting early the following year [17. 3. 45] and he sent a present to Josselin's child a year after that [26. 11. 46]. The Josselins visited him with other relatives in 1651, and he and his wife were also at Earls Colne that year [29. 5. 51]. There was news of him and a letter returned in 1654 [20. 8. 54], and he came for a short stay in 1657, bringing news of his children and sisters [26. 9. 57–1. 10. 57]. There is no reference to further activities, or to his death.

[1] Christened on 9.5.1620 according to the Olney parish register at the B.R.O.

The other member of his wife's family of whom Josselin heard a good deal was her sister Elizabeth. There was news of her marriage [29. 11. 45] and of the delivery of her first son a year later [26. 11. 46]: she seems to have married 'Brother Worrall' as he was termed, to whom Josselin wrote in 1648 [2. 5. 48]. For a while they moved to Ireland and a letter which 'joyd us' came from them in 1665 [9. 7. 65]. Brother Worrall came to stay with the Josselins in 1668 [1. 7. 68] and again in 1676 [13. 9. 76] and was sent away, from the latter visit at least, 'not empty'. In the meantime his wife Elizabeth had spent nearly three weeks at Earls Colne, 'to our joy', during 1670 [15. 7. 70–5. 8. 70]. Clearly the contacts between a wife and her siblings outlasted the death of their parents.

Outside the circle of his wife's nuclear family, the only significant relationship Josselin maintained with her kin was with the Shepherd 'aunt' and 'uncle'. It was at 'Goodwife Shepheard's that he made his proposal of marriage to his wife [1. 1. 40]. Aunt Shepherd promised a gift of £10 at their marriage, not produced in fact for some time [23. 8. 53], though an earlier gift of cloth may also have been part of the wedding present [3. 11. 48]. This aunt was godmother to the Josselin's second child [14. 1. 44]. Josselin took a constant interest in the health of the Shepherds, and in their activities, as when his uncle had a fall from a horse [27. 9. 44]. He also noted his uncle's death, and generally appears to have been closer to them than to any of his own uncles except Ralph and Nathaniel.

The general impression from Josselin's treatment of his affinal relationships is that few visits were made to his wife's distant home, and that interest in his in-laws, except members of his wife's nuclear family, was faint. In the first few years after the wedding Josselin kept in touch with his wife's parents and siblings, but gradually the households drifted apart, though links were not completely broken. Josselin's anxiety when his 'friends at Olny were miserably plundered' [September 1643] during the Civil War, and his affectionate concern for the 'health' of his 'friends at Olny' [e.g. on 21. 5. 48 and 3. 11. 48] is evidence of some continued interest. The fact that Josselin termed his affines 'friends' rather than 'relations' is also significant; they were closer than 'neighbours', but more distant than blood relatives.

9

Ties with godparents, servants and friends

In societies where kinship is a dominant principle of organization, an individual may create important kin ties not only by marriage, but also by 'spiritual kinship' or godparenthood. Sociologists have recently stressed the importance of such spiritual kinship[1] in general, and specific studies have illustrated how significant such links may be in the acquisition of prestige and power.[2] There is some evidence that the godparent had special significance in Anglo-Saxon society,[3] and seventeenth-century diaries show godparents in the role of providers of gifts.[4]

Historians are presented with several problems when considering the position of these 'spiritual kin', and Josselin's Diary throws some light on them. To what extent was godparenthood used to reinforce already existing kinship ties?[5] Was it a mechanism for enlisting the support of higher status 'patrons' as is suggested for the Elizabethan aristocracy?[6] How effective and strong was the relationship; were godparents often appointed overseers to wills;[7] did they often leave property to their godchildren;[8] did they feel any obligation to discipline such godchildren in the event of the parents failing to do so?[9]

[1] For example, Wolf, *Peasants*, p. 85.
[2] There is a good account of the factors in the choice of godparents in Campbell, *Honour and Patronage*, pp. 220–3.
[3] Lancaster, 'kinship in Anglo-Saxon Society', pt I, p. 239 and pt II, p. 369.
[4] Pepys, *Diary*, p. 77. The generosity of John Hales as a godfather is described in Aubrey, *Brief Lives*, p. 203.
[5] Evelyn, *Diary*, pp. 3, 364, indicates that godparents were often kin. Nearly two-thirds of Bethnal Green godparents were siblings (Wilmott and Young, *Family and Kinship*, p. 85).
[6] By the description in Pearson, *Elizabethans at Home*, pp. 83–4. A similar situation exists in parts of Greece where politically advantageous relationships are set up by godparenthood (Campbell, *Honour and Patronage*, pp. 222–3).
[7] An instance of such an appointment is E.R.O., D/AED/1, p. 119.
[8] An analysis of such bequests in the Essex village of Boreham over the period 1503–1620 shows that they were made in 9 out of 78 wills. Usually small sums, averaging about 12*d*. and not exceeding 5*s*. were left. Mike Smythe (E.R.O., D/ABW/34/156) was an exception in leaving small gifts to two godmothers.
[9] Again in the Essex sources, we learn of a case where a godmother, discovering her goddaughter had stolen a chicken, said to her, 'Thou art my goddaughter and suerlie, if thy parents will not convert thee, I will' and so 'then and there she bete her' (E.R.O., D/AEA/2—end pages, no foliation).

Josselin never used the term 'godfather' or 'godmother' but spoke of 'witnesses' at the baptism. For his first child he chose representatives of the three most influential families in the neighbourhood, Mr Richard Harlakenden, Mr John Litle and Mrs Mary Mildmay;[1] the fourth witness was his wife's mother [14. 4. 42]. For his second child he provided only two 'witnesses'; another member of the Harlakenden family, Thomas, and Josselin's wife's Aunt Shepherd [14. 1. 44]. There is little evidence that any of these played a special part in the life of the children involved. Josselin never mentioned his own godparents, nor those of his subsequent children, with the exception of 'Young Mrs Harlakenden' for his eighth child [14. 1. 58].

Only this last godparent is noted as producing christening presents, a silver candlestand and 'porringer cover' some eleven months after the ceremony, on 11 December 1658. None of the Josselin wills mention gifts to godchildren, and the impression is that spiritual kinship, though a useful strengthener of friendships, particularly influential ones, made little impact on everyday life. Obligations to instruct or assist were clearly absent.

It has been suggested that a 'quarter, or a third' of seventeenth-century households contained servants.[2] Such servants, moralists argued, should be treated as part of the family:[3] they should be fed and educated as well as were the children,[4] for both were under government. Although a clergyman should show 'more love than terrour' to his children and 'more terrour than love' to servants, he might take an equal pride in them; he would find 'as much joy in a straight-growing child or servant as a gardiner in a choice tree'.[5] As a result, as Aubrey clearly shows, children and servants might become close friends.[6]

There is apparently little demarcation between farmers and servants either in eating or sleeping arrangements in some modern rural areas,[7] and we may soon know how far this was true of

[1] These families are further described on pp. 151–2 below.
[2] By Laslett, *Lost World*, p. 12; statistics are given on pp. 64, 69 of the same work. An analysis of the Clayworth census, showing that 67/401 of the inhabitants were servants in 1676, is made in Wrigley (ed.), *Historical Demography*, p. 203.
[3] For example, Perkins, *Christian Oeconomie*, pp. 152–6. Another instance is in *George Fox's Journal*, abridged edn, P. C. Parker (1903), p. 34.
[4] Quotations in Hill, *Society and Puritanism*, pp. 450, 443, show this egalitarian attitude.
[5] Herbert, *Priest to the Temple*, pp. 236, 276.
[6] Aubrey, *Brief Lives*, p. 173.
[7] As described for Cumberland, Williams, *Gosforth*, p. 35. This does not necessarily imply equal status, of course.

seventeenth-century England. But as well as the problem of the attitude towards servants, and their treatment, there is the simple question, who were they? Were they related to their masters by blood or marriage? Were they children of friends, or merely strangers? There is some evidence to suggest that among the English upper classes children were put out to be trained in the households of other nobility,[1] but it will be difficult to reach any satisfactory answer to these questions, until much more work has been done at the village level.[2] Societies employ as servants both kin and non-kin for a variety of reasons.[3] There is an added difficulty in deciding what these reasons were in the seventeenth century because of changes in the meaning of the word 'servant', a term which at that period covered a variety of individuals, from farm hands to resident domestic staff.[4]

It was earlier pointed out that the institution of servants and apprentices helped solve the problem of what to do with children between puberty and marriage.[5] This shedding of the young just when they were reaching the age at which they would begin to become producers instead of consumers is one of the anomalies of pre-industrial English society. It would have created a situation of instability unless corrected. After rearing children for between ten and fifteen years at considerable expense, Josselin and many of his contemporaries then sent them away just at the point when they might have begun to make returns on the capital invested in them. Instead of the children giving ten or fifteen years of service to their parents before they themselves married, the young left the home, leaving the ageing parents to raise other children and face encroaching senility on their own.

Nor did the English, like some societies, utilize the extended family—grandparents, grandchildren, brothers or sisters—to deal with this situation. With the very high mortality rates and the frequency of illness and pregnancy, the latter well illustrated in Josselin's family by his wife's inability to run the home for much of

[1] Some Puritans, one of whom is quoted to this effect in Walzer, *Revolution of the Saints*, p. 208, attacked this practice.

[2] The same point is made by Dr Wrigley in Wrigley (ed.), *Historical Demography*, p. 189.

[3] Prestige is suggested as the main determinant by A. Southall (ed.), *Social Change in Modern Africa* (Oxford, 1961), p. 24, when discussing the variations in servant-keeping in Africa.

[4] There is a useful discussion of the meaning of the term 'servant' in seventeenth-century New England, and of master–servant relations in general, in Morgan, *Puritan Family*, p. 109 and ch. 5.

[5] See p. 92 above. Appendix B, pp. 205–10 below, further elaborates the argument in the following paragraph and tries to provide further evidence to see how exceptional Josselin was.

her life, the unit of two adults was too small to survive. An extended family system would have been a means of dealing with this vulnerability, for the old, infirm, and crippled could be cared for by a wide group, and the cost of their care become less of a burden on particular individuals.[1] But, since pre-industrial Englishmen, at least those whom Josselin represents, chose not to use this system, it is arguable that servants partially took the place of the extended kin group. Not only could they be an alternative to such a group of kin, an insurance against illness and a mobile asset in a society in which individuals were constantly moving about, they may also have been crucial in bridging the gap when one or other parent died. If this was indeed the case, Josselin's Diary would indicate their importance. His Diary will also provide evidence on the two questions raised earlier; whether servants were kin, friends, or strangers and what was the general attitude towards them.

Josselin mentioned 'servants' in his Diary on at least thirty occasions. Although he never discussed their personal opinions, or reported their activities, emotions, or dreams, there is evidence that they were regarded as members of the family. This fact is clearly indicated when he comments that one of his maids was 'the first that married out of my family' [5. 8. 44]. His remarks about another of his maids' marriage implies not only interest but concern and a feeling of responsibility: 'I married Mary Potter late my maid to Jo: Penhacke, and it greived mee not to deale bountifully with her, my heart sad to see her match to a person that minds not god, nor likely to bee [a] good housband' [12. 11. 58]. It was in keeping with this affectionate concern that some fifteen years after his father's death Josselin wrote, 'I sent 1s. to an old maide of my father's' [4. 10. 51]. It was a spiritual concern as well as a material one, for he twice referred to blessing servants when they arrived in his household [22. 4. 45 and 22. 12. 50].

'Trouble and greife' are the words Josselin used to describe a servantless household, and his frantic searchings for one, and calls on the Lord to help, indicate how very important servants were in the household economy. 'My mayde went away' he recorded on one occasion [18. 10. 45], and after asking God's help in getting a replacement noted in desperation two days later, 'Many times I sought god for a servant, a mercy I prize'. A year later he was complaining of the 'trouble and greife it would bee to us to bee destitute [of a servant] but a few dayes' [15. 12. 46], and his wife was described as 'tired out without a servant' [20. 10. 64 and

[1] This hypothesis concerning the role of the extended family is well summarized in Goode, *The Family*, pp. 50–1.

25. 5. 45]. Although evidence from other diaries is needed before any conclusions can be reached, these few entries do suggest the urgent need for a servant in a seventeenth-century home of quite modest means.[1]

The Diary gives an ambivalent answer to the other question; were servants kin, friends or strangers? We have seen that Josselin's sister Mary worked as his servant for eight months at one point, and in this connexion his observation 'my sister Mary is come under my roofe as a servant but my respect is and shall be towards her as a sister' [5. 8. 44] indicates that there was a difference in the degree of familiarity accorded to an employee and a member of the family. It also appears that a cousin was employed during Mrs Josselin's delivery in 1658 [24. 1. 58], but in most cases it is impossible to tell whether the maids and male servants in Josselin's home were distant relatives or not, though it seems likely that he would in fact have mentioned any relationship, if there had been one.

The kind of distant bond that might be utilized in choosing servants is illustrated by the will of Josselin's son-in-law Jonathan Woodthorpe, which mentions his apprentice Lawrence Bentall. From the will of Josselin's son John, where Lawrence Bentall is also mentioned, it seems that he was an apprentice in his 'father's sister's husband's sister's husband's' home, a somewhat tortured connexion to say the least![2] It would certainly have presented difficulties to a diarist to describe such relationships, and be difficult to deduce them from parish registers; nevertheless it does seem moderately safe to conclude that the majority of Josselin's servants were neither kin, nor children of particular friends or neighbours. There is no evidence that he himself tried to set up his children in the homes of relatives when he apprenticed them, and he did not refer to such a process among his neighbours. Though considerable care was taken in choosing masters and mistresses for children, the bonds of kinship were not utilized.

It will have become apparent from the preceding discussion that,

[1] Josselin's recorded wages to his female domestic servants are as follows: £1 18s. 0d. p.a. [20. 10. 41]; £2 p.a. and four pairs of shoes [8. 12. 58]; £2 10s. 0a. p.a. [5. 10. 60].

[2] For the relevant wills, see pp. 213–14 below. In diagramatic form the relationship was as follows:

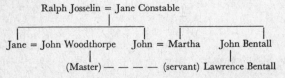

apart from the nuclear family, there was no effective kin 'group' in Josselin's world. Although there were frequent visits and occasional small loans between kin, economic and ritual activities were not carried out by them. When help was needed either in sickness, in economic undertakings, or in the celebration of birth, marriage and death, relatives were only infrequently called upon. We may therefore wonder where such help was found. The answer seems to be, amongst groups of friends and neighbours. The relative contribution of neighbours and kin to Josselin's daily life is partly indicated by the amount of wealth exchanged with each category. An examination of Josselin's property acquisitions showed what a small proportion of his land came from relatives; about only one-tenth in all. Likewise, approximately one-tenth of his money transactions, whether gifts or loans, were with kin. Josselin exchanged at least £90 with his kin, £40 of which was a loan from his father's brother Ralph [19. 4. 49]. Over £1,000 in cash was exchanged with friends and neighbours, either in the form of gifts, or in loans to and from Josselin.[1] As we shall see, neighbours were also relied on to provide the essential group backing for worship and ceremonial, and it was with them that leisure was spent in hospitality.[2]

Josselin usually spoke of 'friends and neighbours' and it is important to keep clear his implicit distinction. Neighbours were those with whom he had daily contact through co-residence: those who came to church to listen to his sermons, who went on perambulations with him, and attended the manor court. Of the many people mentioned by name amongst his acquaintances in Earls Colne the great majority were 'neighbours', people with whom he felt no special bond and with whom he would have ceased to keep in contact if he had moved. They were mentioned only once or twice each in the Diary.

It is possible to plot neighbourly networks and 'friendship' groups when studying modern communities. For example, Professor Williams in his works on Ashworthy and Gosforth has made such analyses and has drawn attention to the important distinction between neighbours forced on the farmer by co-residence and particular 'neighbours' who assume a more vital role and with whom much more intimate relationships are established.[3] For

---

[1] The land which Josselin acquired from his kin is described on p. 64 above; his debts and loans are illustrated in figure 6, p. 56.

[2] There is a good general account of neighbours and neighbourliness in Williams, *Gosforth*, ch. 7.

[3] The distinction between types of neighbour is discussed in Williams, *Ashworthy*, p. 100. A diagram for Ashworthy (*Ashworthy*, p. 102) and Gosforth (*Gosforth*, p. 145), provides useful models for the historian. The need to keep a sharp

Elizabethan women the distinction was noted by a foreigner, 'gossips' being a closer social group than mere neighbours.[1] Neighbours were forced on one and it it was to be hoped that they would be congenial. Thus, when a man moved to his house nearby, Josselin hoped that 'he will bee a very good neighbour' [5. 4. 46]. But friends were chosen and should be carefully selected. When a man married a friend of Josselin's it was noted that he 'desireth my friendship' but that 'freinds are not hastily to bee chosen' [18. 1. 62]. As we have already observed, relations by marriage were collectively termed 'friends'. They were not as close as blood 'kin', but were closer than 'neighbours'.

Contacts with neighbours were of many kinds. Josselin borrowed a cart from 'Goodman Spoone' who 'very lovingly' helped Josselin bring home some logs [23. 6. 49]. Mr Earl gave Josselin 11s. when he left the town for London [21. 12. 46], and his wife gave Mrs Josselin 'some toys'. On another occasion Mrs Haynes sent Josselin's wife four pairs of gloves as a present [8. 9. 58]. Perhaps, as a clergyman, Josselin had an extra incentive to be hospitable to his neighbours for he often seems to have had them to dinner [e.g. 28. 10. 52] and often went out to visit them [e.g. 1. 5. 48]. They helped to bring in his wood [11. 6. 50] and sent him gifts of plums, sugar, capons and other things at New Year [17. 1. 45 and 15. 1. 50]. Josselin, in return, made short-term loans, for instance lending £5 to a Mr Caplyn [24. 10. 51], even to those he considered bad neighbours [15. 1. 49]. Neighbours were entertained at christenings [14. 4. 42] and they also seem to have assisted at funerals [28. 5. 50]. In sickness they were called in; Spooner's wife set the bone in Josselin's son's instep [29. 11. 53]. They acted as amateur midwives for each other, as on the occasion when Mrs Josselin hastened off to attend a neighbour's confinement in 1677 [4. 11. 77]. That the support was emotional as well as practical can be seen from Josselin's first, unfavourable, impression of Earls Colne; 'No neighbour came to wellcome us to our house' he complained. But he revised his opinion when he realized that this was simply a difference in local custom: 'I esteemed it some disrespect and unkindness, but such expressions I perceive now are not so much used in our towne as in others' [20. 10. 41].

Within the wider circle of neighbours Josselin had a smaller, quite distinct, group of close friends, four of whom were of particular importance to him. One of his two real, equal, friendships was with

---

distinction between friends and acquaintances and the tensions inherent in the overlap are discussed in Wilmott and Young, *Family and Kinship*, p. 149 and note.

[1] W. B. Rye, *England as Seen by Foreigners* (1865), pp. 72–3; the same passage is also quoted in Wilson, *Shakespeare's England*, p. 27.

Mr and Mrs Elliston.[1] He dined with them often [e.g. 7. 11. 48], and the children of the two families played together [25. 2. 49]. Josselin showed considerable interest in the proposed marriage of Mrs Mabel Elliston [3. 11. 49], and helped to lay her body in the grave some years later [4. 4. 57]. Economic exchanges between the families were flexible; when Josselin sold Mr Elliston three bullocks on 3 November 1649 he was prepared to wait for payment until Christmas. An even deeper friendship was that with Mary Church.[2] She is first mentioned when she gave Josselin a present of 5s. in 1646 [20. 4. 46], and from then on they often dined together, and she frequently gave him presents, for instance in 1646 and 1649 [31. 12. 46 and 15. 1. 49]. She helped at two of Mrs Josselin's confinements in the late 1640s [18. 2. 48 and 5. 5. 49], and her help was reciprocated when she hurt her leg and Mrs Josselin bled it with leeches [16. 4. 47]. She was referred to as 'kind and tender' as a sister [7. 3. 48] and her death filled Josselin with grief. His heart 'trembled' and he mourned her as 'my deare freind . . . a choyce speciall freind' [4. 6. 50]. Four years earlier she had given him money with which to buy some land [8. 9. 46]. By her will she left £100 to Josselin's daughter and almost all of her considerable estate to Josselin himself.[3] It was obviously a relationship of considerable emotional and financial importance to Josselin in the difficult years when he was building up his estate and getting to know his parishioners.

Two gentry families residing in the vicinity acted as Josselin's patrons and he grew very close to both of them. One of these were the Honeywoods of Marks Hall.[4] Sir Thomas and Lady Honeywood sheltered and fed Josselin on a number of occasions, particularly during the Civil War when his house was plundered [13. 8. 48], Lady Honeywood nursed him when he was ill [27. 1.–10. 3. 73], the two families often dined together, for example in 1652 [30. 12. 52], and Josselin noted both their deaths [1. 6. 66 and 9. 10. 81]. This patronage was second only to that of the Harlakenden family of

[1] Edward Elliston, gent., had a six-hearth house in Earls Colne in 1662; this put him among the dozen wealthiest families in the town and on a par with Josselin (E.R.O., Q/RTh/1).

[2] Mistress Mary Church was the spinster daughter of Mrs Rose Church, widow of Robert Church, D.D. who had been buried in Earls Colne in 1617. Mary was the last of a long-resident family.

[3] The will is transcribed on p. 216 below. The exact nature of the estate, and its importance as a foundation for Josselin's economic expansion, is discussed on p. 63 above.

[4] The position of Marks Hall is shown on figure 2 on p. xi. Sir Thomas Honeywood, one of the Knights of the Shire for Essex, was married to Hester, daughter of John Lamotte. He was a parliamentarian in the Civil War [D.N.B.].

Earls Colne Priory, the patrons of Josselin's living and lords of the manors from which Josselin held his land.[1] In earlier discussions of Josselin's finances we have seen how considerably he depended on Richard Harlakenden for advice, loans, increases to his living, and general support.[2] Josselin often dined with the Harlakendens at the priory [e.g. 30. 12. 48]; he borrowed farm implements from them, for instance a cart [16. 9. 47]; he took a sustained interest in the son's education at Cambridge [18. 6. 49] and carried news of the boy's sickness to his father [26. 9. 50]. Without their goodwill Josselin would have found it impossible to prosper, but there is some evidence, for instance in the intimate and affectionate introduction to a sermon he preached at the funeral of William Harlakenden's wife,[3] that his relations with the family were composed of more than subservience and gratitude. He several times referred to Richard Harlakenden as 'my deare friend', and there seems no reason why he should have put up a pretence in his Diary. His public opinion was expressed in the parish register entry noting the death of 'Richard Harlakenden the elder Esq:'. He was described as 'the good Harlakenden who by deed gave the great tithes of most of the parish to the Church frendes'.[4]

[1] The site of the priory is shown on figure 2, p. xi. Richard Harlakenden was born in 1610. He married twice and had four children by these marriages. He shared Josselin's religious and political views (Morant, *History of Essex*, vol. ii, pp. 212–14).

[2] As described on pp. 34, 37, 55 above.

[3] The sermon is partly printed on p. 221 below.

[4] Earls Colne parish register, 17 September 1677.

IO

The relative importance of kin and neighbours

Analysis of those who attend baptisms, weddings and funerals has often been used to show the range of kinship ties and obligations.[1] Although Josselin never makes a complete list of the guests at these ceremonies, the general impression is that such guests were members of the nuclear family, friends and neighbours. He does not seem to have attended the weddings of his numerous cousins, nor his uncles' funerals. In his case, at least, the nuclear family was the only consistently effective family group to celebrate such occasions. In the same way normal religious life, weekly services, saints days and other festivals, were celebrated together by unrelated neighbours.

Josselin's family left the village before they were old enough to take communion and become full members of the church congregation; the religious group therefore did not reinforce the kinship group. Although he clearly prayed for and with his own children, prayers for more distant relatives are never recorded. Not even his own sisters seem to have been part of his ritual group; there is nothing to show that he attended their weddings or funerals, except in the case of Anne who died in his house. Josselin's spiritual world presents itself as a circumscribed geographical area of his own and neighbouring villages, into which only his closest relatives intruded. Kinship and ritual did not overlap.[2]

Kinship is often the basis for economic exchange and co-operation in pre-industrial societies.[3] Kin are a corporate property group, working and owning land together. They provide insurance in emergencies, and trading partners in extensive ventures.[4] Through

---

[1] Instances are Bott, *Family and Social Network*, pp. 134–5; Williams, *Ashworthy*, p. 174; Firth, *Two Studies*, pp. 51–2.

[2] Firth, *Two Studies*, p. 19, states that there was a great decrease in 'the reciprocal moral and ritual support between family observances and those of the Church' ever since the nineteenth century. Yet Josselin's position, long before then, seems very similar to that of a modern urban dweller.

[3] As R. Firth, *Elements of Social Organization* (1963), p. 52, among others, has pointed out. The importance of extended kinship in labour co-operation in a European community is described in C. R. Arensberg, *The Irish Countryman* (Gloucester, Mass., 1959), p. 66.

[4] Commerce and kinship were obviously linked in some English and New England trading families (Winchester, *Tudor Family Portrait*, p. 76; Morgan, *Puritan Family*, p. 154).

kinship channels occupations are made available to each generation.[1] The picture that emerges from Josselin's Diary, however, does not fit this stereotype. Although the nuclear family appears as a corporate property group, in the sense that those living in it inherited its wealth, no wider group was recognized. Even in the nuclear family labour was not shared; children left home just when they might be expected to contribute, and did not send their earnings home. The effective producing group, in Josselin's case, seems to have been a man, his wife and servants; in the event of extra help or tools being required, neighbours and friends were called upon.

As Professor Gluckman has pointed out, the economic system in many pre-industrial societies allows for little in the way of saving, since products are largely perishable. Annual surpluses are therefore invested in social relationships through gifts, feasts and other forms of 'conspicuous consumption'.[2] Such investment creates a store of goodwill which may be drawn on in emergencies, an insurance against unforeseen loss or shortage. Seventeenth-century England, with a sophisticated monetary economy, literacy and written wills, the private ownership of land safeguarded by a complex legal code, was already at a considerable distance from Gluckman's face-to-face model. There were already extensive facilities for accumulating, storing, and transmitting wealth. Yet the absence of satisfactory insurance mechanisms, with the consequent risk that death, fire, bad harvests, or warfare would suddenly deprive a family of all its wealth, also places a gulf between the seventeenth century and our own age. It was placed half-way between the primitive and the modern, and therefore still shared, to a certain extent, the characteristics described by Gluckman. Josselin's case illustrates this transitional state.

Most of Josselin's income was stored by means of land purchases, but a large proportion was also invested in his children and in improving his other social relationships. This investment outside the nuclear family was not directed towards his extended kin network, but into his pool of friends and neighbours; it was with them that he feasted and exchanged gifts. His friends and neighbours, as well as his own children and servants, provided his primary insurance against loss, old age or ill health. His extended kin group never seem to have helped him and the amount of wealth and labour exchanged with uncles and cousins was insignificant when compared to that

[1] There is some analysis of this topic for eighteenth-century England in Crozier, 'Kinship and Occupational Succession'.

[2] M. Gluckman, *Politics, Law and Ritual in Tribal Society* (Paperback edn, Oxford, 1965), pp. 13-14.

given and received from neighbours. Nor was the group of kin outside the nuclear family included, to any extent, in legacies. In the five wills made by members of the Josselin family and surviving to this day, only one mentioned relatives other than spouses, siblings and children.[1] As in religious matters, the economic grouping did not overlap with kin groups.

As Josselin did not ordinarily turn to his distant relatives in the life crises of birth, marriage and death, nor in economic necessity,[2] we are not surprised to find that he did not call in relatives outside the nuclear family during bouts of illness. We have seen that mothers helped their daughters with confinements, and sister Mary helped sister Jane when the latter was ill. The children also returned home to Josselin's house when they were ill. Neighbours also helped as midwives and bone-setters and when he was ill or homeless Josselin stayed with his friend Lady Honeywood rather than a kinsman. Kin were too far away to offer much assistance.

In the difficult question of how Josselin felt about various categories of neighbours and relatives, perhaps the best index we can use at this late date to judge Josselin's involvement is his reaction to the deaths of relatives and friends. Such feelings are most easily illustrated in a diagram—see figure 11 below.

As far as Josselin's reactions can be judged from his Diary descriptions, the deaths of most of his kin, even siblings, were not deeply felt, especially if we contrast them with the reactions to the deaths of his child Mary and friend Mary Church, both of which shocked him deeply. Next came the deaths of some friends, other children, and favourite kin. Finally, noted without comment, were the deaths of neighbours and the majority of cousins, uncles and aunts. Josselin's 'community of suffering', like his ritual and economic communities, cut across kinship boundaries. The order in which he himself placed various categories of people when praying to God to 'blesse the soules of those I call mine' exactly mirrors the diagram. He prayed for 'wife, children, sisters, friends, kindred, people' [25. 1. 56]. It is especially significant that he should have put 'friends' before kindred.

If we concentrate exclusively on Josselin's kin we are able to see the extent of his recognition of kinship ties. Again, a diagram helps to make things clearer—see figure 12 below.

[1] These wills are summarized on pp. 213–16 below.
[2] The only exception is when Josselin's father died and he was left penniless. Josselin received aid from his uncles and found that 'frends were not so kinde as I expected' [1636]. Josselin was still a young man of nineteen with little to offer to friends and little already invested in such relationships.

From previous analysis of the various categories of kin it will be plain that most individuals fell into more than one classification, depending on whether frequency of visits, mutual aid, or knowledge of activities is used as the prime index. The assignment of positions in the diagram is therefore somewhat arbitrary: a simpler division,

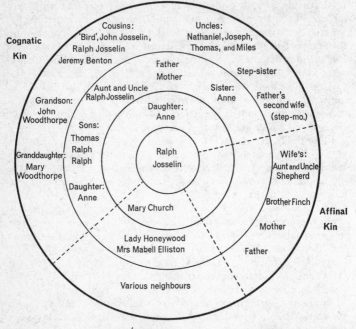

Fig. 11. Noted and lamented deaths in Josselin's environment. At the centre is Ralph Josselin. In the next ring are those whose deaths appear to have shocked Josselin. Then the next ring includes those upon whose death Josselin made some comment of sorrow or affection. Finally, there is a ring of those whose death was noted, without comment, by Josselin.

that indicated by the line between 'intimate' and 'peripheral' kin, is perhaps easier to draw.[1] There are also difficulties in comparing Josselin's recognition of kin ties with those of other investigators. Three obstacles are obvious. Josselin's kinship universe[2] may be

[1] With the former 'social contact' is purposeful, close, and frequent', with the latter 'distant, accidental, or sporadic' (Firth, *Two Studies*, p. 45).

[2] The concept of a 'kinship universe' is suggested in Firth, *Two Studies*, p. 43.

extraordinarily small because it is based merely on references in the Diary. There is little doubt that he could have named many others of his distant kin. The circles reaching as far as 'non-effective' kin are probably fairly complete, but there would probably be many 'unfamiliar kin' of whom he was aware but did not bother to note in the Diary. In the following table, therefore, the category of 'unfamiliar kin' is hardly comparable.

Another difficulty, in the comparison with Elizabeth Bott's material, is that her tables list recognition on the parts of both husband and wife, and as Williams, among others, has pointed out,

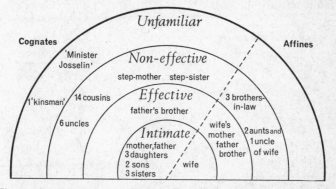

Fig. 12. Josselin's intimate, effective and peripheral kin. The definitions of 'Intimate', 'Effective', 'Non-effective' and 'Unfamiliar' kin are based on the descriptions by Firth (*Two Studies*, p. 45), Bott (*Family and Social Network*, pp. 120–1—an extension and development from Firth), and Williams (*Ashworthy*, p. 168). The following rough definitions are employed: intimate—frequent visiting (at least every six weeks, unless separated by a great distance) and mutual aid; effective—considerable knowledge of activities of kin, but less personal contact and little, if any, aid; non-effective—infrequent contact, some knowledge of activities, no aid; unfamiliar—just name and residence known, no visiting or aid.

kin connexions may be more important to women, and they may recognize a wider range.[1] Both these factors, as well as the omission of husbands and wives of most of those indicated in the diagram, would tend to make figure 12 an under-representation. But this under-emphasis is probably balanced by the final obstacle. Sociologists make their investigations at a certain point in time, and although they may add the number of 'recognized kin now dead', there is undoubtedly a loss of those who in life may have been both recognized and important, and of those who will become important in the future.

[1] Williams, *Gosforth*, p. 72.

In Josselin's case we are enabled to include kin who played some part throughout his life cycle. If, for example, a cross-section of his living 'intimate' kin had been taken on his thirtieth birthday, they would have been reduced from thirteen to six. None of his children had left home (and hence become separated enough to be counted) and both his own parents and his wife's father had been dead for some time. In the same way, a later analysis would have missed his already deceased uncles and aunts and cousins.[1] It seems, therefore, that the following table of comparison may be a rough indication of the relative number of recognized kin in Josselin's circle, and that of two other modern families.[2]

TABLE IX. *A comparison of Josselin's recognition of kin with that of two modern families*

Kin	Josselin		Newbolt		Daniel	
	Nos.	%	Nos.	%	Nos.	%
Intimate	13	27	40	29	3	3
Effective	4	8	29	21	18	20
Non-effective	29	61	63	45	51	57
Unfamiliar	2	4	7	5	18	20
Total recognized living kin	48		139		90	
Recognized kin now dead			17		34	

SOURCE: E. Bott, *Family and Social Network*, p. 120.

Table IX shows that Josselin's recognition was more like the highly mobile and 'narrow range' Daniel family, than either the long-established Newbolts with their forty intimate kin, or the wide

[1] To take but one instance: the Hartley family only had one 'intimate' kin (p. 120) because three of their four parents had already died (Bott, *Family and Social Network*, p. 119).

[2] There are, obviously, very grave problems involved in a comparison of this kind; for example, visiting and presents may have a very different significance in seventeenth-century Essex and twentieth-century London. Nevertheless, a very rough comparison does seem worthwhile. Comparison between Josselin and the figures of 'intimate' and 'peripheral' kin provided by Williams, *Ashworthy*, pp. 164–70, could also be made. For example, one household described by Williams (household C, p. 170) had 215 recognized kin, of whom 94 are 'effective' and 38 'intimate' kin. Such figures cannot, without modification, be included in table IX since the categories are not identical with those of E. Bott. Likewise, Firth, *Two Studies*, p. 42, gives a table of the 'range of kin for Twelve Households'; again the categories are slightly different from Bott's, but the total 'kinship universe', varying between 37 and 246 and averaging (p. 38) 146, would seem to be at least as big, if not much larger, than Ralph Josselin's.

range recognized in Ashworthy. Yet Josselin's total of forty-eight recognized kin may have been small for the period; we know, for instance, that one New England writer named exactly this number of 'cousins' in his diary and letter-book.[1] Only further research will resolve this problem. The general impression from Josselin's case is that his family life corresponded closely to that of mobile modern urban families: 'The range was very narrow, extending vertically to grandparents, although not to the siblings of grandparents, and laterally to first cousins'.[2] Yet there are also significant differences. One of these is the fact that Josselin seems to have known far more about his father's kin than his mother's; it was not the 'matri-central' system described by Professor Firth.[3] How far this was due to circumstances peculiar to Josselin's life, the early death of his mother for example, and how far it was a structural feature of the times we may hope to know after more studies.

Until we do understand more about the factors affecting and affected by kinship in the seventeenth century, it is impossible to generalize with any success about the structure of Ralph Josselin's family life. His Diary suggests that geographical mobility, high age of marriage, low expectation of life, and inheritance concentrated in the nuclear family were some of the major factors militating against the importance of his extended kinship network. The fact that his kinship ties were in many ways like those of a highly mobile modern family suggests also that the existing family structure was already appropriate for industrialization, though we know that there is no necessary correlation between the predominance of the nuclear family and industrial growth.[4] Certainly the above analysis dispels any lingering illusion that the peculiar nature of modern English kinship systems is entirely a post-industrial product.[5]

Perhaps the most important offering that Josselin has to make through his Diary, is that here, and in other similar diaries, is a vast treasury of information about family life in pre-industrial England below the level of the aristocracy. Whether he was representative or atypical; whether, as seems likely, there will be wide variation

[1] Morgan, *Puritan Family*, p. 150.

[2] This description of modern urban families is given by Bott, *Family and Social Network*, p. 128. Josselin's kinship recognition also seems similar to the 'shallow genealogical depth' situation described by Firth, *Two Studies*, p. 37.

[3] *Two Studies*, p. 41.

[4] Sidney M. Greenfield, 'Industrialization and the Family in Sociological Theory', *Am. Jour. Soc.*, vol. LXVII, no. 3 (1961), pp. 312–22, effectively destroys the hypothesis of a necessary correlation.

[5] Such a hypothesis is strongly implied, for example, in Firth, *Two Studies*, pp. 19, 21.

between region and region, highland and lowland England, both in the structure of family life and in the economic and religious context within which it was lived; these questions will only be answered after further studies.[1] The many clergymen, the scattering of merchants and others who sat in their damp houses scribbling their journals, can open up to us their old worlds to enlighten our new one.

[1] Some of the contrasts are suggested in Thirsk, 'The Family', p. 121, for instance those arising out of variations in social class and inheritance patterns. Another broad difference may be between 'fielden' and 'forest' areas; that extended kin were far more important in the former is suggested by Alan Everitt in Thirsk (ed.), *Agrarian History of England*, vol. IV, p. 434.

PART IV

The mental world

II

Attitudes to pain, sin and God

It is clearly desirable to go beyond the previous analysis of the life-cycle and social relationships. The detailed Diary kept by Ralph Josselin enables us to see into the mind of a village clergyman of 300 years ago. The basic structure of his thought is hardly ever directly revealed, yet we may approach it indirectly by piecing together attitudes to particular phenomena and guessing intuitively at the connexions. This 'imaginative leap, is made both easier and harder if the reader is a product of 'Western' society. The gain in understanding from a shared tradition sometimes leads to a loss of perception as to the differences between Josselin's mental world and our own. Only occasionally, in the reference to a witchcraft trial or an apocalyptic vision, are we jolted into the recognition that his perception of the world may have been based on many assumptions totally alien to us.

Although the following attempt to go beyond a conventional discussion of Josselin's religious thought will inevitably produce many distortions and oversimplifications of complex problems, it is hoped that it will also suggest some worthwhile problems for the historian of ideas. The analysis will be centred on his specific responses to phenomena in his environment—death, pain, the weather—and will then move on to an analysis of his dreams and the structure of his thought.

The high mortality rates of pre-industrial England[1] meant that deaths occurred more frequently, and at different points in Josselin's life-cycle, than would be likely in his mid-twentieth-century equivalent.[2] The incidence of deaths in his family is illustrated in table x below.

[1] A rough table of expectation of life at various ages in various places is given in Laslett, *Lost World*, p. 93. Gregory King's estimate for expectation of life at age 0 was 32 years. A sophisticated recent analysis of one parish is given in E. A. Wrigley, 'Mortality in Pre-Industrial England: The Example of Colyton, Devon, Over Three Centuries', *Daedalus* (Spring, 1968).

[2] Although, of course, everyone died, because they died younger it would mean that there was a swifter 'turnover': a particular individual would, for example, witness the death of some of his own children. There is an interesting comparative set of data for another pre-industrial society in D. F. Roberts, 'A Demographic Study of a Dinka Village', *Human Biology*, vol. 28 (1956), p. 399. Roberts writes of the Dinka, 'It appears that by the time the average woman is 50, she has lost at least one third of her children, and about a half of those among her

The effects of these many deaths on Josselin's mentality can only be guessed at this stage. There is not enough evidence yet to see whether the constant cutting short of personal relationships inhibited the growth of deep personal ties;[1] whether the development of individuality was damaged or prevented by such a rapid turnover.[2] It is necessary to remember that there were others, both kin and

TABLE X. *The incidence of death in Ralph Josselin's family*

Years	Josselin's age	Relatives known to have died
1617–26	1–9	mother, sister, sister
1627–36	10–19	father, grandfather, grandmother
1637–46	20–9	wife's father, uncle, uncle, aunt, cousin, grandfather's brother
1647–56	30–9	son, son, daughter, wife's mother, cousin
1657–66	40–9	uncle, aunt, cousin
1667–76	50–9	son, daughter, sister, grandson, step-mother, uncle, uncle, brother-in-law
1676–83	60–8	grandson, brother-in-law

NOTE
The exact dates and relationships are given in the kinship chart, facing p. 234.

neighbours, whose deaths were not recorded in the Diary. It appears that not only was the incidence of death higher, but, measured against Josselin's life-cycle, it occurred at points that diverge widely from the picture presented by modern industrial society. His parents both died before he was twenty; his aunts and uncles were dying off when he was between twenty and thirty; his children between his thirtieth and fortieth years; his grandchildren when he was over fifty.

It is clear that the only loss that moved Josselin deeply was that of a member of his nuclear family (with the exception of one close

brothers and sisters who succeeded in reaching adulthood, besides those who died before doing so; she has also very probably lost her husband'.
[1] An idea suggested by Mr Keith Hopkins when lecturing at the London School of Economics in 1967; see also Ariès, *Centuries of Childhood*, p. 38. Some of the problems and facts are discussed in Hajnal, 'European Marriage Patterns', p. 124, who cites Fourastié as showing 'how rarely parents must have lived to see the marriage of their own children or how frequently men lost their wives'.
[2] The argument, again derived from Mr Hopkins, is as follows: when there is high mortality it is difficult to develop specialized roles and complicated training because the heavy investment in particular individuals thus incurred may all be lost through their death (a problem similar to the modern one of whether to train women whose career may be ended by marriage).

friend), though he frequently noted the deaths of other kin and neighbours.[1] His mother and father had died before Josselin began writing his Diary and we learn of the latter only that 'with greife of heart I layed him in the grave, but my God lives for everymore' [1636]. How intensely he felt his children's death seems to have been directly connected with the age of the child; the ones who died very young, or before they could make emotional ties with their parents, or those who died after they had grown up and left home, were not felt as such a deep loss as the only child who died in the intervening years.[2] A complicating factor may have been that the child whose death so afflicted Josselin was both his first child and a daughter. The father–daughter tie may have been particularly strong at that period in her life.

Josselin's reaction to the death of each child, as reported in the Diary, highlights this unequal emotional response. The infant Ralph, who died at ten days old 'was the youngest, & our affections not so wonted unto it'. Josselin and his wife had already had time 'to bury it in our thoughts; wee lookt on it as a dying child 3 or 4 dayes'. The whole mood of the description is one of quiet resignation; two days before the death his mind was melancholy but not distraught: 'you shallt goe, my infant' he wrote, 'into the land of rest, where there is no sickness nor childhood but all perfection' [19–22. 2. 48]. Resignation was to God's will for 'god shall make mee to see this dealing of his to bee for the best'. The same aura of acceptance surrounds the death of another Ralph, on 2 June 1650 at the age of thirteen months: 'my deare Ralph before midnight fell asleepe whose body Jesus shall awaken; his life was continuall sorrow and trouble; happy he who is at rest in the Lord'.

In the moving account of eight-year-old Mary's death, the resignation is still there, but this time Josselin gave his daughter to his demanding God with more reluctance. The account is too long to quote in full, but excerpts will indicate the poignancy of this loss.

My litle Mary very weake, wee feared she was drawing on; feare came on my heart very much, but shee is not mine, but the Lords, and shee is not

[1] See figure 11, p. 156 above.

[2] This helps to explain, and is given support by, the fact that Essex witches were seldom blamed for the deaths of children under a year old, and usually for those between one and five years old (see the forthcoming book by Alan Macfarlane, *Witchcraft in Tudor and Stuart England* (1970), table 15). The pattern is different to that described for the Comanche, where the grief is directly proportional to the age of the deceased; infants are not mourned, the deaths of grown children 'would cause great grief' but the 'greatest grief of all' is for 'a son just beginning manhood' (A. Kardiner (ed.), *The Psychological Frontiers of Society* (Columbia paperback edn, 1963), p. 80).

too good for her father ... This morning all our hopes of Maries life were gone; to the Lord I have resigned her and with him I leave her ... the Lord make us willing shee should bee out of her paine ... This day a quarter past two in the afternoone my Mary fell asleepe in the Lord ... she was 8 yeares and 45 dayes old when shee dyed; my soule had aboundant cause to blesse God for her, who was our first fruites ... it was a pretious child, a bundle of myrrhe, a bundle of sweetness; shee was a child of ten thousand, full of wisedome, womanlike gravity, knowledge, sweet expressions of God, apt in her learning ... Lord I rejoyce I had such a present for thee ... it lived desired and dyed lamented, thy memory is and will bee sweete unto mee. [22–27. 5. 50]

The contrast with the note on 31 July 1673 recording the death of another Anne is striking: 'This morning after 2 of the clocke my deare Ann in her twentieth year died with mee at Colne; a good child, following her brother to London, & from thence hither, to lie in his grave, loving in their lives & in their deaths they were not divided'. The brother referred to was Thomas, who had died on 15 June 1673: 'About one a clocke in the morning my eldest sonne Thomas and my most deare child ascended early hence to keep his everlasting Sabbath with his heavenly Father, and Saviour with the church above; his end was comfortable'. In the same entry the cry 'he was my hope' implies a deeper dismay about Thomas.

Josselin frequently declared that he had 'resigned' himself to a death before it happened, but how adequate was such preparation, or how long he and his wife were afflicted by their loss it is difficult to say. For a few months, at least, they grieved, and mourning continued, though we do not know whether there were any institutionalized rituals to deal with such grief.[1] Josselin's own antidote against sorrow was simple; the normal 'way to comfort is by running to other imployments, diverting thoughts, bringing in others in their rooms, looking off from them', but he recommended people to face death directly, and to consider the happiness of the deceased; 'the consideration of their state in death is Honey that cureth and asswageth your griefe'.[2] About six weeks after the death of two

[1] The many anthropological accounts of mourning, for instance those by Nadel, *Nupe Religion*, pp. 125 ff., and Schapera, *Married Life*, pp. 310 ff., as well as the analyses of their ritual (Van Gennep, *Rites of Passage*, ch. 8) and social (B. Malinowski, *Magic, Science and Religion* (New York, 1954), pp. 47–53) functions, would provide a good framework for a thorough historical analysis of these subjects. There are many references in historical sources to the length of mourning; for example, Evelyn mourned for one daughter for about a month (*Diary*, p. 429). Excessive mourning should be discouraged argued Robert Burton, *Anatomy of Melancholy* (Everyman edn, 1962), vol. II, p. 180.

[2] The full reference and other extracts from this sermon are printed on p. 221 below.

children, Josselin confessed that 'many times I find the memory of my deare babes bitter as death' [14. 7. 50]. When his wife was sick some two weeks later he attributed it to grief [4. 8. 50]. Thirteen months after the death of Mary his daughter he could write 'I have thoughts of my sweetest Daughter now with comfort, who have had thoughts of her like the bitterness of death' [sic].[1]

Yet, as already suggested, once dead the children or ancestors were given no institutional recognition in any kind of cult. Mourning was not to be too intense, or the memory of individuals to be retained too long, 'for God would have us forget the dead . . . this forgetfulness is not of the graces and vertues of the dead . . . but it is of their persons'. It is not 'uncomely to wet the Herses of our dying friends, with tears' but sorrow must be 'moderated', we must not grieve 'as others which have no hope' [sic].[2]

Death seems to have been viewed as an absolute separation; the dead were no longer in communication with the earth, though they continued to exist as individual souls. The problem of keeping them 'alive', and yet keeping them from interfering with the living, was resolved by sending them on to another plane or dimension—heaven. Josselin's infrequent Diary references to heaven suggest that he held an Old Testament vision of it. There was a gate to be opened when the mortal soul was admitted; 'before you open the grave for me' [28. 11. 74], Josselin reminded God, 'open heaven gate'. It was also above the earth, his mother 'being received up into heaven' [1618]. For the dead there was first a sleep, from which they awoke in heaven: 'my Mary fell asleepe in the Lord; her soule past into that rest where the body of Jesus, and the soules of the s[aint]s are' [27. 5. 50]. Rest, health, 'no sicknes nor childhood but all perfection' [19. 2. 48], this was the prospect, though for a time soul and body would be separated, 'the body goes downward and the soul upward', the bones were buried whilst the soul lived 'in thy and my gods sight'. Eventually 'soule and bodye shall assuredly arise to injoy god, and these eyes of mine shall see it' [22. 2. 48]. There was no cause to mourn, for 'Your Wives, your Husbands, your Sonnes and Daughters, whose departing you so much lament, are but stept aside into their retiring rooms, their cool Summer-parlours, the shady cool Grove of the Grave to take a little rest by sleep, and when they awake they shall return again'.[3]

Until such time, however, the enduring soul was of no especial concern to the living. Josselin believed that all his children would go

---

[1] See p. 221.

[2] As he put it in a funeral sermon (see appendix C, p. 221 below).

[3] See the same sermon, p. 221 below.

to heaven, which was a comfort when he was facing their loss; the more he missed them the more he stressed his certainty that God needed their company. Nevertheless, belief in the after-life does not play an important part in his private thoughts as recorded in the Diary. There is not a single direct reference to hell or to damnation. It thus seems that a Puritan clergyman, who might have been expected to use heaven and hell as threats or inducements to himself and his congregation, showed the most tepid interest in both.

Heaven's function as a substitute, a recompense for the afflictions of temporal life was not especially considered by Josselin either;[1] only once does he hint that the scales of suffering in this life might be weighted down by extra ease in the next. Two years from his death, looking back over his life, he asked that 'god give a good harvest; by my troubles here I hope a better porcon' [31. 7. 81]. The fields of this life which he had sown with tears would, he hoped, yield him an extra harvest of eternal bliss. But his thoughts were seldom extended in the direction of that eternity; the sanctions and explanations he sought were this-worldly. Death was the end of everything imaginable, beyond it the merest speculation.[2] Thus the 'this-worldly' orientation of his economic activities, with their concentration on investment in material rather than spiritual goods, found its counterpart in his philosophy.

Josselin's attitude to his own death combined both his belief in its blessings, and confusion about its exact meaning for him personally. Sometimes his Calvinistic confidence in his pre-elected salvation deserted him, and he considered the possibility that he would not get to heaven. 'I have frequent thoughts and feares of death', he wrote on 14 December 1656, 'which if I should miscarry, and be eternally miserable, how sad would bee my condition'. This was when he was nearly forty-two years old, but ten years later when he was ill with 'gripings' he cried out 'oh how willing I was to die, and bee with Christ which is best' [1. 9. 67]; and on another occasion he

---

[1] The situation seems similar to that described by Firth, *Elements of Social Organization*, p. 209, where 'ideas of the afterworld place so little emphasis on punishment for the guilty soul' because, Firth suggests, members of the society have other, more effective, social controls—among them the belief, shared by Josselin, that sin and physical misfortune are somehow linked.

[2] The very great degree to which the after-life might have mirrored this world is shown, for example, by the description of tribal beliefs in Burling, *Rengsanngri*, p. 60. One wonders how far this was true in various parts of pre-industrial England: did the representation of hell as filled with 'Landlords and puritanes and Sheriffs' bailiffs' remain merely at the level of social satire in seventeenth-century Westmorland (Campbell, *English Yeoman*, p. 162)?

remarked that for himself he was not concerned with the consequences of dying, but felt he should stay alive for the sake of his
children [4. 12. 68].

Then, as death approached with more inevitability, fear returned;
in his last illness he was pleading with God 'to remove the fear of
death' from him [25. 2. 83]; he had been relieved of such morbid
misgivings before [25. 4. 75]. How much of his life was spent under
fears of this kind and how far his behaviour was determined by
them it is impossible to say; nor do we know whether he considered
with John Donne that it was 'a sinne of feare' to doubt the power of
God to save and redeem him. That he was a confused and anxious
man, his imagination troubled in all aspects of his life, emerges
clearly from many entries.

Whatever he felt about his own death, his attitude towards the
man who deliberately brought about his own end was mild. Although
the church might, in accordance with ecclesiastical law, refuse burial
to the suicide, Josselin treated this offence gently.[1] He never seems
to have contemplated taking such a step himself, but showed neither
anger nor horror when someone else committed this, theoretically,
most heinous offence. On three occasions he merely noted that
someone had drowned or hanged himself [24. 4. 58, 23. 9. 65,
1. 1. 68], and added no comment. In the other cases his instinctive
response was pity. He spoke of 'the sad end of one Rust, who drowned
himselfe' [8. 5. 46], and of 'sad sins, judgements, one made away
himself for feare of want' [31. 1. 56].

In theological terms his explanation for suicide is somewhat
ambivalent. In one case he proposed that an attempt on his life
was the outcome of a man's being 'left to himselfe' and without God
[20. 11. 64]. Another time he thought it might be a direct judgement
from God: a man living with a separatist drowned himself and
Josselin, approved that 'Lord thy judgments are secret and righteous'
[4. 11. 44]. There is no suggestion that the pressure to commit
suicide came from the 'seduction of the Devil' as the coroners'
inquests put it, except, possibly, on one occasion when Josselin
visited a sick man 'who was much troubled in mind upon his life:
he had strong temptacons from Sathan' [3. 9. 44], temptations that
may have been towards suicide.

It is interesting that Josselin thought it worth entering suicides

---

[1] These regulations are cited, for example, in R. W. Muncey, *The Romance
of Parish Registers* (1933), p. 92. But from the cases quoted on the next page
of Muncey it is clear that the actual attitude and the letter of the law might
diverge.

in his Diary, but we do not know what proportion of those of which he heard he did in fact note down. As a minister he may have been in a position to encounter more than the normal amount; seven suicides and one, possibly two, attempted suicides seems a high figure with which a mid-seventeenth-century Essex vicar should have personally come into contact.[1]

Interlinked with high mortality was a high incidence of physical distress arising from the many incurable diseases of pre-industrial society. Only a reading of the actual Diary will bring home to the reader the constant, almost obsessional, discussion of pain and sickness. We have already seen how Josselin's wife spent eight and a half years of her life undergoing debilitating pregnancies, and even at the end of her child-bearing life she was subject to illness. She was 'ill' in March 1667, October 1667, and had a 'quartain ague' in October 1668 which continued through December and into February 1669. It returned on 20 March 1670. She was the subject of 'a very strange fitt' on 14 December 1677 and was so ill that Josselin thought there was little hope of her recovery on 10 October 1680: one of the many aspects of the insecurity of the era was an inability to judge the severity of an illness.[2]

Josselin himself had trouble in his eyes [15. 6. 45], suffered a 'sciatica' pain [27. 11. 72], had a 'listless, restless illness in my left kidney' [12. 4. 74] and, in his last illness which lasted intermittently from 1675 until his death in 1683, suffered a constant running sore in his leg; for instance, he noted on 23 January 1676 'My leg runs, sadly painful'. The children, of whom five predeceased their father were also beset by a variety of ailments. As babies they had ring-worm [1. 12. 44], and were 'livergrowne' [7. 5. 50]. As adolescents four had smallpox and recovered,[3] and they were in constant danger of plague: during the epidemic of the Great Plague of 1665 the Diary is almost entirely devoted to reports of the latest number of the dying in London and Colchester. The Diary also shows the whole

---

[1] None of the four named suicides are recorded as buried in the Earls Colne parish register, although they may have been buried elsewhere. Laslett, basing himself on Graunt's figures, suggests a suicide rate of 2.5 per 100,000 for the mid-seventeenth century (Laslett, Lost World, pp. 137–8). The original calculations by Graunt, and a discussion of some of the contemporary literature are contained in S. E. Sprott, The English Debate on Suicide: from Donne to Hume (La Salle, Illinois, 1961).

[2] The position of Mrs Josselin is very different from the situation of women in modern Bethnal Green, for example, where women are reported to be seldom incapacitated by illness (Wilmott and Young, Family and Kinship, p. 55).

[3] Tom [12. 6. 59]; John [18. 4. 69]; Elizabeth [3. 11. 78]; Rebecka [27. 5. 80].

family variously afflicted; on 15 June 1645 Josselin noted: 'My eyes troubled with rheums, my daughter with her cough, and my wife ill'. It is hardly surprising that during another of his wife's disorders he reflected that 'this life is a bundle of sorrows' [3. 11. 67].

As well as the contagious and infectious diseases and numerous painful troubles affecting the backs and stomachs of people living with poor sanitation in damp houses, there were hosts of small accidents which might, without modern remedies, lead to a painful death. Josselin saw all around him dangers that were hard to avert and lurked in almost any situation; for instance there was the man who pricked his thumb with a thistle and was likely to die of gangrene [10. 2. 56]. This awareness of the precarious world he lived in makes his Diary at times a catalogue of all the disasters that might have happened but were narrowly avoided. Whenever he went on a journey he praised God for bringing him safely home; when his horse slipped he rejoiced that he had been saved broken bones. His everlasting anxiety, mixed with relief and gratitude to God, is well illustrated in an entry for 26 August 1644:

leaping over the pales I scratched my face, but God be praised I had no further hurt though I might if providence had not preserved mee, & also in our fall when my wife and I pulling downe a tree with a rope with our pulling all fell together, but no hurt God bee praised: such falls my children have many times & yett safe; Mary fell out of the parlour window with her face against the bench & had no hurt; a strange providence, all the wit of the world could not have given such a fall & preserved from hurt, to God bee the praise.

The possible range of counter-actions against illness and accident were limited, institutionalized insurance policies were, of course, unknown. The frequent threats of fire, particularly with young children in the house [e.g. 19. 3. 46], were only one of the menaces to a man's security; such fire could reduce a person overnight to penury. We have already suggested in an earlier section that one way to avert disaster was to invest part of one's wealth in social relationships, particularly in co-operation with neighbours. This provided a partial solution to the problem of economic loss. Yet there were still wide areas which relief of this kind could not reach. Political events rebuffed Josselin's hopes many times, yet for this kind of unpredictability there was only one remedy: 'in all shakings God is the same' [14. 10. 59] Josselin assured himself. This sense that nothing was secure, except one's relationship to God, was expressed in many Diary entries, for example 'A bullock died almost suddenly. Lord there is nothing sure but thy selfe' [21. 2. 74].

As far as physical pain was concerned, Josselin was prepared to make some effort to cure his own and his family's illnesses—he visited the healing waters at Tunbridge for his bad leg for example [11. 7. 75]—but his experience made it clear that contemporary medicine could do very little. A neighbour might be able to set a bone in his son's instep [29. 11. 53], but the vast majority of ailments must await the restoring hand of God. 'The Lord I looke unto to bee my phisitian' Josselin declared [1. 2. 74], and, again, 'healing is thy blessing, you hast and wilt doe it' [23. 1. 76]. Sometimes he took both precautions; 'Advised with a surgeon for my leg, but my hope is in God' [29. 10. 76]. This reliance on an inscrutable God explains Josselin's lack of interest in the secondary causes of disease. He rarely speculated on this subject: in pages of description devoted to the Great Plague he never discussed the possible secondary causes; during an earlier outbreak of the 'spotted' fevers he had merely repeated the current opinion that 'distempered and infected air' might have something to do with the outbreak [15. 8. 47].

Pondering about *why* God should have seen fit to visit an infliction, rather than concentrating on the problem of *how* sickness spread and could be prevented, may have been the cause, or the effect, of high mortality rates.[1] The primary problem for Josselin was to reconcile pain and misfortune with an immediately involved and basically benevolent godhead. He asked the old question, 'why did this have to happen to me?' and provided answers for himself from a mind conditioned to submission and acceptance. The problem he faced was nowhere better expressed than in his reaction after the deaths of his daughter and of his friend, both called Mary [4. 6. 50]. 'When Mrs Mary dyed, my heart trembled, and was perplexed in the dealings of the Lord so sadly with us, and desiring God not to proceed on against us with his darts and arrows; looking backe into my wayes, and observing why God hath thus dealt with mee'.

One of his answers was simply to side-step the suffering and to concentrate on the remarkable recovery of the victim. When he was stung by a bee he was grateful that 'providence' prevented it swelling badly [5. 9. 44], but did not stop to wonder at the providence that allowed the sting. He told how 'I found God had gratiously kept my daughter Mary who was strucke with a horse' [7. 10. 44], but avoided the suspicion that it was less than gracious of God to have allowed the kick in the first place. Near-disasters were used as evidence of God's care, for how much worse things could have been

[1] The classic discussion of the distinction between explanations of 'why' and 'how' is contained in E. E. Evans-Pritchard, *Witchcraft, Oracles and Magic among the Azande* (Oxford, 1937), pp. 63–83.

without it; when a neighbour's dog bit one of his hogs and killed it, 'blessed bee God it was not a child' [4. 9. 55] was his reaction. His long account of the plague of 1665 shows up this attitude very clearly. For every abatement 'God's name be praised' [27. 10. 65] but when the numbers of the dying rose, there was no word of reproach.

There emerges here a principle of thought of considerable importance; the principle that pain and evil came from God. There is no hint in the Diary that Josselin envisaged an alternative source of evil, Satan for example. Again and again he traces his own and the nation's troubles back to God. 'The Lord's hand is abated in the distempers of the small pox' [13. 4. 51], shows that he considered the other great killer, apart from plague, to be God-given. 'The Lord giveth and the lord taketh' [30. 7. 52], he wrote when a neighbour's daughter died, and in a time of personal suffering faced up to one of the world's great dilemmas when he asked himself 'Shall I receive good at gods hand and not evill?' [22. 8. 50]

Josselin never wavered from his faith in a good God, so his assurance was that, in a sense, God could not send evil; he could not, without betraying his nature, be malicious, he would not 'meditate unkindnes, or lie in waite to bruise a poor reed' [23. 5. 64]. As Josselin wrote to a friend, 'The Lord doth not willingly afflict the sons of men, he doth not envy us our wives . . . and our children'.[1] Therefore any apparent unkindness must be part of a benign plan since one of Josselin's firmest convictions was that nothing happened by accident. Mere mortals would not always understand the plan, and Josselin himself was often at a loss. The success of the Quakers, for instance, puzzled him, for they 'seeme to be swarming and increased, and why Lord y[ou] onely knowest' [30. 6. 61]. Usually the only course was to accept what came, whether it was simply the scab on the children [21. 3. 52], or something worse, and wait for God to turn away his wrath 'when it pleases him' [15. 9. 44].

Yet it was also important to try to find out particular causes for God's displeasure, for once these were known his anger might be averted; 'now when this God striketh, he taketh notice how we eye him that holdeth the Rod, and whether we enquire how he was provoked to do thus, that seeking his face he may discover it unto us'.[2] A constant stream of prayers flowed from Josselin to his 'dear angrie Lord' in an effort to control the misfortunes apportioned out for him. Sometimes these succeeded, as when a child was saved [14. 11. 51], or when the plague missed him and his family after

[1] The funeral sermon from which there are abstracts on p. 221 below.
[2] The funeral sermon, sig. A6ᵛ, full reference on p. 221 below.

repeated intercessions [e.g. on 8. 10. 65]. Sometimes the child died, and then there was some recompense in the thought of the after-life. But still there was a great load of suffering to be borne, a burden which might be expected to crush the religious system of a pre-industrial society, but instead acted as one of its most powerful supports. To stay well, to stay alive, involved placating and, in a sense, outwitting God, and at the same time it involved ever stricter conformity to social norms.

Basically Josselin seems to have accepted that pain was either divine purge, as in the story of Job, or a punishment; in either case it might be interpreted as a 'blessing' [30. 12. 66] for it would lead the conforming Christian back to the right path, or morally strengthen him. 'God doth not alwayes knit his brows when he striketh . . . Affliction is one way of evidencing love'. Often suffering could be used to bring people to more 'watchfulness, holiness, to more unpright walking with him'.[1] On another level, God might simply be trying to give practical advice. This could lead to perplexity as to God's intentions; for instance, when Josselin found his parishioners increasingly unwilling to support him, he searched his heart 'to see whether it bee rather a punishment on mee for my sin, or a providence of God withall to remove mee from them' [12. 9. 48]. On this occasion he finally decided that, though he could not 'but acknowledge many iniquities', events could be interpreted as a hint from God that he should leave.

His general hope was that suffering would be salutary to his soul: 'Much troubled with my leg and backe with pains. it may bee god doth it to better my soul—thats my hope' he wrote [5. 11. 82]. But pain and sin did not, he felt, automatically cancel each other out, still the search for the reason for God's anger must go on, the restless self-analysis for root causes; 'afflictions slay not sin, its grace must mortifie them' [1. 4. 77]. Suffering would lead to a search for the sin which had precipitated it, and when that sin had been 'sensibly felt and truly bemoaned' it would do a person good in 'making us cleave closer to Christ'.[2]

Two principles upon which this search for the link between pain and behaviour was conducted emerge clearly from the Diary. The first concerns the time at which the search occurred. It was not until the misfortune had happened that Josselin searched round for an explanation. He does not seem to have awaited punishment for particular lapses, at least not consciously. The exception to this rule

---

[1] Funeral sermon, sigs. A7-A7ᵛ; full reference on p. 222 below.
[2] These remarks are to be found among Josselin's 'sayings' at the start of the manuscript Diary (p. 5).

occurred when he was castigating the nation generally for its godlessness, behaviour which he felt sure would lead to disaster. Normally, and without exception in his private life, it was the misfortune that occurred first, then came the search for explanations. The other principle was that the size of the explanation was proportionate to the size of the misfortune. If the misfortune was a general calamity affecting the whole nation, the explanation must lie in a sin committed by the whole nation. If it was a private loss, it was a private sin. Thus Josselin wrote 'The nacons sins are many and sad, Lord lett publike ones be pardoned; the nacons judgments are, 1: continual raine to the spoyling of much grasse, and threatning of the harvest. 2: the sad charge by warre to the undoing of the country; the sad decay of trade' [16. 8. 48]. The weather could be judged a sure sign of God's displeasure: 'Among all the severall judgment on this nacon, God this spring, in the latter end of April, when rye was earing and eared, sent such terrible frosts, that the eare was frozen and so dyed . . . as if the Lord would continue our want, and penury, wee continuing our sins' [9. 5. 48]. General political defeat, too, 'speaks our sins aloud' [9. 9. 44].

To draw such connexions was the accepted fashion of all the governing and literate classes; public fasts in times of pestilence were frequent, for example, that recorded by Josselin on 30 September 1657. Only infrequently does he hint at the sort of general failing that might lead to a general catastrophe; on 5 August 1644 he prayed that plague be kept away 'and lett not our sins, our covetousness and pride of the poore in the plenty of their Dutch worke [i.e. cloth industry] cause thee to bee angry with us'. The suggestion is clear that the new economic enterprises might disrupt the spiritual life of the nation, and out of an angry heaven retribution descend in the shape of drought, disease, or flood.

On the personal level we have already seen how Josselin linked his failures, his abandonment by his parishioners, and his illness. On 24 January 1647 he wrote 'my little daughter aguish, the lord raise her up, & pardon my many failings'; here the implication is that punishment could be deflected on to a member of his family, innocent and young though she might be, and in one most curious passage this implication is carried to its logical conclusion; that God should kill one of his children because of his fondness for chess. The passage is so revealing that it is worth quoting in full; the whole entry is for 23 February 1648.

As often times before, so on this day did I especially desire of God to discover and hint to my soule, what is the aime of the God of heaven more especially in this correction of his upon mee; and when I had seriously considered my heart, and wayes, and compared them with the affliction and sought unto God, my thoughts often fixed on thes particulars:

Whereas I have given my minde to unseasonable playing at chesse, now it run in my thoughts in my illnes as if I had beene at chesse; I shall be very sparing in the use of that recreacon and that at more convenient seasons.

Wheras I have walked with much vanitie in my thoughts and resolved against it and have served divers lusts too much in thoughts, and in actions, wheras both body and soule should bee the Lords who hath called mee to holynes, God hath taken away a sonne; I hope the Lord will keepe my feete in uprightness that I may walke alwayes with him, and I trust it shall bee my endeav[o]ur more than ever:

And also that I should bee more carefull of my family to instruct them in the feare of God, that they may live in his sight and bee serviceable to his glory.

God was seen as a stern father figure, who punished human failings on the human level; Josselin had taken himself from God, therefore God 'hath taken away a sonne', a terrible reciprocation. Guilt would be the constant companion of a man who held such views, self-examination an almost daily occurrence as he strove to live up to the ideals he had set himself.

Guilt in fact greets us from nearly every page of the Diary, for Josselin blamed himself for almost everything that happened, and if something as simple as chess was not at hand, an earnest introspective regard was turned on to each thought and action. Almost one suspects that, like George Herbert, he was too happy in his unhappiness, turning his purge to food. When his wife was ill he admitted that 'its hard to find out the particular cause of our troubles, but what good wee omitt, or ill wee doe that is hinted to us, its safe to reforme' [8. 7. 56]. Whatever the hints were, they were produced from his own mind, and there corrected.[1] Thus pain, even when it was not visited on himself but on his family, was not a disruptive element, but a cohesive one. It drew him to his God, abased and repentant, even if he was not sure what for. This is illustrated when, on 4 June 1650, he was meditating on the death of his child Ralph and his dear friend Mrs Mary Church.

My heart trembled, and was perplexed in the dealings of the Lord so sadly with us, and desiring God not to proceed on against us with his darts and arrows; looking backe into my wayes, and observing why God hath thus dealth with mee, the Lord followed mee with that, 'sin no more, lest a worse thing happen unto thee'; and the intimacon of God was that he would proceed no farther against mee or mine, and he would assist mee

[1] The mechanism thus seems equivalent to the modern 'conscience', without which 'guilt' is absent.

with his grace if I clave to him with a full purpose of heart, which I resolve; oh my God helpe mee. oh my God faile mee not! for in thee doe I put my trust.[1]

Clearly a holy life was not only a spiritual benefit, but a very practical necessity. To sin was to court disaster, and not only for oneself. The ungodly could expect to be struck down and their children with them, for God would certainly take sides, as in an incident concerning the Quakers, of whom Josselin was obviously afraid.[2] The entry is for 15 December 1674:

Quakers increased; John Garrod their head in our town, building them a meeting place, appointing to meet once a week; I am not over solicitous of the effect, having seen Abbotts meeting house left, expecting God will appear for his truth, and I hope in perticular for mee in this place who truly desire to feare his name. I doe not determine why, but this morning viz 26, that Garrods wife died, within 6 weeks of the use of that house; I onely desire to feare and tremble, but doe not question the downfall of that sect under the feet of Christ and his servants.

Disasters and sudden deaths were so frequent that they could be woven into almost any pattern to justify any belief.

In one sense the linking of pain and sin can be seen as a conservative force. It justified Josselin in his resistance to the Quakers; it may, in times of plague, have made people 'resort to the word' [6. 5. 66], forcing them back to a God they were beginning to abandon. Too much deviation was dangerous for it led to physical punishment. But the effects of such a belief may also, indirectly, be radical. The constant need to prune away sinful behaviour and to cling closer to the Calvinist God may well have provided Josselin with the energy and single-heartedness without which his ministry might have collapsed. Like other ministers whose militant Puritanism was changing the structure of seventeenth-century thought and institutions, he needed support for his minority views and this he seemed to find in the hard hand of God. Although the connexion between pain and sin was an old one, it was, as it had always been, a neutral weapon. In new hands it might lead to added conformity and strictness in certain sections of life, but an added confidence and radicalism in others.[3]

In theory Josselin believed that he deserved all the punishment

[1] The punctuation has been slightly altered to improve the sense.
[2] There is a fuller discussion of Josselin's relationship with the Quakers on pp. 26–7 above.
[3] This is similar to the use made of witchcraft prosecutions. In some societies they prevent change, in others they are a means of destroying old values (Macfarlane, *Witchcraft in England*).

he received and was grateful for even a day's respite from it, as when he noted 'God good to mee this day, though I sinfull and unworthy' [7. 9. 51]. This sinfulness was his great preoccupation but, unfortunately, he never makes clear what his temptations were, or even whether they were materialistic, spiritual or sexual. The adjectives he uses to describe his temptations could be applied to a number of different offences: he is 'corrupt', 'lustful', 'vile', 'unclean', 'worldly'. A few quotations from the Diary will illustrate his endless struggle against his lower nature. Writing of his childhood, he describes his 'prodigious uncleane lusts', suppressed but causing him 'to loath and abhorre my selfe' [1618]. On 1 September 1644 he pleaded with God to 'helpe mee against vaine thoughts and imaginacons' and despite receiving some help [10. 8. 51] he was still 'easily yielding to corrupt meditacons', his heart 'full of its old pranks' [15, 29. 9. 50].

Usually he seems to have seen his faults as part of the chronic corruption of the human condition; the roots of evil he placed firmly in the human heart, his own erring heart particularly: 'my heart was dead and drowsy and wonderfully tost with corrupt imaginations' [16. 8. 50]. The only hope for this soul-sickness was the hand of God; 'Oh what mercy is this that god hath not lett my corrupcons loose, and made them too strong for mee' [2. 10. 48]. The temptations might also come from without, as when he delightfully described that 'I find Sathan like the lapwing crying before mee with one temptacon or vanitie, to drawe my minde from my god of my salvacon' [10. 9. 48]. Sometimes he visualized the world dangerously astir with evil and thanked God that he had given him 'a spirit more free from annoyances of Sathan, I have been a thoroughfare for many vile uncleane, worldly thoughts' [19. 1. 51]. Generally speaking though, the weakness was already within, waiting to be used by the powers of evil.[1]

Josselin's preoccupation with personal sin appears to have declined rapidly after 1652 when he was thirty-seven years old. From the age of twenty-nine, when the Diary became detailed in 1644, entries about his failings are frequent, but the period of real crisis was between 1648–51. This was a crucial time in the building

---

[1] The internalization of sanctions through self-examination is revealed in Puritan diaries (e.g. Knappen, *Two Puritan Diaries*, p. 55). It has also been discussed by historians, for instance Hill, *Society and Puritanism*, p. 244 and ch. 6 *passim*; Tawney, *Religion and Capitalism*, pp. 106–7. The process deserves further study and comparison with the situation in many other pre-industrial societies; for example the external sanctions in Greece (Campbell, *Honour and Patronage*, p. 326). Reasons for such internalization could also be investigated (some suggestions have already been made by Riesman, *Lonely Crowd*, pp. 15–16, xxv).

up of his estate and it may have been the conflict between his spiritual and secular roles that caused him to lament his 'vaine thoughts'. This anxiety is apparent in part of his long self-analysis entered at the date 12 September 1648: 'what a distraction it is for men to be intangled with thoughts of providing for their tables, when we should be attending our studdyes'. Probably the economic pressures eased, and perhaps the godly standards imperceptibly dropped as he reached his late thirites.

Another possibility is that the temptations were partly, at least, sexual. Two remarks hint at this; 'I find a wantones in my heart, and private converse with my wife' [18. 11. 55] and 'My mind very full of roving thoughts in my wives absence' [23. 5. 69]. Whatever the failings, real or imaginary, Josselin was a man at war with himself. This conflict may have arisen partly out of the demands of different roles; father of his family bound to provide for his children, and father of his parishioners obliged to feed their souls. There was also a clash between his duty towards the poor and an equal duty towards his own relatives. He explained the pulls of his various commitments quite clearly. He must be 'hospitable and mindfull of the poore; Titus 1:8: and our Towne is full of poore' but he was also 'bound to provide for his family, and lay up for them' [12. 9. 48]. Yet the general impression from the Diary is that, although Josselin was tormented by anxiety no less than by physical pain, the conflict he felt most was between the material and the spiritual; purity of thought and feeling as expected of a minister, as opposed to the physical and emotional desires of an ordinary, fallible, man. The result of the conflict was an everlasting striving towards godliness in an attempt to overcome anxiety; in this sense his soul was in a state of 'productive tension'.[1] However anxious, he did not resort to communing with angels to assist himself, as he seems to have believed that other troubled people did [27. 7. 55].

There is enough material in Josselin's Diary for a book entirely devoted to his relations with God; only a few of the many insights he affords can be mentioned here. God was envisaged as an immediate and personal force, present in every puff of wind; when Josselin arrived at another village to find that a fire had just started he 'saw the danger to his great barn, and praying to god the wind a little wheeled which much tended to secure it, a wonderfull answer of prayer' [6. 3. 63]. God watched over the swelling of bee stings, and plucked children from fires, and saw that trees fell in the right

[1] The phrase is from David Riesman, *Selected Essays from Individualism Reconsidered* (paperback edn, New York, 1954), p. 5.

direction. When even his almighty availability was stretched, there were the angels to whom he could delegate smaller tasks as when he was 'good in preserving An in a milke bowle, and Jane from swouning who let her fall in, and John in falling from the top of the schoole staires; God give his angels charge over us' [1. 9. 54]. Mary Church was similarly saved by angels when 'throwing out a bason of water, threw her selfe out of her doore. She had a sad fall, yett gods angells keepe us in many dangers' [24. 9. 44]. Josselin himself, though believing in angels, went straight to God when he wanted spiritual assistance.

Communion with the almighty was not only a spiritual enrich-ment, but a day-to-day requirement. Healing came from his hand as we have seen, and as he controlled the weather and growth, life itself depended on his blessing. Such a belief was so deeply embedded that it is seldom as clearly stated as on 26 January 1659 when Josselin noted that he was 'full of busines about my farme, the Lord plante, worke with mee, or all is vain'. It seemed obvious that God was as keen to bring in the harvest as were the farmers, for had he not given an extra 'hay day' when one had to be missed because of a fast [8. 7. 66]?

God could be contacted either through the medium of ritual or through prayer. The intensity of emotion at the communion service is shown in the graphic account of one such service; the sense of the personal presence of God was undoubtedly heightened by the long-awaited solemnization after a considerable period when no com-munion had been held. As Josselin described it:

Wee all sat round and neare the table; the bread was broken not cutt in blessing it; the Lord poured out a spirit of mourning over Christ crucified on me and most of the company, and my soule eyed him more than ever, and God was sweete to me in the worke . . . Received an account from many of our society of the sweete and comfortable presence of God with them, the livelynesse of the actions in breaking the bread, and in powring out the wine. [23. 2. 51]

Yet his most highly charged meetings with his Maker seem to have taken place during private intercession rather than in public ritual. During the two weeks before the communion described above he had two such meetings. On 11 February 'before I did anything, I sought God in private, and he sweetly answered mee "who art thou that art afraid of a man and fearest not mee", and on the 13th 'I sought God, he answerd not; I was resolved to rest on his former answer; I sought again, and he answered, "I will never faile thee nor forsake thee", the which word came with power, and commanded my heart'.

Whether Josselin really believed that he heard a voice, or whether his mind seemed to move towards a biblical text, there is no doubt that his belief gave him confidence.

When he needed guidance in taking any important decision he turned to God, for instance when he was deciding whether to leave Earls Colne [12. 9. 48]. In affliction God was a refuge; 'how happy are they that have a god in their difficulties to goe unto' [14. 7. 50] he exclaimed, reconciling this with his belief in God as the afflicter. Lonely, estranged, or threatened, he felt protected, for 'the Lord is a shield to mee who never sought the wrong of others' [22. 7. 60]. When 'not one person spake to mee, coming out of the church' there was the comfort that 'my confidence is in thee, and with quietnes I roule my self on thee' [8. 10. 71]. Public opinion was still a powerful force, but deviation from it was thus made possible.

God was, of course, present at all the major rituals of the life-cycle, at baptism, marriage and burial. He was also exhorted at times of public fasts and at weekly services to preserve the faithful from sickness and to bless the crops. Unfortunately no clear impression emerges from the Diary of the degree to which agricultural and ritual calendars overlapped; for instance we do not know how important was the blessing of the ploughs on Plough Monday, or the sanctifying of the harvest at the Harvest Festival.[1] Nor are the rituals themselves, the behaviour that characterized them, or the social group which participated, even described in detail, though we have seen that it was the nuclear family and the neighbours who constituted the ritual group.

God, as Josselin saw him, was huge and inscrutable, the sum of the universe, who both worked through natural laws and outside them; 'when god once breakes the course of nature, wee and our reason is silenced' [29. 11. 46]. He was the one secure feature in a shifting world, the nearest equivalent Josselin knew to an insurance company, bank, and welfare state, who could be invested in with some degree of confidence; 'I had something to lend to the Lord' he wrote, 'which he in his time will repay' [3. 3. 47]. But though unchallenged ruler of the universe—and Satan was never suggested as an effective rival—he took a personal concern in everyday activities.

---

[1] Anthropologists have, for some time, been aware that the ritual and agricultural calendars are not *necessarily* linked, the one a reflection of the other, as Durkheim had once argued (Nadel, *Nupe Religion*, p. 71). Yet we might still expect agriculture and religion to be closely blended. Josselin's prayers for rain (20.4.45 is an example) and the belief that workers would be singing psalms at their work (Herbert, *Priest to the Temple*, pp. 244–6) are merely two of the possible links. Some suggestive remarks on the many problems needing investigation here are made in Thomas, 'Work and Leisure', pp. 52–3.

His purposes were human purposes, he was there to save the family from accidents, help with the harvest, discomfort adversaries, discipline a recalcitrant son [12. 2. 71]. Josselin managed to overlook the logical difficulties in his image of this strict, demanding, vengeful, yet thoughtful and merciful almighty father. Certainly he received great reassurance from him, and the whole impetus of his existence was in his faith.

12

Dreams,[1] imagery and the structure of thought

Many societies use dreams as a method of interpreting the divine will, but Josselin's Diary gives no hint that its author employed them for this purpose in his religious exercises.[2] This was not for lack of dreams. We know from his entries of thirty-four of his own; but beyond describing them he did not carry out any sort of sophisticated analysis of their content, probably because their meaning was self-evident. He believed that the future could be predicted from dreams and hoped he 'might even forseeingly dream' [5. 1. 79], though perhaps not like the woman he quoted who was warned of her death in a dream [14. 9. 56]. He felt he had dreamt correctly about future political developments [22. 1. 55] and also predicted that three of his children would die but be replaced [25. 1. 58]. These modest successes made him interested enough to note down the contents of many dreams and to speculate on strange ones to see whether they 'tended . . . to my good' [4. 11. 77]. Also he was interested in the theory that 'they say dreames declare a mans Temperament' [12. 9. 44].

Josselin's own 'Temperament', or subconscious life, has to pass through a double censorship before it reaches us; that of his own memory in recalling the dream on waking, and that of the energy and interest he had in noting it in his Diary. He may have written down only a small proportion of dreams and omitted the more personal and illuminating ones; that he did omit a certain number

[1] Modern studies on the subject of dreams suggest that they are not, as Freud maintained, symptoms of subconscious anxiety states or sublimated desires, but more a computer type 'run through' of the mind's activities in order to discard the superfluous. Whichever theory is proved correct, dreams do point to the mind's pre-occupations and a discussion of them seems worthwhile.

[2] Three ways of regarding dreams—as 'outside' objective facts, visions of the wandering soul, or symbolic messages, are discussed in E. R. Dodds, *The Greeks and the Irrational* (California, 1966), p. 104. The whole of ch. 4 of the same work provides a useful analysis of dreams in pre-industrial cultures. George Fox (*Journal*, p. 10) followed contemporary opinion when he divided dreams into carnal, diabolic, and 'speakings of God to man'; Josselin does not seem to have made such a division, at least not explicitly. One example of the many books on dream interpretation at this period is Thomas Hill, *The most pleasaunte arte of the interpretacion of dreames* (1576).

we can be sure, for on 26 May 1678 he remarked that during a period of illness his 'head [was] light and dreams troublesome', yet nothing of such dreams appears in the Diary for that year. Despite the difficulties in analysing his dreams—the most dream-filled periods of his life may be missing, the subjects which gave him the greatest anxiety in his dreams simply omitted—it does seem worth making the effort since historians have seldom discussed the dreams of pre-industrial Englishmen.

The date and type of dream recorded in the Diary, based on a very rough classification into four types, is given in table XI below.

TABLE XI. *The dreams of Ralph Josselin*

Date	Religious	Religio–political	Political	Personal
1644–9				12.9.44
1650–9	7.8.53		12.12.50	13.8.53
	8.6.54		12.9.52	
	22.11.54		15.2.54	
	3.2.55	4.1.55	22.11.54	
	23.3.56	7.9.56	25.1.55	16.2.56
	3.10.56	12.4.57	13.3.55	5.4.56
	22.10.56		23.3.55	30.6.56
	15.2.58		5.10.56	7.10.56
				25.1.58
				30.6.59
1660–9	20.12.63		21.3.69	
1670–9		5.1.79	27.1.79	30.4.76
1680–3	30.11.82			
Totals:	10	4	10	9

NOTE

Josselin recorded one other 'very strange' dream on 4.11.77 but this is not included in the table since he did not describe its content.

Analysis will show that the classification in table XI is not entirely satisfactory and that a few of the dreams might be placed in more than one column. Basing impressions on the Diary references, Josselin's greatest interest was in political and religious dreams. If his selection of dreams was roughly in proportion to his total of remembered dreams, it is interesting that public affairs should have played such a large part in his private and subconscious mind. The other feature of general interest is that twenty-six of the thirty-three recorded dreams in the table occurred between 1650–9, when Josselin was aged between thirty-five and forty-five. There could be several explanations for this concentration. The two most likely are that the 1650s were a time of particular political and religious upheaval, a disturbance reflected in his dream life; or that Josselin was especially interested in dreams at this period. The two are not unconnected. In a period of unrest dreams may have assumed a more than ordinary significance.[1]

Either explanation would fit the fact that it was only in the 1650s that Josselin recorded the dreams of other members of his family. On 2 March 1651 his daughter of five

> dreamd that Jesus Christ was in our church, and went up into my pulpitt, and that he stayed a while, and then he came down and came into bed to her; she sayd to him, why dost you come to me, and he answered her, to sleep a little with thee, and he lyd downe and slept; and again she dreamd that Jesus Christ told her that he should come and rayne upon the earth 10000 years.

The main interest of this dream is in the evidence it provides for Josselin's curiosity about current millenarian beliefs, and for the fact that a young child could also be influenced by such beliefs and have her dreams on them taken seriously. The same features are illustrated by a recorded dream of son Thomas, who was just over eleven years at the time. The way in which millenarian beliefs mingled with childish fantasies is excellently illustrated.

> Tom dreamed he saw a wonderful house in the aer, very fine and shiny like the inside of oister shells; a great man as big as a house came out, with a great fire in his head, he came to the ground; the house was vanisht to a snaile, and he and sister crept in the ground like frogs. [3. 2. 55]

It was the same curiosity that prompted Josselin to record in great detail a dream of his wife's on 26 November 1654 in which she saw the sky filled with light and flames. Only four days before he recorded another dream in which she and her husband were 'familiar' with the protector, Cromwell.

Josselin's own religious dreams were also much occupied with apocalyptic revelation; the five such dreams were written down in 1654, 1655 and October 1656. 'This night in my dreame', he began one account, 'I thought I saw a blacke cloud directly in the fashion of a stagge, and a man sitting on him, his face to the West, and [it] noted the speed of a great person in his conquests' [3. 10. 56]. That this combined both a national and personal interest in millenarianism will appear later. His other religious dreams seem to reflect the day-to-day preoccupations and worries of a country clergyman. In the

---

[1] It is hoped that experts in the field of dream interpretation will use the references in table XI to provide the material for a proper comparative analysis of Josselin's dreams.

first he thought that an Anabaptist was throwing stones at him [7. 8. 53]; in the second he was present at a sermon by 'Mr Sams' which took place in a 'bushy' lane, and in which he had to prompt the preacher who forgot his text [8. 6. 54].[1] In another he found himself in a pulpit without his collar or surplice on and unable to sing the psalms or find the places in the bible [23. 3. 56]. This is a familiar dream situation, but in his case may have reflected his anxiety about a general scorn for the ministry.

A still more anxious and serious dream on this subject was that of 1658 that he had been condemned to 'die for religion', a sentence which at first dismayed him, but which he later found 'very comfortable' [15. 2. 58]. It was shown earlier that after the Restoration Josselin went through a period of considerable insecurity, uncertain whether he would be ejected for his non-conformist views. His optimistic dream of 1663 in which he 'dreamd the church w[h]ere I preacht full, multitudes standing without at windows' reveals, if nothing else, the poor attendances of his waking life [20. 12. 63]. Finally, a few months before his death, the reading of Job reminded him of dreams he had had 'often this summer and last night' in which, on his friends' advice, he had given up his ministry, and was afterwards 'always grieved and troubled for it' [30. 11. 82]. In this case, dreams may have fortified his decision not to abandon his vocation.

Josselin's political dreams were almost entirely grouped round the years 1654 to 1655 when Cromwell attempted to rule with various types of government and was rumoured to be meditating the assumption of the royal title. 'I thought something appeared', Josselin wrote of a dream on 23 March 1655, 'I saw nothing distinctly, but I thought it was Cromwell, who told mee he had taken the prince, would have me dispose him. I told him, I would not, but he had enough that would'. A 'religio-political' dream described how 'one came to mee and told me that Thurlow[2] was turned Jew. I answered perhaps it was a mistake, he might declare he was a Jew born, the Jewes having lived here' [4. 1. 55]. Among other slightly bizarre dreams was one in which Josselin became 'familiar' with the pope [22. 11. 54]. What he believed to be the threatened destruction of parliament in the late 1670s again set him dreaming.

[1] John Sams (Sammes) came from New England to Kelvedon in Essex as minister on 9 October 1647. He was at Coggeshall by 1654, but was ejected for nonconformity in 1662 (Smith, *Ecclesiastical History*, p. 391).

[2] John Thurloe (1616–68), Cromwell's secretary of state from 1652; there is a good short biography of him in the *D.N.B.* (by Charles Firth).

Of his personal dreams, only the first showed him kicking against the constraints of his tightly controlled conscious behaviour. He dreamt that he 'was in wondrous passion with a man that wrongd mee and my child' [12. 9. 44]; he was duly ashamed. His next recorded dream with its obviously acquisitive symbolism, could be interpreted as a promise of either worldly or spiritual harvests.

At night musing on the afflictions on the ministry and church of god, I dreamed that one sent mee a bushel of wheate, and in the mouth of the sacke was a bundle of mony, which I conceived was 10s.; it proved 13 at first telling; thinking I was mistaken I told it over againe and still it increased; more halfe crownes and more 1s. so that I could not reckon it ... awaking I thought presently of god's providing for us unexpectedly and by way of wonder, and that his should not want though the young lyons famish. [13. 8. 53]

The practical working out of this provision was also reflected in dreams; dreams about ditching his lands [30. 6. 56], about purchasing lands [7. 10. 56] about visits to Colchester [5. 4. 56], and about the help he was giving a friend in a law suit [16. 2. 56]. Only twice did he dream about his family, once the prophetic dream, already mentioned, in which he foresaw the death and replacement of three of his children [25. 1. 58], the second time about the death of his son-in-law [30. 4. 76]. The other personal dream was in the form of a nightmare about being attacked by a dog [30. 6. 59]. In all, it seems that Josselin's personal dreaming was uncomplicated, sometimes employing easily comprehended symbolism, usually a direct narrative of events. Their concentration between 1653 and 1659 may have meant that these dreams reflected his greatest period of anxiety over his rapidly increasing estate.

Josselin's verbal imagery is striking and a deeper analysis of it would be rewarding. He was extremely fond of concrete images to link the spiritual with the physical world; when a bee stung him he asked 'Let not sin oh Lord that dreadful sting bee able to poyson mee' [5. 9. 44]. And the cherries he brought to his wife inspired the pious wish that 'The Lord make mee to himself as ripe early fruit' [3. 6. 47]. Affliction was 'a thorn in my side' [23. 4. 76], and his wife 'as merry as the pleasant roe' [20. 6. 47], his dead child offered to God as 'a bundle of myrrh ... a box of sweet ointment' [27. 5. 50]. The influence of the King James Bible is apparent, but further studies might reveal how deeply natural phenomena were observed in educated circles in the seventeenth century, and produce useful material on the classification of such phenomena; which processes were thought of as alike, which sharply differentiated. The placing of the boundaries between the physical and spiritual world often appears strangely alien to the mid-twentieth-century reader. Some of Josselin's imagery has also lost much of its force for a town-dwelling population, but it is easy to see how biblical stories and metaphors would have a rich meaning for Josselin's country audience. Josselin's own farming experiences linked him with the world of the New Testament. Thus he described how 'This morning found my lost sheep with 2 lambs . . . oh that my stray sheep might return to thee oh God' [10. 2. 74]. When he gathered in the harvest he asked for grace 'to prepar our selves as wheate . . . to bee gatherd into his [i.e. Christ's] granary' [6. 8. 82], and spoke of a dead friend as 'ripened in faith by many Afflictions . . . and now like a rick of Corn brought in, in due season'.[1]

Biblical cadences are present too in the many analogies Josselin drew from the human reproductive cycle; he asked that people might be 'weaned' from their old enjoyments [25. 12. 47] and from sin [3. 4. 53], as the Psalmist had likened his soul to a 'weaned child'.[2] He prophesied that 'the troubles of the world shall come on them suddenly as paines of a travailing woman' [6. 1. 52]; and he optimistically hoped that God would make the returning Charles II as a 'nursing Father to thy people' [10. 6. 60]. The social world and the natural world were also linked; marriage negotiations were seen as 'ripening' [12. 5. 47] and an unusually large congregation reminded him that 'its good fishing where many are; catch some, oh Lord, I pray thee' [28. 5. 65]. The image for the Devil, 'I find Sathan like the lapwing crying before mee' [10. 9. 48], probably drew on popular folklore which represented the bird as evil and treacherous.[3] The image is as concrete as that evoked when Josselin, speaking of his old temptations, described how 'sometimes they show their hornes, but Gods carpenters are ready to cutt them off' [10. 8. 51].

It seems unlikely that Josselin delighted in natural phenomena for their own sake, yet some of his descriptions strike the modern reader as full of appreciation. For example he wrote one January 'grasse springing, herbes budding, birds singing, plowes going' [3. 1. 75]. The general feeling from the Diary is of a fluid world, with the

---

[1] The final quotation is from the funeral sermon summarized on p. 221 below, sig. A3.

[2] Ps. 131, vs. 2.

[3] Also on the lapwing's strategy in drawing away people from its nest by false pretences.

material holding spiritual meaning, the spiritual merging with and informing the solid presences of natural objects. There was a vast symbolism abroad—in clouds, in birds, in unseasonable showers. 'The heavens for some time have mourned over us' [15. 6. 73], he wrote at the death of his son.

Weather was 'sad' or 'sweet' and its vagaries were studied to discover what omen or threat they held. Ultimately this symbolism found its counterpart in every aspect of life. 'The war damps all trade; the Lord drive his spiritual trade' [11. 11. 66], may have been another pious analogy, but more likely it reveals the feeling Josselin held that trade, like everything else, took place on several levels. As physical pain and behaviour were linked, so were the natural worlds of weather and growth and economic activity with the moral forces that swayed them. The great linker was God; his vitality worked in and through the whole universe and like a great wind swept away any barriers that man sought to erect.

God's main weapon was the weather, which he used to threaten, to confuse and often to punish: 'a wett night, and a wettish day, as if God would have called men to his w[orsh]ip, but their [sic] was no regard of the same', Josselin wrote anxiously on 30 August 1648. The rain that fell on his roof that night was a threat, but on 23 April 1650 'it rained a most sweete showre; God is opening his hand to fill us with his bounty', he recorded. Bad weather at a critical time could have a catastrophic effect on prices, as we saw in an earlier section. Always there was a great feeling of insecurity; even a young rook falling out of its nest was described in the Diary as a strange omen [23. 10. 44].[1]

This mental world, so full of omens and symbolic nuances, contained few barriers against rumours of witchcraft and the millennium, of monstrous births and meetings with the devil. Analysis of the Josselin family's dreams has already shown that during the 1650s they dreamt fairly frequently of strange fires and figures in the sky, which seemed to fit in with the prophecies in the Book of Revelation concerning the Second Coming. Interest in millenarianism was widespread in England at the time.[2] Josselin first recorded his meditations on the subject on 17 November 1650 when 'his thoughts [were] much that god was beginning to ruine the kingdom of the earth, and bringing christs kingdom in'. Earthquakes, at

[1] The use of the weather as a portent by yeomen-farmers is described in Campbell, *English Yeoman*, p. 369.
[2] See, for example, Norman Cohn, *The Pursuit of the Millennium* (Mercury edn, 1962), pp. 321–78, and Christopher Hill, *Puritanism and Revolution* (Mercury books edn, 1962), pp. 323–36.

various places including Geddington, Northamptonshire, and floods in Flanders and Paris during the summer of 1650 must 'portend something' he thought [24. 1. 51]. On 30 March 1651 he noted apocalyptic rumours concerning the year 1655, which were circulating from Poland.

How early he began to study the subject seriously we do not know, but on 3 February 1653 he had a letter from an uncle urging him to carry on with his 'apocaliptiq studdies', and it was within the next three years that he recorded his three dreams on the subject, though whether such beliefs influenced his behaviour or sermons is not apparent. He was certainly not prepared to swallow whole the wild conjectures circulating at the time, and was sceptical of the many fringe prophets about. A book of 'Welsh prophecies, which asserts that Cromwell is the great Conqueror that shall conquer Turke and Pope' struck him as excessive in its claims. Cromwell would be 'most great' he admitted, but the book generally 'giveth mee no satisfaction' [12. 12. 57]. His mixture of interest and scepticism was most marked in the year 1656. In his first entry for the year he noted that 'some think their very world would end in 56 [26. 1. 56], and a few months later he spoke of 'that stupendous yeare of 1656, of which men have had strange thoughts' and although he was 'not of their minde' yet he expected 'notable effects' [24. 3. 56]. Awake and asleep he was interested in millenarianism, but with common-sense scepticism.

His reporting at second hand of other odd phenomena show him assuming the possibility of their existence, though again with common-sense precautions that each case must be judged on its merits. When he told of 'a monster born in our town' [28. 4. 72], he may have meant little more than that the baby was hideously deformed in some way, or he may have meant that it was like the 'monster borne about Colchester, first a child, then a serpent, then a toad which lapped', of which he heard when visiting Lady Honeywood [8. 5. 46]. He had no trouble in trusting an account of a man who was 'heaved into the water by one in the shape of a bull' which 'passed by him and as a wind with a rustle it beat him down into the road' [16. 7. 55].[1] The man in question possessed an evil character according to Josselin, and the supernatural force that bore down on him, bull-like or wind-like, was certainly a personification of the devil.[2] This he would not argue about; that the devil

[1] This is very reminiscent of the even more extraordinary story of the invisible powers which transported Francis Fry, as described in Aubrey, *Brief Lives*, pp. 196–9.

[2] The man, Guy Penhack (or Pennocke) was heaved into a brook just beside

could take human or beastly shape he firmly believed, and a much clearer account of such a personification is given. Returning home one day, a man called Stephens visited him, 'who had the divell appearing to him; the greediness of mony, made him desire it, and god sufferd it; he [i.e. the devil] appeared in a blacke gown, and then in red; he tooke his bloud on white paper'. Four days later 'I was with Stephens and Mr R[ichard] H[arlakenden]; he was afraid the divel was coming in upon us; I thought he might [i.e. the devil might come] but trusted Christ would secure us in whose worke wee were' [10 and 14. 6. 55].

This was Josselin's closest brush with the devil, nor did he personally meet any angels though his friends told him of 'the passages of those that have communion with angels' among them 'Mr. Sadler, M[aste]r of requests to the protector', who 'had a vision and trance 3 days togither' [27. 7. 55].[1] The skies were generous with visions too; on 20 August 1656 'a remarkable cross' was seen, and on the 12th of the same month 'two armies were seen in the aire fighting'.

Monsters, angels, sky-symbols, the devil, these were part of every-day living, and therefore it was with no difficulty that Josselin could conceive of old women with the power to inflict injury in their curses. No prosecutions for witchcraft have been discovered for Earls Colne after 1587, yet Josselin twice notes informal suspicions concerning this offence. In 1656 'one J. Biford was clamoured on as a witch, and Mr C. thought his child ill by it'. Josselin took the suspect 'alone into the feild, and dealt with him solemnely, and I conceive the poore wretch is innocent as to that evill' [30. 8. 56]. The following year,

Mr. Clarke, the minister of Gaines Colne, told us that he saw one An Crow, counted a witch, take something out of a pot and lay by a grave. He considered what was to do; when he drew near he espied some baked pears and a little thing in shape like a rat, only reddish and without a tail, run from them and vanish away that he could not tell what became of it. The partie said she laid them there to cool. She was under the window

---

Josselin's future property at Stonebridge meadow (see figure 8, field 7). Penhack seems to have been notorious in the village. Baptized on 24.8.1618 according to the parish register; he was summoned to the quarter sessions for 'begetting with child Judith Neale of Stistead, singlewoman' (E.R.O., Q/SR 330/58), an event described by Josselin in his Diary for 24.8.46. He was the same man who, when sick, had been 'much troubled in mind upon his life: he had strong temptacons from Sathan' (3.9.44). These temptations were obviously the prelude to the events described above.

[1] John Sadler (1615–74), one of the masters in chancery. In 1662 he accurately prophesied the plague and fire of London (*D.N.B.*).

where we exercised. I pressed her what I could; she protests her innocency. [19. 7. 57]

Josselin obviously accepted the possibility that witchcraft was at work, that witches could make other people's children ill, that they had small animals as 'familiars'. Yet, in the particular cases which he examined, he was not convinced that the suspects were 'witches'. Nor, when interpreting the afflictions of his own existence, did he ever seek to explain them in terms of the malign will of another human being. Yet it was a natural counterpart of his faith in the power of prayer, that he should also believe in the power of a curse. So when Potter's windmill burnt down, and he knew that 'the woman often wisht it were on a light fire', Josselin accepted that 'god sometimes gives persons their curses' [14. 7. 59].[1]

From our present standpoint it was in many ways a differently arranged world that Josselin inhabited, and it might appear even more remote if there was enough material in his Diary to enlighten us on other attitudes; to time, for instance, and to space. Did he see time as repetitive or as forever renewed, as qualitatively varying, or merely as a quantitative and uniform progression as a series of units?[2] Did he see space and distance in a way that is familiar to us, or was it demarcated differently, sacred spaces lying beside dangerous ones in an order of a wholly imaginary, but solid, significance? How did he regard travel? With a great deal of trepidation on setting out and relief on returning as appears in every entry where he refers to it, but was this simply a question of bad roads and robbers or was there some other factor which eludes us?

Standing back from Josselin's opinions, both his assumptions and his certainties as recorded in his Diary, the general picture we receive is of a figure far removed from the contented, adjusted personality, free from the strains and conflicts of modern life, which some historians would have us believe inhabited seventeenth-century England.[3] An examination of his economic and social life by itself, of his close ties to the soil and to his parishioners, might have

[1] For a further discussion of contemporary beliefs in witchcraft and the power of cursing in Essex at this time, see Macfarlane, *Witchcraft in England*.

[2] Among the many anthropological discussions of these opposed concepts of time, one of the most stimulating is Pierre Bourdieu, 'The attitude of the Algerian peasant toward time', in *Mediterranean Countrymen*, ed. J. Pitt-Rivers (Paris, 1963).

[3] People, we are told, 'belonged to a more satisfying world—despite its physical hazards and high mortalities—than that which we inhabit' (W. G. Hoskins, 'Provincial Life', in *Shakespeare Survey*, *17*, ed. A. Nicoll (Cambridge, 1964), p. 20).

justified such an impression; but to listen to his daily discussion of accident, pain and death is to find him as anxiety-ridden, as insecure, as many of his modern counterparts. His fierce introspective battles against temptation might well help to label him as a 'neurotic' by modern standards.

Josselin may, of course, have been exceptionally sensitive and anxious as a Puritan clergyman, though it is arguable whether the anxiety was more the cause or the effect of his Calvinistic beliefs.[1] Yet he never went mad or became 'distracted' as did at least six of his parishioners and neighbours.[2] His Diary indicates, however, that a worthwhile analysis of mental breakdown and mental strain could be undertaken for seventeenth-century England. The conflicts between roles, between the ideal of his religion and the exigencies of daily living, between his desire to serve God and his need for the help and comfort of his congregation and friends, all are well illustrated in the Diary.

One of the chief causes for his constant state of watchfulness and worry, was that the world of phenomena was seen as purposeful and comprehensible; a long enough search would discover the source of almost every event. The universe was a moral one, full of divine purpose and meaning, and it was the task of the conscientious Christian to unravel the meaning and tailor his living to the purpose. It was relevant to ask 'Why did it rain today?', 'Why did my hog die?', for nothing, however trivial, was haphazard. An integral part of this attitude was that all phenomena were personalized; human beings were not surrounded by 'dead' material, to be shifted about in a meaningless fashion. Divine power informed every corner of the earth, an immanence that in its pantheistic form later found most perfect expression in the works of William Wordsworth. Thus emerges the paradox that in an insecure world, beyond comprehension or control, everything from fire and water to the Quakers was potentially controllable through the godhead that could be petitioned within it.

In this entirely moral universe, tranquillity and an end of suffering could only be achieved if man became part of the divine harmony. Pain and pestilence were seen as signs of God's displeasure; personal and social morality were interconnected with physical events in a

[1] A helpful discussion of the relationship between anxiety and Puritanism, clearer than the same author's later book on the subject, is given in Michael Walzer, 'Puritanism as a Revolutionary Ideology', *Hist. Th.*, vol. iii, no. 1 (1963), pp. 77–9.

[2] Cases of mental disturbance of one sort or another are recorded under the following dates in the Diary: 26.8.44; 1.4.46; 28.12.46; 9.5.47; 9.4.56; 2.2.58; 30.1.64; 18.3.75.

way that, though not always clear, was never in question.[1] That this was so in an increasingly literate and far from 'face to face' society, where there were already many impersonal relationships in an area of enormous geographical mobility, is of considerable interest.[2] The best way, it was felt, to manipulate the physical environment was through manipulation of social relationships, which in their turn strengthened ties with God. Such strategy became both a sanction and guide to behaviour. As sure as night followed day, disaster would follow wrong-doing, though the culprit might not always be openly known.

One obvious effect of this strongly held conviction was that it acted as a distraction from the 'real' cause of disturbance. Instead of seeking a remedy for physical sickness on the physical plane, people moved into the spiritual world to find it. Such a system carried built in 'fail-safe' devices, for if there was no response in the form of improvement, it simply implied a wrong diagnosis; it was therefore very difficult to break out of. The general tendency of the Puritans, if Josselin is at all representative, was to uphold the old persuasion that linked the physical and spiritual spheres, thereby blocking experiments.

Another effect was the need, an absolute need, for conformity of both conduct and will. Hostile attitudes could disastrously react on to the whole community. This high level of conformity is reflected in the system of open confessions and penances, and the unchallenged concern each felt in the thoughts and private behaviour of others.[3] It was a simple logical step, from the assumption of an alliance between the physical and spiritual, to the certainty that godliness and success were similarly interdependent. The poor were sinful in some way not always discernible; the rich, in spite of moderate afflictions, were reaping the rewards of their good living. This bears

[1] Such an interconnection has been noted in many societies; for example, quarrels between people will disturb the crops, the Sherpas believe (Fürer-Haimendorf, *The Sherpas of Nepal* (1964), p. 108). The idea that the disruption of social, moral and physical planes may be interlinked in pre-industrial societies is stimulatingly argued in Max Gluckman, *Custom and Conflict in Africa* (Paperback edn, Oxford, 1963), pp. 94–5, and the same author's *Politics, Law and Ritual*, pp. 242–3.

[2] It has been suggested, for instance by Gluckman, *Custom and Conflict*, p. 95, that such an interblending of natural and supernatural is a product of a relatively static and highly 'personalized' society.

[3] The change from a situation where actions alone were controlled, to that where motives were also under supervision is described by Riesman, *Lonely Crowd*, p. 15. In both cases, however, kin and neighbours are vitally interested in conformity for the deviance of one individual will affect them all (a situation suggestively described by George Foster, 'Peasant Society and the Image of Limited Good', *Am. Anth.*, vol. 67, no. 2 (1965), p. 297).

out the old theory that Calvinists, with their obsession to prove to themselves and others that they were saved, became highly 'achievement-orientated' in a society where this may have been unusual. The problems such a theory posed for the failures must have been acute, for spiritual conviction could not long have survived complete material failure.[1]

As the social, spiritual and physical could not be split apart, on their union rested another of the basic principles of Josselin's thought, that of reciprocity. Every thought, act or outward occurrence had an echo. Josselin's sanguine expectation, both in his economic and social life, was that the more he lent to the Lord, via his neighbours, the more would one day be returned; and conversely he was careful to avoid unkindness, which would return to him unkindly. We can be in sympathy with such a supposition, but in Josselin's thought the principle of reciprocity worked across the artificial boundaries demarcating the social, physical and spiritual worlds, for to him no thought or action could be solely so classified. Kindness to a neighbour involved spiritual concern, and could express itself in physical support; as far as this we can follow him. Where we would hesitate to do so is in his belief that reciprocation might return along a different plane from that on which it departed.

Witchcraft trials of the day illustrate this belief very clearly. A small physical act, such as refusing to give a penny to a neighbour, could be reciprocated both on the physical and spiritual level in the form of supernaturally mediated sickness.[2] Words could move between the two worlds with ease; on one level humdrum, squandered sounds, on another malevolent or solicitous expressions of inner thought which, arranged into the right order, could be used as prayers or curses and gave to the user control of the power every-

[1] The whole problem of the interdependence of physical and spiritual riches is a highly complex one, too immense to be adequately discussed here. Tawney, *Religion and Capitalism*, pp. 122–3; Hill, *Puritanism and Revolution*, ch. 7 (especially p. 227); Hill, *Society and Puritanism*, ch. 7, provide the standard view on the correlation. That there was no uniformity of views in the seventeenth century is illustrated by Burton, *Anatomy of Melancholy*, vol. II, p. 145, and it seems that even Puritan writers such as John Dod provided a loophole by admitting that 'for poor Christians their Father kept the purse, but the rich Christians keep the purse in their own hands' (quoted in Haller, *Rise of Puritanism*, p. 60). Nor is the connexion between poverty and sin confined to Calvinist societies; for example, we are told that a group of (tenuously) Greek Orthodox shepherds believe that 'there must always be something morally wrong with a very poor man' (Campbell, *Honour and Patronage*, p. 273).
[2] This process is described at greater length in Macfarlane, *Witchcraft in England*.

where available.[1] Josselin's constant intercessions with God on behalf of his family and town shows him trying to release this power; casting his bread upon the waters as forcefully as he could was his daily concern, for there was no telling in what form it would return to him.

Further problems, far too complex for discussion in this context, await the historian who tries to relate Josselin's mental structure to his social and physical background, to see for example, whether his religious beliefs were 'appropriate' in his cultural surroundings. Yet it does not seem too optimistic to predict that if other sources are as adequate as the one Diary investigated in the preceding pages, it should one day be possible to discover the ways in which the mental, social and economic structures of the pre-industrial period were linked. In such an endeavour we will need not merely the pains-taking demographic and economic analysis of the new schools of social and local history, but also the awareness of comparative material, and the constant pressure to investigate new and basic problems which can only be acquired through a detailed study of anthropological and sociological literature.

The endeavour will be made lighter if other diarists lay themselves as disarmingly open to our scrutiny as the Reverend Ralph Josselin, 1617–83.

[1] Although some Puritans attacked the idea that words had an intrinsic 'power' (for example, William Perkins, *A Discourse of the Damned Art of Witchcraft* (Cambridge, 1608), p. 134), it is clear that many during this period believed that, as spells and prayers showed, words were efficacious. The popular belief was given intellectual standing by the widespread neo-platonist doctrine that words had 'power'.

Appendixes

A

The fertility of Ralph Josselin's wife

The Diary provides three types of evidence on which to base conclusions about fertility. Firstly there are the births recorded in the
text, often with the hour of birth stated. Secondly there is the fact
that Josselin often noted when his wife began 'breeding', information
he appears to have obtained from his wife, as his statements show.[1]
Thirdly there is a list of 'The times of the births of my children by
Jane my loving wife' amongst the miscellaneous notes at the
beginning of the manuscript Diary.[2] These are numbered from 1 to
10, the first 6 are uninterrupted and agree with the dates elsewhere
in the Diary, but then appears the following list:[3]

7. Anne Josselin born 20 June 1654.
0. June 1656 my wife miscarried about 2 months gone with child.
8. Mary Josselin born 14 January 1658.
0. May 1659 my wife miscarried about 2 months gone with child.
9. Elizabeth Josselin born 20 June 1660.
0.0.0. miscarried thrice by 24 December 1661.
10. Rebekah Josselin born 26 November 1663.

Evidence from these three sources may be combined to throw
light on questions which are of particular current interest, namely
the attitude to having children and the possibility that birth control
was practised in the mid-seventeenth century. Enthusiasm for
children might be expected to decline after a sufficient number had
been produced to ensure the survival of heirs. There are two ways,
neither of them conclusive but both suggestive, of discovering
whether this was so. Firstly there is the degree of interest shown by
Josselin in his wife's possible state of pregnancy. Secondly there are
the birth intervals, the presumption being that these would grow
longer as the desire for children diminished, though other factors
such as age have to be taken into account. Table XII below combines
the three types of information. It shows the relationship between the

[1] It may have been common for women to tell close relatives of their pregnancy,
for example *The Diary of the Lady Anne Clifford* (1923), p. 107, shows that Lady
Anne told her two sisters and her husband. Josselin himself 'heard from my
daughter Smith that she is about 5 months gone' (on 25.7.78).
[2] The list of births and miscarriages is on page 6 of the original MS. Diary. It is
omitted in the edited Diary and in the E.R.O. transcript.
[3] The entries have been slightly modified in form, though not in substance; the
entry of the triple miscarriages is written in different ink from the rest.

TABLE XII. *Fertility of Ralph Josselin's wife*

Date of conception	Interval between live births	Recognition of pregnancy
July 1641	17½ months after marriage	wife 'breeding' [July 1641]
March/April 1643	20½ months	wife 'breeding' [spring 1643]
Feb. 1645	23 months	wife 'confident shee was breeding & supposed it a daughter' [4. 4. 45]
May 1647	25½ months	[wrong] 'My wife concluded shee was with child, now gone 7 weekes with a boy. She useth not to be mistaken' [20. 3. 47]
August 1648	15 months	'my deare wife very ill ... I hope it was only about her quickening' [7. 11. 48]
Jan. 1651	29 months	'my wife she thinks shee breeds' [23. 8. 50] 'apprehendeth shee breedeth' [16. 11. 50] 'concluded she was with child with a sonne' [21. 11. 50] 'she is now certaine she breedeth not' [24. 11. 50]
Sept. 1653	33 months	'she breedeth with difficulty' [30. 10. 53]
April 1656	— —	'thought she miscarried' [18. 6. 56]
April 1657	43 months	'my wife guessed that shee was with child and about 3 weeks gone' [16. 5. 57] 'wife onely very ill, but concludes it is childing, and a girle' [2. 5. 57] 'my wife quickned shee concludeth a son' [23. 6. 67]
March 1659	— — — —	
Sept. 1659	29 months	'my wife was so quiet shee thought she might not bee with child, shee was not as yet so confident as formerly, nor with her as formerly' [4. 6. 59]
3 miscarriages, 1661	— —	
Feb. 1663	41 months	— — — —

NOTES
1. The date of conceptions is only approximate, being based, in the case of live births, on the subtraction of 9 months from the date of birth.
2. Conceptions terminated by miscarriages are italicized.

dates of conception, both of live and dead births, and the recognition of pregnancy

The most obvious fact indicated by this table is that Josselin failed to note the first signs of pregnancy in the last two live births, or in any of the conceptions leading to miscarriages. His wife was able to recognize her own pregnancy within two months of conception, though what methods she used we are not told; she also tried to predict the sex of the future child.[1] Josselin's interest in her information remained strong until the conception of the ninth live birth, when he already had five children alive, two boys and three girls. By then his zeal for offspring may have waned as the economic burden increased.[2]

Whether he or his wife then took any measures to limit their family is a matter of guesswork and of reading between the figures. It is clear from the following table that gaps between births widened, the last five coming after longer intervals than the first five. It is also worth noting at this point that miscarriages coincided almost exactly with the earliest point at which Josselin's wife could have known she was pregnant, and have used some form of abortion. We can compare in table XIII the figures for birth intervals with those established for another area in the same period, though statistics obtained from one woman cannot be used to draw firm conclusions. The average

TABLE XIII. *Birth intervals (in months): Josselin and Colyton compared*

Births	0–1	1–2	2–3	3–4	Last	1–4 combined	7–10
Josselin	17.5	20.5	23	25.5	41	21.6	36.5
Colyton							
1560–1646	11.3	25.2	27.4	30.1	37.5	27.5	—
1647–1719	10.3	29.1	32.6	32.1	50.7	29.1	–

SOURCE *for Colyton figures*: E. A. Wrigley, 'Family Limitation in Pre-Industrial England', *Econ. Hist. Rev.*, 2nd series, vol. XIX, no. 1 (1966), p. 93, table 8.

interval between the first four births in Josselin's family (21.6) is far lower than the mean for Colyton during the earlier period (27.5) and strongly suggests that there was no control of fertility at this stage.

A partial explanation for birth intervals is their relation to

[1] The date of conception appears to have been accurately and quickly discovered at this period. Lady Clifford (*Diary*, p. 60) spoke of her sister who was '13 weeks gone with child', and a doctor told a man that his wife was with child in January when, from the subsequent birth exactly 8 months later, she could only have been about four weeks gone (Blundell, *Diary*, pp. 19, 24). Contemporary manuals for midwives gave lists of methods by which to tell not only whether a woman was pregnant, but also the sex of the future child (e.g. R. C., *The Compleat Midwife*, pp. 78–82).

[2] This economic burden is shown diagrammatically in figure 5 on p. 47 above.

weaning habits, but here we are faced with the difficulty of deciding whether a woman weaned her child because she thought herself pregnant or became pregnant because she stopped breast-feeding. All that we can attempt to show here is that conception and weaning certainly seemed to overlap in the case of Ralph Josselin's wife, at least in time. This can best be demonstrated by another table.

TABLE XIV. *Weaning and conception dates in Josselin's family*

Date at which child was weaned	Date of conception of subsequent child	Gap between weaning and conception (months)	Age of child at weaning (months)
1. March/April 1643	March/April 1643	0	c. 12
2. 30 Jan.–9 Feb. 1645	c. Feb. 1645	0	13
3. May 1647	c. May 1647	0	c. 18
4. Died at 10 days, Feb. 1648	c. August 1648	6	(10 days)
5. Died at 13 months, June 1650	c. Jan. 1651	7	(13)
6. April 1653	c. Sept. 1653	5	19
7. Oct. 1655	c. April 1656	6	16
8. Jan. 1659	c. March 1659	11	—
0. stillbirth, May 1659	c. Sept. 1659	4	—
9. June 1661	c. Feb. 1663	3 miscarriages in 6 months after weaning	12*

NOTE

* is an approximate age at weaning, since no information is given about the date of weaning the eighth and tenth children.

It will be seen that the time of weaning coincided almost exactly with the date of conception in the first three cases. If we compare these three cases to the dates at which pregnancy was recognized, as indicated in table XIII, it seems evident that Mrs Josselin did not stop breast-feeding because she thought herself pregnant: in case 3 she weaned her child in May 1647 although she had concluded on 20 March 1647 that she was '7 weekes with a boy'.[1] Nor does she appear to have waited until she felt herself to be pregnant before she weaned a child: in case 2 she could not possibly have been pregnant on 30 January when she began to wean the child since the next birth was not until 25 November. It was, indeed, not until 4 April, two months after weaning had been completed, that she was

[1] Alice Thornton went on suckling one of her children until two weeks before the delivery of her next child, which suggests that there was no wide-scale prohibition on this practice (Thornton, *Autobiography*, p. 145).

'confident shee was breeding'. It is of interest to note in passing that in the one case where breast-feeding was cut short at ten days because of the death of the infant, the gap before the next birth was the shortest in the whole series. This is a phenomenon that has been noted for other parts of England.[1] There was still a gap of fifteen months, however.

Breast-feeding for between twelve and nineteen months helps to explain some of the intervals between births.[2] The longer gaps between the births of the last four children are largely accounted for by the miscarriages which, naturally, go unrecorded in the parish register. We may wonder, also, whether Josselin included all his wife's miscarriages in his private list. It seems likely that, if there were three such miscarriages before 24 December 1661, there would have been others in the following fifteen months which elapsed before the final child to be born alive was conceived.

Nor do we know whether miscarriages were consciously induced as a form of birth control. It is clear that abortifacients were known in England and were used.[3] Given their availability it might seem more than a coincidence that these miscarriages occurred suddenly at the end of Mrs Josselin's child-bearing period, when she had previously been free from them. Also, as pointed out earlier, at least two of them occurred at the earliest point at which she could have been certain that she was pregnant.[4]

[1] For example in W. G. Howson, 'Plague, Poverty and Population in Parts of North-West England, 1580–1720', *Trans. Hist. Soc. Lancs. & Ches.*, vol. CXII (1960), p. 46.

[2] Nag, *Factors Affecting Human Fertility*, p. 79, refers to an unpublished study which indicates that 'breast feeding tends to prolong the intervals between pregnancies'. The effect is not a completely infertile period and it only lessens the chance of conception by about 25%. A number of societies also have a taboo on intercourse during the breast-feeding period, and there is some evidence that this was so in seventeenth-century England, at least during the early months after the delivery (some of the evidence is summarized in Macfarlane, 'The Regulation of Marital and Sexual Relationships', ch. 7; Nag, *Factors Affecting Human Fertility*, pp. 78–9, 188–90, usefully draws together information on such prohibitions from a number of societies).

[3] A number of references to their use are contained in Macfarlane, 'The Regulation of Marital and Sexual Relationships', p. 154.

[4] It is well known, of course, that miscarriages increase at the end of the child-bearing period (e.g. F. Lorimer *et al.*, *Culture and Human Fertility* (UNESCO, 1954), p. 306). It is also known, as a seventeenth-century writer put it, that 'Women are most subject to suffer Abortion, or Miscarriage, in the first two months of their Conception' (Nicholas Culpepper, *A Directory for Midwives* (1658), p. 111), a tendency possibly accentuated, as another writer argued, by the 'common opinion, that a woman several moneths gone ought to walk very much' (R. C., *The Compleat Midwife*, pp. 8–9). But it is also true that it is very

The first miscarriage caused Mrs Josselin considerable pain and sickness. On 15 June 1656 Josselin noted 'my wife very ill' and on the 18th, 'This morning my wife thought she miscarried, lord a miscarrying womb is a sad affliction, keepe us from a miscarrying heart'. Eleven days later, although still only 'indifferent well', Jane was able to attend church; she became worse again, however, and was described as 'very ill' on 3 August. The last of the sequence of three miscarriages in the second half of 1661 was also noted in the Diary, but Josselin now seemed almost relieved that his wife had miscarried. On 22 December he wrote: 'my wife if breeding feareth miscarrying, the lord looke after her' and the following day, 'At night my wife miscarried, of a false conception, a mercy to be free of it, and I trust god will preserve my dear ones life; the conception was reall, god raiseth her up again'. It is tempting to speculate on what he meant by a 'false conception', and it would be easy to deduce that he meant an unwanted or unexpected one, since he explicitly stated that it was a 'reall' conception, and not 'false' in that sense. Perhaps evidence from other sources will solve this problem.[1]

easy for women to induce miscarriages, for instance by wearing a very tight belt. There is a discussion of the ease of such methods in Kingsley Davis and J. Blake, 'Social Structure and Fertility: An Analytic Framework', *Economic Development and Cultural Change*, vol. 4, no. 3 (1956), p. 230 (note 43).

[1] Figures for miscarriages and stillbirths in pre-industrial societies are extremely unreliable, but they probably fall within the range indicated in the table of 'foetal wastage' in Nag, *Factors Affecting Human Fertility*, pp. 222–3, that is between 2.9% and 23.1% of all conceptions. Hair guesses that there was a rate of over 10% loss in all conceptions during the seventeenth century (P. E. H. Hair, 'Bridal Pregnancy in Earlier Centuries', *Pop. Stud.*, vol. xx, no. 2 (1966), p. 235). All these estimates are a good deal lower than the (minimum) 33% loss of Josselin's wife. Other diaries of this period also frequently record miscarriages, for example: *The Diary and Will of Elias Ashmole*, ed. R. T. Gunther (Oxford, 1927), p. 118; *Mrs Elizabeth Freke, Her Diary, 1671 to 1714*, ed. M. Carberry (Cork, 1913), p. 23; *The Autobiography of Anne Lady Halkett*, ed. J. G. Nicholas, Cam. Soc., new series, vol. xiii (1875), p. 18; Lucy Hutchinson, *Memoirs of the Life of Colonel Hutchinson*, (2 vols. 4th edn, 1822), vol. i, p. 98; Pledger, 'Diary', p. 65; *Diary of Walter Powell*, transcribed J. A. Bradney, p. 19. William Sampson in *The Rector's Book, Clayworth Nottinghamshire, 1675–1700*, eds. H. Gill and E. L. Guilford (Nottingham, 1910), p. 125, noted a miscarriage in which the foetus was 'about the bigness of a Garden Bean'.

B

Children and servants:
the problem of adolescence

Analysis of his Diary has shown that Josselin's children left home at between the age of 10 and 15 years. Some went to be educated away from home; others to be servants and apprentices. Their absent labour was replaced by the hiring of other, unrelated, servants.[1] The purpose of this appendix is to see how representative a pattern this was; to discuss whether it was usual for the nuclear family to start shedding its members as they reached puberty. Any widespread tendency in this direction would have important consequences for seventeenth-century society. At the level of family life it would be a mechanism for separating the generations at a time when there might otherwise have been considerable difficulty. Both men and woman had to wait roughly ten years, on average, between puberty and marriage in seventeenth-century Europe; we might well have expected that such a delay would lead to sexual competition within families.[2] Incestuous temptations, however, would be minimized by the virtual absence of more than two co-residing adults of the same family. Another source of tension, the changes in patterns of authority as the children approached adulthood, would also be diminished. Children would be disciplined by strangers, outsiders who found it easier to perform this task in the absence of intimate and already fixed emotional ties. Such outsiders could also extend and broaden the education of their charges, teaching them skills and providing them with contacts which were beyond the reach of the children's own parents. Finally, the risks inherent in family life with the prevailing high mortality rates would be decreased. Children would be dispersed and would not be entirely dependent on parents who were always likely to die before the children grew up.

Apart from these and other consequences, there are more prosaic reasons for wanting to discover when children left home. Current analyses of parish registers and censuses depend heavily on assumptions about how long people stayed at home. For example, Dr Wrigley argues that 'As long as the child at that date is under 10,

[1] See pp. 146–8 above.
[2] The classic discussion of the 'unique' European late marriage pattern is Hajnal, 'European Marriage Patterns'.

or even under 15, there is a strong probability that he is still living with his parents.[1] This, obviously, would be an unsafe deduction in Ralph Josselin's case. In order to discover how correct such an assumption is in general a brief survey has been made of three types of evidence. Other diaries and the comments of travellers and educationalists indicate what happened in certain instances and what was believed to be the practice. Evidence from the biographical details given as church court depositions and from listings of inhabitants supplements this impression.

The most revealing description of the English custom of sending their children away from home is that written by an Italian visitor to England in about the year 1500. Although it is already well known it warrants full quotation.

The want of affection in the English is strongly manifested towards their children; for after having kept them at home till they arrive at the age of 7 to 9 years at the utmost, they put them out, both males and females, to hard service in the houses of other people, binding them generally for another 7 or 9 years. And these are called apprentices, and during that time they perform all the most menial offices; and few are born who are exempted from this fate, for every one, however rich he may be, sends away his children into the houses of others, whilst he, in return, receives those of strangers into his own. And on inquiryng their reason for this severity, they answered that they did it in order that their children might learn better manners. But I, for my part, believe that they do it because they like to enjoy all their comforts themselves, and that they are better served by strangers than they would be by their own children . . . That if the English sent their children away from home to learn virtue and good manners, and took them back again when theyr apprenticeship was over, they might, perhaps, be excused; but they never return, for the girls are settled by their patrons, and the boys make the best marriages they can.[2]

Naturally this pattern changed during the sixteenth century. New forms of education, private schools and universities, gained popularity. But, as in the case of the putting out of children to be servants among the poorer classes, the effect was the same; children left home before or at puberty, seldom to return. For the yeomanry upwards, a formal education became an established form of age ritual. After two or three years at a 'petty' school near their home, boys, and a few girls, would go to grammar school. The educational writer Brinsley indicates how early parents sought to rid their home of their children. 'For the time of their entrance with us', he writes 'in our countrey schooles, it is commonly about 7 or 8 yeares old:

[1] 'Mortality in pre-Industrial England', p. 549.
[2] C. A. Sneyd (trans.), *A Relation or rather a True Account of the Island of England . . . about the year 1500*, by an Italian, Cam. Soc., vol. xxxvii (1847), pp. 24–5.

six is very soone'. But some began at the age of 6 years, 'if any beginne so early, they are rather sent to the schoole to keepe them from troubling the house at home, and from danger, and shrewd turnes, than for any great hope and desire that their friends have that they should learne any thing in effect'.[1] Then, at about 15 years old, the wealthier boys would go to university.[2] How far such a pattern was actually practised, and what the great proportion of boys and girls who never went to grammar school did, we may now investigate.[3]

Evidence from diaries confirms that it was usual for boys from wealthier households to have left home for boarding school by the age of 10 and that girls would have been boarded away from home at about the same age. Elias Pledger went to school in London at the age of 6 or 7 and sent his son off to school at the age of 8; the future Sir John Bramston went away to school at the age of 8; Simon Forman was the same age when he was boarded out at school, as was the son of Mrs Elizabeth Freke.[4] The girls seem to have been a year or two older when they left home. Lucy Hutchinson's mother-in-law was taken off to court at the age of 9 and one of the daughters of John Dee was 'put to Mistress Brayce' at the same age. A female cousin of Oliver Cromwell was sent off to school in London at the age of about 12 and Lady Margaret Hoby was brought up in the household of the countess of Huntingdon and, in turn, a cousin 'brought his daughter Jane, beinge at the age of 13 yeares auld, to me, who, as he saied, he freely gave me'.[5] Other instances could be cited to show that children were sometimes sent away earlier or later than the above examples. The earl of Cork sent his son away

[1] John Brinsley, *Ludus Literarius: or, the Grammar Schoole* (1627), p. 9.
[2] This ideal picture of educational progress is described, for example, by M. H. Curtis, 'Education and Apprenticeship', in *Shakespeare Survey*, 17, ed. A. Nicoll (Cambridge, 1964), pp. 59–62.
[3] Despite Professor Jordan's estimate that there was at least one school for each 4,400 of the English population in the early seventeenth century, so that, M. H. Curtis estimates, half the boys in England had some formal education (*Shakespeare Survey*, 17, pp. 58, 62), it is probably more likely that, as in a Kentish parish (C. W. Chalkin, 'A Kentish Wealden Parish (Tonbridge)' (unpublished Oxford B. Litt. thesis, 1960; Bodleian Library), p. 99), only roughly one-fifth of the boys in country villages and an even smaller proportion of the girls, would receive a formal, institutional, education.
[4] Pledger, 'Diary', fols. 2ᵛ, 83; *The Autobiography of Sir John Bramston*, ed. T. W. Bramston, Cam. Soc., vol. XXXII (1845), p. 99; *Autobiography and Personal Diary of Dr Simon Forman*, ed. J. O. Halliwell (1849), p. 4; Freke, *Diary*, pp. 24, 31.
[5] Hutchinson, *Memoirs*, vol. I, p. 67; Dee, *Diary*, pp. 11, 34; Anon, *Religious Diary*, fol. 214; *Diary of Lady Margaret Hoby*, 1599–1605, ed. Dorothy M. Meads (1930), pp. 5, 202.

from Ireland to England 'to be bred there' when the child was only 6¾ years old. The Rev. Thomas Compton, on the other hand, was brought up by his aunt until he was nearly 13 and Marmaduke Rawdon seems to have remained at home until he was aged 16.[1]

While it seems fairly certain that children from families of a status equal to, or higher than, Josselin's would be expected to leave home at between 7 and 13 years of age, diaries give little evidence as to how far down the social order such a pattern spread. Occasionally, as in the case of the Westmorland yeoman James Jackson, we discover that it was customary among the yeomanry for children to be boarded out when they went to school.[2] For the most part, however, it is necessary to turn to local records for further information about the bulk of the village population. Local studies are beginning to show a movement away from some villages of children in their early teens. On the basis of parish register material for the period 1642–1851, Dr West has concluded for the Lincolnshire village of Wrangle that 'perhaps the greatest drain on the parish was the departure of boys and girls at about the age of 13'.[3] Similarly, early movement is indicated in the depositions at archdeaconry courts in the sixteenth and seventeenth centuries. On the basis of 200 depositions in Sussex between 1580–1640, Julian Cornwall concludes that 'a good deal of movement occurred fairly early in life ... Well over half appear to have done so [i.e. moved] between the ages of eleven or twelve ... and thirty'.[4] An analysis of similar material to that used by Cornwall, the archdeaconry depositions for the archdeaconry of Essex between 1586 and 1600, indicates that people were imprecise about their earliest movements.[5] In an attempt to overcome the failing memories of older deponents, 16 depositions by men and 2 by women, all aged 30 years or younger, were selected. Five of these claimed to have remained in their town or village of birth all their lives; of the others, all except 2 had left their village by the age of 20, 8 out of the total 18 had definitely left their natal village by the end of their 16th year.

[1] Cork, *L. P.*, vol. II, p. 101; 'Rev. Thomas Compton, Rector of Great Holland, 1725–1761', by John Taylor, *Ess. Rev.*, vol. 9 (1900), p. 34; *The Life of Marmaduke Rawdon of York*, ed. R. Davies, Cam. Soc., vol. LXXXV (1868), p. 5.

[2] 'James Jackson's Diary, 1650–1683', selections by F. Grainger, *Trans. Cumb. & West. Ant. & Arch. Soc.*, new series, vol. 21 (1921).

[3] 'The Social and Economic History of the East Fen Village of Wrangle, 1603–1837' (unpublished Ph.D. thesis, 1966; Leicester University Library), p. 56.

[4] 'Evidence of Population Mobility in the Seventeenth Century', *Bull. Inst. Hist. Res.*, vol. XL, (November, 1967), p. 149.

[5] The sources, deposited at the E.R.O., are D/AED/3 (96 examinations) and D/AED/4 fols 1–42 (to the end of 1600), 35 examinations.

A more satisfactory method of estimating when people left home is to use the occasional early listing of inhabitants. Two preliminary analyses have been made of such material, the first of the 1599 Ealing listing, the second, as a contrast, of the 1695 listing of Kirkby Lonsdale in Westmorland.[1] The Ealing census may be analysed in a number of ways to show that boys normally left home at between 8 and 15, girls between 9 and 14, and that they were then replaced by servants, male and female. There were in the village 29 'sons' aged between 5 and 14, and only 8 such 'sons' between 15 and 24. If we omit the 8 wealthiest families, and 2 households where widows had their sons living with them, there were only 4 out of 76 households with 'sons' aged between 15 and 24 in them. Similarly with girls. Some 24 'daughters' aged 10–14 were residing with their parents, but the number of the following 5-year group aged 15–19 had shrunk to 6. In the years between puberty and marriage approximately ⅔ of the males and ¾ of the female children seem to have been living away from their parents.

Yet analysis of the age and sex structure of this listing does not indicate a gap in the years between 15 and 24. This is because the missing children were replaced by other people's children acting as servants. There were only 11 servants aged between 10 and 15, while there were 35 such servants, male and female, aged between 16 and 21.[2] But the replacement was not symmetrical: those who lost children after investing a considerable amount of time and money in them, did not necessarily get servants in return. All the top 15 families of yeoman status and above had servants, usually between 2 and 5 for each household. But of the other 71 families, only 12 had 1 or more servants. The institution of servanthood might, therefore, be regarded as a disguised means whereby wealth and labour flowed from the poorer to the richer: husbandmen and their families were left precariously devoid of any adult support, while the households of the wealthier villagers were stabilized against the effects of illness

[1] There is a description and transcript of the Ealing listing by K. J. Allison, 'An Elizabethan Village "Census"', *Bull. Inst. Hist. Res.*, vol. xxxvi (1963). Analysis of the Kirkby Lonsdale listing (the original is in the Cumberland and Westmorland Record Office, Kendal depository, *Fleming* Papers, WD/Ry) was undertaken by Mrs Iris Macfarlane. The figures, based on a comparison of the listing with the parish register, are only at a preliminary stage and will be revised and expanded in a future publication.

[2] There is a preliminary analysis, by sex and age categories, of the Ealing listing in Wrigley (ed.), *English Historical Demography*, p. 194. Particularly difficult to place are the occasional young male husbandmen living in various households. They were not stated to be servants, but they were probably performing this role and have been included as servants in the above calculations.

and death by the presence of young men and women whom they had not raised, and who replaced their absent children.

The Kirkby Lonsdale listing shows the same pattern. There were 55 male children aged between 5 and 14 years living at home, and only 9 such children in the next 10-year age group, from 15 to 24. Similarly with girls, where the figure dropped from 66 to 7 between the two 10-year periods. The shedding of children is most striking in the middle group termed 'farmers' in the listing, consisting of 31 households. Up to the age of 12 there were 32 children living at home; thereafter, up to and including the age of 24, there were none. The two extremes—gentry/yeomen and 'poor'—seem to have more often kept adolescent children at home, but even with them this was the exception rather than the rule. As in Ealing, the gap caused by the departure of children was partially filled by servants; the majority of Kirkby Lonsdale servants were aged between 13 and 20 years old. They worked for the wealthier families, as in Ealing.

How far children went in search of employment; the motives of parents in sending them away; the degree to which they expected to benefit from their children's earnings; the psychological effects of boarding children out at the age of 8 onwards; the degree to which the whole process was a form of age ritual, a way of demarcating off age-boundaries by movement through space; all these and other problems will, it is hoped, be explored by future social historians. The preceding brief discussion has merely shown that Josselin's children were not exceptional in their mobility. If further illustration is still needed it is neatly provided by an autobiographical poem by Sir John Gibson in 1655 which shows the way in which each stage of life was separated off by physical space:

> Crake it had my infancye,
> Yorke did my youth bringe up,
> Cambridge had my jollitie,
> When I her brestes did sucke.
> London brought me into thraule
> And wed me to a wife.
> Welburne [co. York] my carefull time had all
> Joyn'd with a troubled life.[1]

[1] 'Autobiography of Sir John Gibson, 1655' in *North Country Diaries* (2nd series; Sur. Soc., vol. CXXIV, 1914), p. 52. Illustrations of the exchange of children and a discussion of the possible reasons for such activity are contained in Morgan, *Puritan Family*, pp. 75–8. There is also some discussion of this subject in Goode, *The Family*, p. 54.

C

Extracts from records relating to the Josselin family

Note on transcription: some punctuation has been added to make the sense clearer. 'J.' has occasionally been used after a Christian name as an abbreviation for 'Josselin'.

WILLS

Will of Ralph Josselin
E.R.O. D/ACR/10/144. Made 1 June 1683; proved 5 November 1683.

In the name of God Amen. I Ralph Josselin of Earls Colne clerke, being sick, commend my soule into the hands of God that gave it, trusting assuredly through the meritts of my blessed Saviour Jesus Christ to enjoye an Inheritance in Glory among his sanctifyed ones.

Item I give and bequeath unto my only wife Jane, the wife of my youth, my freehold land called Springs Marsh as also a certaine parcell of Coppiehold Land called stulps [sic] being inclosed w[i]th the s[ai]d Marsh during the terme of her Naturall life, and Imediately after he[r] dec[ease]d I give both the s[ai]d closes free & Coppy to Elizabeth one of the daughters of the s[ai]d Ralph and now wife of Mr Gilbert Smith of the parrish of St Martins in the Feilds colour man, her heires and Assignes for ever; as also I give and bequeath to my beloved wife the freehold Meadow called Stonebridge meadow togeather with the bridge to be laid for the convenient ingress and egress of the same during the terme of her Naturall life.

Item I give and bequeath to my said wife Jane for her better maintenaunce all that Silver and gold I have formerly given her and to her heires and Assignes for ever togeather with all wearing apparrell, the furniture of the Chamber wherein I now Lodge as also the furniture in the Grey Chamber togeather with w[ha]tsoever brass, plate, pewter, Iron, Steel, linnen and w[ha]tsoever else of my Goods shall be needfull for her prop[er] use, togeather w[i]th her dwelling in three or foure Roomes of the Mancon house wherein I now dwell together w[i]th free ingresse, egress, and regress out of the same into the yards according to all her occasions, w[i]th all the wood logge, broom, coale, or w[ha]tsoev[er] in the Yard is Layd is for fyering during her Naturall life togeather with all the Pullin in the Yards.

Item, I give unto my daughter Mrs Mary Josselin, the wife of Mr

Edward Day of Great St Martins in the Feilds, all that my messuage or freehold Tenem[en]t on Colne Green wherein I now dwell togoather w[i]th all the barnes, Stables, Outhouses, hovels, Yards, somer house and orchard therunto belonging, wh[ic]h containe halfe an acre more or less from a little below the barne cross to the New hedge that parts the Orchar[d], togeather w[i]th those Coppyhold lands called now by the name of App[er] Coes or by w[ha]tsoever names the s[ai]d lands are or were knowne by, w[hi]ch said Coppyhold lands begineth at a little bridge next the freehold Tenem[en]t of one Mole and now in the tenure or Occupacon of Henry Wiseman or his Assignes and so abutte on the Green till it meete w[i]th the s[ai]d freehold Tenem[en]t & then it takes in a parcell of Wast lying before the s[ai]d tenem[en]t and p[ar]t of the Garden thereto belonging and from the Gate at the End of the Land it lyeth North on the road leading of[f] Colne Green towards Colne engaine, untill you come to a chase way that goeth out the s[ai]d road to certain free land belonging to a farme called Prachnetts & from & about the middle of that lane the s[ai] Coppyhold lands is p[ar]ted by a fence or hedge from lands called Lower Coes lying on the North, which said fence goeth to lands called Bayleys being Coppyhold belonging to one Robt. Harris on the East & on the North of the s[ai]d Bayles & so the s[ai]d Coppyhold Lands abutts on the freehold lands that belongeth to one Mr Sibley on the East it comes up by the East to lands lying on the free lands of the s[ai]d Mole & comes up there to the little bridge above said, all w[hi]ch s[ai]d Coppyhold lands containe by Estimacon twenty acres more or less and are to pay yearly and every year twenty shillings quittrent to the Lord of the Manor of Colne Pryory all w[hi]ch said Messuage I do give and bequeath to my daughter Mrs Mary Day & her heires for ever; and in case the s[ai]d Mrs Mary dec[ease]d w[i]thout the s[ai]d heires, then I give and bequeath all the said dminished p[re]misses unto the s[ai]d Mr Edw[a]rd Day during the terme of his Naturall life and in case they shall have heires of the bodyes and here disposed to sell the premises, they shall offer it to some of the heires of the said Ralph for such a summe of lawfull money of England as shall not exceed foure hundred pounds. Also I give unto my said daughter Mrs Mary Day, one hundred pound of Lawfull English money to be paid unto her or the said Mr Edward Day within foure monthes after my deceased by my executrix within mencioned.

Item, I do give and bequeath forty pounds unto my daughter Mrs Jane Woodthorpe, to be paid to her out of a bond she oweth to me and my Executor & in the meane time during Naturall lives of me and my wife Separately she is to pay unto us forty shillings yearly and every year.

Item, I give & bequeath during her Naturall life to my beloved wife Mrs Jane Josselin My two lower broome fielde called the Lower Coes or by whatsoever names they are called by which said field abutts on the land that goeth downe Pracknetts Close on the West & on the North on a field belonging to the said Pracknetts and to the lands also on the North which I bought of Mr Fletcher and his wife in Colne.

Item, I give to my daughter Mrs Elizabeth Smith and my daughter Mrs Rebecca Spicer each ten Shillings to buy them rings as my last legacie to them.

Item, I give to my beloved wife Jane Josselin, my debts and funerall expences being first paid, all my debts, chattles, bills, bonds, whatsoever, togeather with my bullocks, cheep, cowes, hoggs, two young Mares, corne threst and unthrast [unthreshed], hay, straw, chaffe, whom I make sole and alone Executrix of this my last will and testament. all other of my Lands unbequeathed I give and bequeath unto my onely son John Josselin to enter on them September the 29th next after my decease, togeather with Inhams, Herne lays, & love land that I bought of Mr and Mrs Fletcher, but on this express condicon, that he suffer his mother to lay what corne and hay she please in the boarded barne & one end of the other barne at Fishers. And that he suffer her or her Executors quietly and peaceably to dispose of [for] the[ir] owne use all the cattle, hay, grass, corne, growing on all my lands whatsoever untill Semptember 29th next after my decease; which Condicon being truly performed on his part, I appointe his mother to give him my fallow in Hobstevene and all the harness, my waggone, plows, tumbrells & all things pertaining to them. My body I appointe to be buried according to the law, with as much privicy as may be. My Library I give as it now Stands (with the good liking of my Executrix herein named) I give to one or two of my Grandchildren who shall first divote to the Ministry. My houshold goods I leave at my Executrices pleasure to be divided into five parts, to be chosen by them according to their age.

In witness, I set my hand 1st June 1683   Ralph Josselin.
in presence of Jas. Ludgater, Richard Potter, Humphrey Rugels.

Will of John Josselin, gent. [son]

E.R.O. D/ACR/10/334. Proved 20 March 1691.

John Josselin of Earl's Colne, weak in body but sound in mind, his body to be buried 'as neer my brother Thomas as can be'.—Property [freehold and copyhold held of the manor of Colne Priory] to go to 'Martha my loveing wife' and then to be equally divided between children when they reach the age of 20.
Executor—Martha and 'loving brother-in-law' John Ben[t]all.
Witnesses. John Cressener, George Toller, Lawrence Bentall.

Will of Jonathan Woodthorp [son-in-law]

E.R.O. D/ABR/11/308. Made 19 October 1683; proved 14 June 1684.

I, Jonathen Woodthorp of Lexden, tanner,
—to my daughter Jane W. copyhold land worth £100 at 21 or marriage.
—to my daughter Mary W.   „   „   „ £200   „   „   „
— „   „   „   Elizabeth „   „   „ £200   „   „   „

—to 'my dear wife Jane W.' my plate and household stuff.

—to brother Edward W. twenty shillings p.a. for five years.

—to servant John Baldwin twenty shillings.

—to Laurence Bentall my apprentice, twenty shillings when his apprenticeship ends.

Wife to be executrice and three daughters to be residuary legatees. Overseers to be my cousin Edward Woodthorp of Hadleigh, gent. and William Ellis the younger.

Witnesses. John Eldred, William Wilshire, John Foulsham.

Will of Thomas Constable [father-in-law]

B.R.O., Act Book, 1648, fol. 68. Made 2 June 1643; proved 2 May 1648.

Thomas Constable of Olney, tailor, being weak in body, made the following will.

—to daughter Jane Josselin twenty shillings.

—to grand-daughter Mary Josselin one ewe and one lamb.

—to son Jeremy half of the house where I now dwell and half the land purchased of Philip Osborne at the age of 24, but if my wife Anne Constable re-marry, these to go to him at her marriage. The other half of the above to go to him at Anne's death. If he has no heirs, to go to my daughter Elizabeth Constable, and if she have no heirs to my daughter Jane Constable. Household furniture and tools also to Jeremy.

—to daughter Elizabeth Constable, a tenement and close, when she is 22 or marries, unless Anne can pay her £50 instead; also beds, curtains, sheets etc.

—all the rest of goods and chattels to my beloved wife, who is also the executrice.

Overseers to be my brother-in-law Lawrence Shepherd and William Geynes.

signature of testator.

Will of Joseph Josselin [uncle]

E.R.O. D/AER/20/161. Made 7 November 1642; proved 6 December 1645.

I, Joseph Josslyn of Cranham, yeoman, bequeath my soul to God, believing myself to be 'one of the number of the Elect' ... Ralph J. of Roxwell, my father, yeoman, in his will devised to Simon Josselyn his son, my elder brother, 4 parcels of land in Roxwell on the condition that Simon paid to me £103 within two years of the death of Simon J. of Cranham, my uncle. I devise this £103 as follows:

—to Richard J. my brother £40.

—to Nathaniel J. my brother £10.

—to Daniel Hudson, my brother-in-law, £20.

1111111111111111111111111111111111

—to Anne Hudson, my sister, £5, (and also another £15 of the £103 given me by my uncle Thomas J. deceased).
—to Mary Gill, my cousin, now wife of Thomas Gill of Cranham, £20.
—to the four children of Daniel Hudson, namely Daniel, Simon, William and Elizabeth, £5 each.
—to John Hudson, my cousin, the son of the aforsaid Daniel, £10.
—to Thomas J., my brother, £10.
—to the three daughters of John J., my eldest brother, £5 (viz. Dorothy (40/-), Anne (40/-), Mary (20/-).)
—to John Owting of Cranham, £4.
—to Ralph and Simon J., my brothers, a pair of gloves each.
Executors to be my brother Richard J. and brother-in-law Daniel Hudson.

mark of testator.

Will of Ralph Josselin [uncle]
Somerset House, 1657, Ruthen 511. Made 27 November 1656.

I, Ralph Josselin, yeoman, of Cranham Hall, Essex.

Whereas there is owing to me by Mr Forn, minister of Great Warley, upon bond £100, I give this to my daughter Dorothy and her heirs provided that she gives to my daughter Grace the sum of £20 and provided also that Grace and Dorothy pay to my 'nephew' Ralph Josselin minister of Earls Colne the sum of £6 'as a testimony of my love to him'. All other property not bequeathed I give to my daughter Elizabeth, provided that my said daughter shall not dispose of herself in marriage without the consent of Dorothy and Grace her sisters and of my 'Cozen' Ralph Josselin. The executors are to allow her the yearly profits from the estates until she marries. If she marries without the above consent she is to be given the profits of the estates as above after marriage, and the actual estate is to be divided up at the executors' discretion between her children. If she dies before marriage, the goods are to be divided between daughters Grace and Dorothy and some £20 is to go to my 'cousin' Ralph Josselin.

Memorandum, an added codicil. 21 March 1656/7.
£20 is to be given to my daughter Grace Johnson (now the wife of Robert Johnson) which is now in the hands of Captain Stracy.

Will of Ralph Josselin [grandfather]
Somerset House, 1632, Audley 57. Made 4 August 1626; signed 3 September 1628; proved, 4 May 1632.

I, Ralph Josselin of Roxwell, yeoman.

—to Dorothy, my wife, a yearly rent of £20 and lodging.
—to Simon J., my brother, a life annuity of £25 and lodging.

—to John J., my son, already given his portion of £800, he is to have a further £10, which is to go to his son Ralph if he dies before receiving it.

—to son Thomas, £5; to daughter Mary, £5; to daughter Anna, £10.

—to son Richard, £200 (if executors default on this he is to have part of Highfield in Roxwell, some 20 acres).

—to son Joseph, £160 (if executors default he is to have land called Woodfeildes, Spicers Croft, Bollinghatch, Grave, Mottshott).

—to son Nathaniel, £100.

[All three above legacies were in recompense for a £15 legacy left to each son by their Uncle Thomas.]

—to daughter Elizabeth, sufficient food and apparell for life.

—to poor of Roxwell, 20/-.

Executors and residuary legatees are sons Ralph and Simon, who are to have a farm called Bollinghatch in Roxwell and Writtle.

If Simon dies without heirs, the above to go to Nathaniel.

If Ralph dies without heirs, the above to go to John.

Overseer to be Nathaniel.

Will of Mary Church [friend]

E.R.O. D/ACW/15/280. Made 17 May 1650; proved 9 July 1650. The will was originally written in the hand of Ralph Josselin.

I, Mary Church, of Earls Colne, gentlewoman.

—to Rose Church, my mother, a copyhold tenement called 'Clarks' and 5 parcels of land thereunto belonging; and another piece of copyhold called 'Gates croft' in Earls Colne, now in the occupation of Henry Thompson. After her death these are to go to Ralph Josselin and his heirs for ever upon these conditions:—that he will pay unto the said Rose £30 before the next court day after the testator's death, and pay £20 six months after the court, and £5 to the poor on the day of the testator's burial, and to pay unto his daughter Jane Josselin £100 when she reaches the age of 21.

—to Ralph Josselin: the title of my copyhold 'Readings' and another croft called 'Stonebridge Croft' which is copyhold on condition that he pay unto John, the son of John Church, my kinsman of Earls Colne, £100 within four years after the death of Rose Church. If John Church (the son) dies, the money is to go to Bartholomew Church his brother (son of John); Josselin is also to pay £10 to John Church aforesaid to Earls Colne, gent., also to pay £10 to Rose Briant, widow, my kinswoman, also to pay £50 to Elizabeth, daughter of John Church, my kinsman aforesaid.

Witnesses. Sam Burton and Christopher Mathews (mark of).

signature of Mary Church.

PARISH REGISTER ENTRIES

Bishops Stortford

H.R.O.

Baptisms:

1622	31 March	Elizabeth Josslyn, da. of John/Anne.
1624	28 Nov.	Rebecka J.,	da. of John/Anne.
1631	20 Jan.	Rebecka J.,	da. of John/Hellen.

Burials:

1624	22 Nov.	Elizabeth J.,	da. of John/Anne.
1624	29 Nov.	Anne J., wife of John J. Ma[u]ltster.
1624	16 Dec.	Rebecka J., chrisom child of John and Anne.

Cranham

At Cranham, Essex.

Baptisms:

| 1636 | 1 May | Elizabeth, da. of Ralph/Grace J. |
| 1638 | 18 May | Anne, da. of Ralph/Grace J. |

Burials:

| 1640 | 29 May | Mary, da. of Ralph J. |
| 1646 | 6 June | Grace, the wife of Ralph J. |

Earls Colne (only items omitted in the Diary)

E.R.O. D/P 209/1/1–3.

Baptisms:

1648	18 Feb.	Ralph, second son of Ralph J.
1673	21 Oct.	Jane, da. of Jonathan/Jane Woodthorpe.
1683	3 May	Ralph, son of Mr John/Martha J.
1686	20 April	Jane, da. of John/Martha J.

Burial:

| 1683 | 30 Aug. | Mr Ralph J. the Minister of this parish near 44y [sic] was buryed by me Perkins. |

Marriage:

| 1661 | 25 July | Robert Finch widdower and Mary J. single. |

Kelvedon

E.R.O. T/R 12.

Burial:

| 1672 | 2 Jan. | John Joscelyne of Feering (gent). |

Lexden

E.R.O. D/P 233/1/3.
Baptisms:

1676	30 Apr.	Mary, da. of Jonathan/Jane Woodthorpe.
1678	7 July	Frances, da. of Jonathan/Jane Woodthorpe.
1680	28 Oct.	Elizabeth, da. of Jonathan/Jane ,,

Burials:

1680	16 May	Frances, da. of Jonathan/Jane Woodthorpe.
1683	11 Dec.	Jonathan Woodthorpe.

Olney

B.R.O. D/A/T/144.
Baptisms:

1620	9 May	Jeremy, son of Thomas Constable.
1621	26 Nov.	Jane, da. of Thomas Constable.
1623	1 Jan.	Mary, da. of Thomas Constable.

Roxwell

E.R.O. T/R 81.
Baptisms:

1590	8 July	Ralph Joslin.
1600	16 July	Joseph, son of Ralph J.
1602	29 Aug.	Nathaniel J.
1604	23 Sept.	Elizabeth J.
1611	30 June	Mary, da. of John J.
1617	18 Feb.	Ralph, son of John J.
1643	3 Oct.	Theba, da. of Richard J.
1654	9 Jan.	Mary, da. of Richard J.
1656	18 Aug.	Anne, da. of Richard J.
1658	2 Feb.	Richard, son of Richard J.
1663	7 July	Thomas, son of Richard J.

Burials:

1634	16 Oct.	Widow Joscelyn.
1656	6 Oct.	Anne, da. of Richard.
1668	— —	Richard J.

Marriages:

1583	21 May	Ralfe Joslin and Marie Bright.
1667	28 Nov.	John Battle and Theabald [sic] J.
1687	13 Oct.	William Turnage and Mary J.
1695	27 Oct.	Richard J. and Elizabeth Sumners.

COURT CASES

Assize

P.R.O., Assizes 35/111/1, no. 5 (transcript at the E.R.O.). At the assizes held at Chelmsford, 14 March 1670.

Gilbert Tingle labourer and Eliz. his wife and Anne Seamor, wid., all of Earls Colne, on 11 Dec. 21 Charles II, at about 2 a.m. broke into the house of Thomas Joslyne and stole 'forty two pounds weight of browne thredd' worth £8 8s., 'twenty foure pounds weight of black thredd' worth 48s., 'twelve grosse of hancke thredd' worth 30s., 'ten thousand needles' worth 13s. 4d., 'seven hundred and twenty yards of Manchester filletting' worth 30s., 'seaven hundred yards of other filletting' worth 33s. 4d., 'a hundred and sixty yards of tape' worth 20s., 'six hundred yards of holland tape' worth 18s., 'foure hundred yards of Cadiz for shoestrings' worth 32s. 4d., 'an hundred and forty foure yards of cotten ribbon' worth 10s., 'a thousand thredd laces' worth 40s., '280 thimbles' worth 12s. Pleads not guilty; all guilty, to be hanged.

Witnesses. Thomas Joslyn, Peter Dore, John Chapman, James Lucy.

Chancery

P.R.O., C.10 38/110. The answer of Ralph Josselin the elder, one of the defendants, to the Bill of Complaint of Daniell Hudson and Richard Josselin, the complainants. Subscribed 28 November 1646. The defendant rehearses the conditions of the will of Ralph Josselin his father [see the abstract of this will of the diarist's grandfather, Ralph, on p. 215 above for these conditions]. The total estate left by his father was worth about £3,000. The will was proved.

And about twelve or thirteen years since this defendant Ralph J. and Simon J. did suffer a common recovery of the said messuage and land called Bollinghatch (dated indenture 6/6 Chas. I), as unto the said field called Highfeild to the use and behoofe of this deft. and his heirs upon conditions that if this deft. and Simon J. should not pay unto the Complainant Richard J. the sum of 200 pounds then the said recovery should be [returned] to Richard J. and his heirs ... The defendant says that he did pay unto the Complainant Richard J. the sum of 200 pounds according to the purport of the said Indenture and the will of his father & enjoys the land called Highfield—but left the other land completely to the other defendant Simon J. And he confesseth it to be true that Dorothy this defendants mother dyed divers yeares since and that Simon J. this defendants uncle her survived and dyed about three yeares since, and [he] believeth that the said Joseph Josselin is likewise dead. And [he] hath heard that before his deathe he made his last will and Testament in writing [printed on p. 214 above] and made the complainant his executor and thereby did despose of the said £160. He admits that the defendants did ask him for £160, but he not having Woodfield, Spicers Croft and Bollinghatch Grove did not pay it. And he says that the farm Bollinghatch being purchased joyntly by Simon Josselin this defendants uncle and the said Ralph Josselin this defendants father, this defendant doth believe that the said Simon Josselin did release to the said Ralph J. this defendants father all his estate and interest in the said messuage and farme. And he does not know what profits have been raised on the said lands called Woodfield and other premises for settling the £160 having left the matter to the other defendant Simon Josselin. And [he] says that he and the other executor have paid out more than all his personal estate did amount unto.

MANORIAL RECORDS

Rental of Earls Colne and Colne Priory, 19 March 1671

(E.R.O. D/DPr/113 (extract re lands of Ralph Josselin).

	rent		
	£	s	d
Ralph Josselin, clerk, or one of his children holds by Copy a tenement, sometime two tenements, which were of Richard Kemp and late of Thomas Wade	00	02	00
The same, a tenement and yard called Brittens lying on Colne Green . . . late of Richard Burton	00	00	10
The same . . . Doddipole Hoe . . . 1½ acres	00	01	00
The same . . . Spriggs Marsh . . . 1½ acres	00	00	10
'Ten Acres now divided into two peeces of land called Reddings and one Croft called Stowbridge', plus Clarks and 5 crofts	01	01	10
The same . . . Cattcroft	00	01	08
[all the above are copyhold lands]			
Vickers Style, freely held, ½ acre	00	00	06
Little Bridgmans 3 acres	00	04	00
Sawyers 3 acres	00	04	00
Wastlindale Mordens, late Churches	00	00	05
As vicar of Colne, freely held croft	00	00	08
The same for a part of vicarage garden	00	00	04
Messuage and lands called Hobstevens (23 acres), and certain lands called Pitchards (18 acres)	02	05	09
	04	04	01

EXTRACTS FROM JOSSELIN'S TWO SURVIVING SERMONS

1652

Dr Williams's Library, London, 1023, N.8.

The State of the Saints departed, Gods Cordial to Comfort the Saints remaining alive. A Sermon Preached at the Funeral of Mrs Smythee

Harlakenden Wife to William Harlakenden Esq., 28 June 1651. By
Ralph Josselin. Pastor at the Church at Earls Colne in Essex.
John II 2. vs. 12: Our Friend Lazarus Sleepeth.
              Lord if he sleep he shall do well.
Printed London, 1652.

Epistle Dedicatory. To the Worshippfull William Harlakenden.
[A2] Sir,

  God giveth counsel that Friends should shew pity to their afflicted
Friends, especially when the hand of the Almighty toucheth them: this
act of God shooting his Arrows into your bed and bosome, and wounding
to death your dearest outward enjoyment, was not a touch but stroke,
that pierceth deep into the hearts of your Friends ... [A2ᵛ] [these
meditations] I send them to you ... that they might be a Handkerchief
of Gods sending to wipe away those remaining tears ... But if your
thoughts should be hereby to keep her in your eye ... you will but injure
your self, for God would have us forget the [A3] dead, and her much
more ... she is present with Jesus, gathered to Jesus, ripened in faith by
many Afflictions ... and now like a rick of Corn brought in, in her due
season ...

  [A4] Sir, I said before, Gods providence leadeth us to forget the dead,
and time doth of it self concoct those sorrows ... but this forgetfulness is
not of the graces and vertues of the dead ... but it is of their persons,
which in time passe from us, and we scarce retain their image in our
minde ... (Christians should work themselves into a state where they
[A4ᵛ] can think about the dead without too much sorrow) ... you can
consider, here I was wont to see my dear Wife; here to enjoy her delightsome imbraces; her counsel, spiritual Discourses, furtherance, encouragement in the wayes of God, I was wont to finde her an help to ease me of
the burthen and trouble of household-affaires, whose countenance
welcomed me home with joy, [A5] and the delight in whom eased me
from many sorrows ... [A5ᵛ] when others go to the Tombs and Graves
to mourn, Christians go to the graves to rejoyce, this is such a way ...
[A6] if their sting you, the consideration of their state in death is Honey
that cureth and asswageth your grief, our way to comfort is by running
to other imployments, diverting thoughts, bringing in other[s] in their
rooms, looking off from them (but if you can consider their present state)
... you will finde your tears not [A6ᵛ] brinish, but pleasant, this Sir, I
have found and do finde an experienced truth, and not a notion, I have
thoughts of my sweetest Daughter now with comfort, who have had
thoughts of her like the bitternesse of death.

  But yet, Dear Sir, this is not all your work, but one great piece is to
see why God contendeth with you, *The Lord doth not willingly afflict the
sons of men*, he doth not envy us our Wives like Vines, and our Children
like Plants and Branches compassing our Beds and Tables ... now when
this God striketh, he taketh notice how we eye him that holdeth the Rod,
and whether we enquire how he was provoked to do this, that seeking

his face he may discover it unto us, sometime we shall not need search farre, some evil or other presents it self at first view, that God would [A7] have us to repent of, and utterly abandon. Afflictions of this nature with yours now, God many times useth to wean his from the Creature, and discover its emptiness and nothingness, he hereby sometimes arouseth his to more watchfulnesse, holinesse, to more close upright walking with him; Sometime God doth not point at what he intendeth, but its more dark, and then we must seek his face, and intreat that he would shew us . . . [A7ᵛ] and in this Enquiry, and Search, I humbly intreat you, let not your spirituall eye be removed from Gods love and tendernesse; God doth not alwayes knit his brows when he striketh . . . he chastiseth us with the same heart-love . . . as when he dealth out his mercies . . . Affliction is one way of evidencing love, and it is the note of a Bastard, that he endureth not correction . . .

The sermon

The sermon, some forty-three small pages ($5'' \times 2\frac{1}{2}''$), dwells on the analogy between sleep and death.

[6] First, as concerneth their bodies. 1. They sleep in Jesus, they [7] are at rest in his bosom, in his arms, they take rest of sleep. 2. Though in the dust, cast or laid up in the grave, yet they shall be rais'd again . . . [14] Their death is not separation either of soul or body from God and Christ; tis a separation of soul and body from each other that they may more closely enjoy the communion of Jesus Christ: a wicked mans death is a departing from God, a separating of soul and body from God for ever . . . [15] Your Wives, your Husbands, your Sonnes and Daughters, whose departing you so much lament, are but stept aside into their retiring rooms, their cool Summer-parlours, the shady cool Grove of the Grave to take a little rest by sleep, and when they awake they shall return again . . . [41] 2. But you eye your losse, your misse and want of them, Oh when I returne home, Oh my childe that met me, hugged me, is dead; my wife that came forth to welcome me with joy, is gone for ever, Oh how naked house [42] and family is unto me! . . . Did not God make thy Wife and thy Daughter whom thou bemoanest more for himself then for thee? . . .

1669

E.R.O. Diary of John Bufton of Coggeshall, ACC 4121. One of the small Ms. written by John Bufton (no. 6) was entitled 'Notes on 39 sermons' and no. 11 among these was 'The Notes of the Sermon preached at the Buriall of Old Mistriss Porter by Mr Joslin November the 11th 1669'. It is written in a minute hand from memory and contains about 1,250 words.

Text. Hebrews 11.5. 'By faith Enoch was translated that he should not see death, and was not found because god had translated him: for before this translation he had this testimony, that he pleased god.'

He was translated, which is a peculiar way of going out of this world into the other world. But the ordinary way is death, when life is either worne asunder by length of time, or many weaknesses: or cut asunder by some violence; & so the body goes downward and the soul upwards . . .

But what must we do that we may have gods testimony before we go from hence . . . 2. Live a life of faith . . . Do not take care upon your selves, but roul all upon god, and that is a pleasing life to god, when we submit to gods will, and do not murmur at him; but when we are satisfied at our heavenly fathers carving, this is pleasing to god: when we can Submit & say, The lord gives, & the lord takes, & blessed be the name of the lord, this is very pleasing to god . . . 3. Saies the apostle in 1 Timothy 5.4. If any widdow have children or nephews, let them learne first to shew piety at home, & to requite their parents: for that is good & acceptable before god; this is pleasing to god. The word carries with it such a goodness that has such a beauty in it, as may be a patterne for all to follow. Now to requite, is when that we do, carries a proportion to what we have received. Now what have we received from our parents? We received from them our life under god, & our bringing up, & education, with a great deal of care & labor, & with all love & tenderness, Now to returne that love & tenderness to your parents with all willingness, this is to requite them; & this is well pleasing to god. Oh then children, requite your parents for the cost they have laid out about you, follow their counsells, & chear up their sperits in their gray haires . . .

Bibliography

UNPUBLISHED SOURCES USED IN STUDY

Diary of Ralph Josselin

The original Diary is in the possession of Colonel G. O. C. Probert, Bevills, Bures, Suffolk.

At the E.R.O.

Transcript (full) and microfilm of the original Diary, T/B 9/1, 2.
Wills deposited at Chelmsford, as referenced in appendix C.
Parish registers of:

> Earls Colne, D/P/209/1/1–4;
> Kelvedon, T/R 12;
> Lexden, D/P/223/1/3;
> Rettendon, D/P/251/1/1;
> Roxwell, T/R 81.

Estate and manorial records. Of principal value were the following:

Full index to the Rolls, 1624–85, D/DPr 42;
Register of admissions to Colne Priory lands, D/DPr 100;
Rental of Earls Colne and Colne Priory, 1671, D/DPr 113;
Abstracts of Titles, 1598–1810, D/DPr 619;
Map of Earls Colne parish, made 1598, recopied 1810, D/DSm P2.
(Other records among the D/DU and D/DPr collection were also used.)
Transcript of assize records, 1646–84.
Transcript of quarter sessions records, 1641–54.
Transcript of Essex Ship Money, T/A 42.
Essex Hearth Taxes of 1662 and 1671, Q/RTh/1 and 5.
Earls Colne Tithe Map and Award, 1838, D/CT 101 and 101A.
Diary of John Bufton of Coggeshall, no. 6 (uncatalogued).

Ecclesiastical court records deposited at Chelmsford covering Josselin's ministry: only D/ACA 55 was of real value, though D/ACA 54, D/ACV 6, D/ABA 10 and D/ABV 2 were also searched.

At the B.R.O.

Olney parish register and wills relating to the Constable and Shepherd families.

At the H.R.O.

Bishops Stortford parish register (first).

At Cranham, Essex

Cranham parish register.

At Somerset House, London

Prerogative Court of Canterbury wills relating to the Josselin family, references in appendix C.

At Dr Williams's Library (14 Gordon Square, London, W.C.1)

A sermon by Ralph Josselin, published in 1652, 1023 N.8.

At the P.R.O.

Chancery case concerning Josselin family, C.10 38/110.

At the B.M.

Various unpublished diaries, as indicated in the following pages.

LIST OF PUBLISHED WORKS REFERRED TO
IN THE TEXT

(Unpublished diaries have also been listed here, alphabetically by name of diarist, for ease of reference.)

Allison, K. J. 'An Elizabethan Village "Census"'. *Bull. Inst. Hist. Res.*, vol. XXXVI. 1963.

Ambrose, Isaac. *Complete Works*. 1674.

Anon. 'Religious Diary, 1690–1702'. B.M. Add. MS. 5858, fols. 213–21.

Arensberg, C. R. *The Irish Countryman*. Gloucester, Mass., 1959.

Ariès, P. *Centuries of Childhood*. Translated, 1962.

Ashmole, Elias. *The Diary and Will of Elias Ashmole*. Ed. R. T. Gunther. Oxford, 1927.

Assheton, N. *The Journal of Nicholas Assheton of Downham, Lancs*. Ed. F. R. Raines. Chet. Soc., vol. XIV. 1848.

Atkinson, J. C. *Forty Years in a Moorland Parish*. 1891.

Aubrey, John. *Brief Lives*. Ed. O. L. Dick. Peregrine edn, 1962.

Beadle, John. *The Journal or Diary of a Thankful Christian*. 1656.

Becon, Thomas. *Workes*. 1560.

Blundell, N. *Blundell's Diary: Comprising selections from the diary of Nicholas Blundell Esq. from 1702 to 1728*. Ed. T. E. Gibson. Liverpool, 1895.

Bott, E. *Family and Social Network*. Tavistock Publications, 1957.

Bourdieu, P. 'The attitude of the Algerian peasant toward time'. In *Mediterranean Countrymen*. Ed. J. Pitt-Rivers. Paris, 1963.

Bramston, J. *The Autobiography of Sir John Bramston*. Ed. T. W. Bramston. Cam. Soc., vol. XXXII. 1845.

Brinsley, John. *Ludus Literarius: or, the Grammar Schoole.* 1627.

Browne, Sir T. 'Urn Burial' and 'Christian Morals' reprinted with *Religio Medici.* Everyman edn, 1962.

Burling, R. *Rengsanggri; Family and Kinship in a Garo Village.* Philadelphia, 1963.

Burn, Richard. *Ecclesiastical Law.* 4 vols. 4th edn, 1781.

Burrell, Timothy. 'Extracts from the Journal and Account Book of Timothy Burrell'. *Suss. Arch. Coll.*, vol. III. 1850.

Burton, Robert. *Anatomy of Melancholy.* 2 vols. Everyman edn, 1962.

Campbell, J. K. *Honour, Family and Patronage.* Oxford, 1964.

Campbell, M. *The English Yeoman.* New Haven, 1942.

Cellier, Mrs E. 'A Scheme for the Foundation of a Royal Hospital'. *Harleian Miscellany*, vol. IX, pp. 191–8. 1810.

Chalkin, C. W. 'A Kentish Wealden Parish (Tonbridge)'. Unpublished B. Litt. thesis, 1960. Bodleian Library.

Clifford, Lady A. *The Diary of the Lady Anne Clifford.* Introductory notes by V. Sackville-West. 1923.

Cogan, Thomas. *The Haven of Health.* 1589.

Cohn, Norman. *The Pursuit of the Millennium*, Mercury edn, 1962

Compton, T. 'Rev. Thos. Compton, Rector of Great Holland, 1725–1761'. John Taylor in *Ess. Rev.*, vol. 9. 1900.

Connell, K. H. 'Peasant Marriage in Ireland: its Structure and Development since the Famine'. *Econ. Hist. Rev.*, 2nd ser., vol XIV, no. 3. 1962.

Cork, earl of. *The Lismore Papers* (1st series). Ed. A. B. Grosart. 5 vols. 1886.

Cornwall, J. 'Evidence of Population Mobility in the Seventeenth Century'. *Bull. Inst. Hist. Res.*, vol. XL. November, 1967.

Coverdale, Myles. (trans.) *The Christian State of Matrimony.* 1543.

Crosfield, T. *The Diary of Thomas Crosfield.* Ed. F. S. Boas. 1935.

Crozier, D. 'Kinship and Occupational Succession'. *Soc. Rev.*, new series, vol. 13, no. 1. 1965.

Culpepper, N. *A Directory for Midwives.* 1658.

Curtis, M. H. 'Education and Apprenticeship'. In *Shakespeare Survey*, 17. Ed. A. Nicoll. Cambridge, 1964.

Davis, K. and Blake, J. 'Social Structure and Fertility: An Analytic Framework'. *Economic Development and Cultural Change*, vol. 4, no. 3. 1956.

Dawson, W. R. *A Leechbook or Collection of Medical Recipes of the Fifteenth Century.* 1934.

Dee, John. *The Private Diary of Dr John Dee.* Ed. J. O. Halliwell. Cam. Soc., vol. XIX. 1842.

Dictionary of National Biography. Ed. Sidney Lee. 1909.

Dod, J. and Clever, R. *A Godlie Forme of Household Government.* 1612.

Dodds, E. R. *The Greeks and the Irrational.* California, 1966.

Epstein, A. L. (ed.) *The Craft of Social Anthropology.* 1967.

Erikson, Erik. *Childhood and Society.* Pelican edn, 1965.

Evans-Pritchard, E. E. *Witchcraft, Oracles and Magic among the Azande*. Oxford, 1937.

Evelyn, John. *The Diary and Correspondence of John Evelyn, F.R.S.* Ed. William Bray. No date.

Eyre, Adam. *Adam Eyre, A Dyurnall*. Ed. H. J. Morehouse. Sur. Soc., vol. LXV. 1875.

Fell, Sarah. *Household Account Book of Sarah Fell of Swarthmoor Hall, 1673–8*. Ed. N. Penny. Cambridge, 1920.

Finch, M. E. *The Wealth of Five Northamptonshire Families, 1540–1640*. Northants. Record Soc., vol XIX. 1956.

Firth, Raymond. *Human Types*. Revised edn, 1956.

——. *Elements of Social Organization*. 1963.

——. (ed.) *Two Studies of Kinship in London*. 1956.

Forman, Simon. *Autobiography and Personal Diary of Dr Simon Forman*. Ed. J. O. Halliwell. 1849.

Fortes, M. 'Kinship, Incest and Exogamy of the Northern Territories of the Gold Coast'. In *Custom is King*. Ed. L. H. D. Buxton. 1949.

Foster, George. 'Peasant Society and the Image of Limited Good'. *Am. Anth.*, vol. 67, no. 2. 1965.

Foster, Joseph. *Alumni Oxonienses*, 4 vols. Oxford, 1891–2.

Fox, George. *George Fox's Journal*. Abridged by P. C. Parker. 1903.

Freke, Elizabeth. *Mrs Elizabeth Freke, Her Diary, 1671 to 1714*. Ed. M. Carbery. Cork, 1913.

Fürer-Haimendorf, Christoph von. *The Sherpas of Nepal*. 1964.

——. *Morals and Merit*. 1967.

Gaule, John. *Select Cases of Conscience Touching Witches and Witchcrafts*. 1646.

Gibson, J. 'Autobiography of Sir John Gibson, 1655'. In *North Country Diaries* (2nd series). Sur. Soc., vol. CXXIV. 1914.

Gluckman, Max. *Custom and Conflict in Africa*. Paperback edn, Oxford, 1963.

——. *Politics, Law and Ritual in Tribal Society*. Paperback edn, Oxford, 1965.

Goode, William J. *The Family*. New Jersey, 1964.

Gouge, William. *Of Domesticall Duties*. 1622.

Greene, John. 'The Diary of John Greene'. Ed. E. M. Symonds. *Eng. Hist. Rev.*, vol. XLIV. 1929.

Hair, P. E. H. 'Bridal Pregnancy in Earlier Centuries'. *Population Studies*, vol. XX, no. 2. 1966.

Hajnal, J. 'European Marriage Patterns in Perspective'. In *Population in History*. Eds. D. V. Glass and D. E. C. Eversley. 1965.

Halkett, Lady. *The Autobiography of Anne Lady Halkett*. Ed. J. G. Nichols. Cam. Soc., new series, vol. XIII. 1875.

Haller, William. *The Rise of Puritanism*. New York, 1957.

Halpern, Joel M. *A Serbian Village*. New York, 1967.

Harrington, William. *The Commendacions of Matrymony*. 1528.

Herbert, George. *A Priest to the Temple*. 1652; Everyman edn, 1908.

Heywood, Oliver. *Rev. Oliver Heywood's Diary, 1630–1702.* Ed. J. Horsfall Turner. 4 vols. Brighouse, 1882.

Hill, Christopher. *Puritanism and Revolution.* Mercury edn, 1962.

——. *Economic Problems of the Church.* Oxford, 1963.

——. *Society and Puritanism in Pre-Revolutionary England.* Mercury edn, 1966.

Hill, Thomas. *The most pleasaunte art of the interpretacion of dreames.* 1576.

Hoby, Lady M. *Diary of Lady Margaret Hoby, 1599–1605.* Ed. Dorothy M. Meads. 1930.

Homans, G. C. *English Villagers of the Thirteenth Century.* New York, 1960.

Hoskins, W. G. *Essays in Leicestershire History.* Liverpool, 1950.

——. *Local History in England.* 1959.

——. *Provincial England.* 1963.

——. *The Midland Peasant.* Papermac edn, 1965.

——. 'Provincial Life'. In *Shakespeare Survey*, 17. Ed. A. Nicoll. Cambridge, 1964.

——. 'Harvest Fluctuations and English Economic History, 1620–1759'. *Agric. Hist. Rev.*, vol. 16, part 1. 1968.

Howson, W. G. 'Plague, Poverty and Population in Parts of North-West England, 1580–1720'. *Trans. Hist. Soc. Lancs. & Ches.*, vol. CXII. 1960.

Hutchinson, Lucy. *Memoirs of the Life of Colonel Hutchinson.* 2 vols. 4th edn, 1822.

Isham, Thomas. *The Journal of Thomas Isham of Lamport, Northants, 1671–3.* Ed. W. Rye. Norwich, 1875.

Jackson, James. 'James Jackson's Diary, 1650–1683'. Selections by F. Grainger. *Trans. Cumb. & West. Ant. & Arch. Soc.*, new series, vol. 21. 1921.

Jolly, Thomas. *The Note Book of the Rev. Thomas Jolly, 1671–1693.* Ed. Henry Fishwick. Chet. Soc., new series, vol. XXXIII, 1894.

Josselin, Ralph. *The Diary of the Rev. Ralph Josselin, 1616–1683.* Ed. E. Hockliffe. Cam. Soc., vol. XV. 1908.

Kardiner, Abram (ed.) *The Psychological Frontiers of Society.* Columbia paperback edn, 1963.

Knappen, M. M. (ed.) *Two Elizabethan Puritan Diaries.* 1933.

Lancaster, L. 'Kinship in Anglo-Saxon Society'. 2 parts. *Brit. Jour. Soc.*, vol. IX, nos. 3 and 4. 1958.

Laslett, Peter. *The World we have lost.* University paperback edn, 1965.

——. and Harrison, John. 'Clayworth and Cogenhoe'. In *Historical Essays presented to David Ogg.* Eds. H. E. Bell and R. L. Ollard. 1963.

Leach, E. R. *Pul Eliya, A village in Ceylon.* Cambridge, 1961.

Loder, Robert. *Robert Loder's Farm Accounts, 1610–1620.* Ed. G. E. Fussell. Cam. Soc., 3rd series, vol. LIII. 1936.

Lorimer, F. *et al. Culture and Human Fertility.* UNESCO, 1954.

Macfarlane, A. *Witchcraft in Tudor and Stuart England.* Coming in 1970.

——. 'The Regulation of Marital and Sexual Relationships in Seventeenth Century England'. Unpublished M.Phil. thesis, 1968. London University Library.

Malinowski, B. *Magic, Science and Religion*. New York, 1954.
——. *Sex and Repression in Savage Society*. Paperback edn, 1960.
Manningham, J. *The Diary of John Manningham, 1602–3*. Ed. J. Bruce. Cam. Soc., vol. XCIX. 1868.
Maquet, J. *The Premise of Inequality in Ruanda*. Oxford, 1961.
Martindale, Adam. *The Life of Adam Martindale*. Ed. R. Parkinson. Chet. Soc., vol. IV. 1845.
Matthews, A. G. (ed.) *Calamy Revised*. Oxford, 1934.
Matthews, William. *British Diaries*. Cambridge, 1950.
——. *British Autobiographies*. Berkeley, 1955.
Mead, Margaret. *Sex and Temperament in Three Primitive Societies*. 1935.
——. *Coming of Age in Samoa*. Pelican, 1963.
Mildmay, Lady. 'The Journal of Lady Mildmay, circa 1570–1617'. *Q.R.*, vol. CCXV. 1911.
Moore, Giles. 'Extracts from the Journal and Account Book of the Rev. Giles Moore' by R. W. Blencoe. *Suss. Arch. Coll.*, vol. I. 1847.
Moore, Percivall. *Marriage Contracts or Espousals in the Reign of Queen Elizabeth*. Ass. Arch. Soc., vol. XXX, pt. I. 1909.
Morant, Philip. *The History and Antiquities of the County of Essex*. 2 vols. 1816.
More, Rev. John. 'Extracts from diaries, 1694–1700'. B.M. Add. MS. 25463, fols. 197–9.
Morgan, E. S. *The Puritan Family*. Harper Torchbook edn, 1966.
Muncey, R. W. *The Romance of Parish Registers*. 1933.
Nadel, S. F. *Nupe Religion*. 1954.
Nag, Moni. *Factors Affecting Human Fertility in Nonindustrial Societies*. Yale University Publications in Anthropology, 66. New Haven, 1962.
Newcome, Henry. *The Autobiography of Henry Newcome*. Ed. Richard Parkinson. Chet. Soc., vol. XXVI. 1852.
Northumberland, Henry Percy, ninth earl of. *Advice To His Son*. Ed. G. B. Harrison. 1930.
Notestein, Wallace. *English Folk*. 1938.
——. *English People on the Eve of Colonization*. New York, 1954.
——. *Four Worthies*. 1956.
Obeyesekere, G. *Land Tenure in Ceylon*. Cambridge, 1967.
Osborne, F. *Advice to a Son*. 5th edn, Oxford, 1656.
Pearson, L. E. *Elizabethans at Home*. Stanford, 1957.
Pepys, Samuel. *The Diary of Samuel Pepys from 1659 to 1669*. Ed. Lord Braybrooke. No date. Also consulted was *The Diary of Samuel Pepys*. Ed. H. B. Wheatley. 8 vols. 1904.
Perkins, William. *A Discourse of the Damned Art of Witchcraft*. Cambridge, 1608.
——. *Christian Oeconomie*. 1609.
Phaire, Thomas. *The Boke of Chyldren*. 1545; reprinted 1965.
Pledger, E. 'The Diary of Elias Pledger of Little Baddow, Essex'. Unpublished. Dr Williams's Library, London.
Ponsonby, A. *English Diaries*. 1923.
——. *More English Diaries*. 1927.

Powell, Walter. *The Diary of Walter Powell, 1630–1654.* Transcribed by J. A. Bradney. Bristol, 1907.

Power, Eileen. *Medieval People.* University paperback edn, 1963.

Quintrell, Brian. 'The Government of the County of Essex, 1603–1642'. Unpublished Ph.D. thesis, 1965. London University Library.

Radcliffe-Brown, A. R. 'Introduction' in *African Systems of Kinship and Marriage.* Ed. A. R. Radcliffe-Brown and D. Forde. Oxford, 1950.

A Rational Account of the Naturall Weaknesses of Women. By 'a Physician'. 2nd edn, 1716. B.M. 1177 c.l.

Rawdon, M. *The Life of Marmaduke Rawdon of York.* Ed. R. Davies. Cam. Soc., vol. LXXXV, 1868.

R.C. *The Compleat Midwife's Practice Enlarged.* 1659.

Redfield, Robert. *The Little Community.* Paperback edn, Chicago, 1960.

Rich, Mary. 'The Diary of Mary Rich, Countess of Warwick, 1666–72.' B.M. Add. MS. 27351–5 and 27358.

Riesman, David. *Selected Essays from Individualism Reconsidered.* Paperback edn, New York, 1954.

——. *The Lonely Crowd.* Abridged edn, New Haven, 1961.

Roberts, D. F. 'A Demographic Study of a Dinka Village'. *Human Biology,* vol. 28. 1956.

Rous, John. *The Diary of John Rous.* Ed. M. Green. Cam. Soc., vol. LXVI. 1856.

Rowse, A. L. *Tudor Cornwall.* 1941.

Rye, W. B. *England as Seen by Foreigners.* 1865.

Sampson, William. Author of *The Rector's Book, Clayworth Nottinghamshire, 1675–1700.* Eds. H. Gill and E. L. Guilford. Nottingham, 1910.

Schapera, I. *Married Life in an African Tribe.* Reprinted, 1966.

Scot, Reginald. *The Discoverie of Witchcraft.* 1584; reprinted, Arundel, 1964.

Sharp, Mrs Jane. *The Midwives Book.* 1671.

Shaw, W. A. *A History of the English Church During the Civil Wars and Under the Commonwealth, 1640–1660.* 2 vols. 1900.

Simpson, Alan. *The Wealth of the Gentry, 1540–1660.* Cambridge, 1963.

Slingsby, Henry. *The Diary of Sir Henry Slingsby of Scriven, Bart.* Ed. D. Parsons. 1836.

Smith, Harold. 'The Diary of Ralph Josselin'. *Ess. Rev.,* vol. XXXIV. 1925.

——. *The Ecclesiastical History of Essex.* Colchester, no date (about 1930).

Sneyd, C. A. (trans.) *A Relation, or rather a True Account of the Island of England . . . about the year 1500.* By an Italian. Cam. Soc., vol. XXXVII. 1847.

Southall, A. (ed.) *Social Change in Modern Africa.* Oxford, 1961.

Sprott, S. E. *The English Debate on Suicide: From Donne to Hume.* La Salle, Illinois, 1961.

Stapley, Richard, 'Extracts from the Diary of Richard Stapley, Gent.' By Rev. E. Turner. *Suss. Arch. Coll.,* vol. II. 1849.

Steer, Francis W. *Farm and Cottage Inventories of Mid-Essex, 1635–1749.* Colchester, 1950.

Stirling, Paul. *Turkish Village*. Paperback edn, New York, 1965.

Stone, Lawrence. *The Crisis of the Aristocracy, 1558–1641*. Oxford, 1965. Ch. II.

——. 'Marriage among the English Nobility in the 16th and 17th Centuries'. *Comp. Stud. Soc. & Hist.*, vol. III, no. 2. 1961.

Stout, William. *The Autobiography of William Stout of Lancaster, 1665–1752*. Ed. J. D. Marshall. Manchester, 1967.

Styles, Philip. 'A Census of a Warwickshire Village in 1698'. *Univ. Birm. Hist. Jour.*, vol. III. 1951–2.

Tawney, R. H. *Religion and the Rise of Capitalism*. Pelican edn, 1961.

Thirsk, Joan. 'The Family'. *P. & P.*, vol. 127. 1964.

——. (ed.) *The Agrarian History of England and Wales*. Vol. IV, 1500–1640. Cambridge, 1967.

Thomas, Keith. 'History and Anthropology'. *P. & P.*, vol. 24. 1963.

——. 'Work and Leisure in Pre-Industrial Society'. *P. & P.*, vol. 29. 1964.

Thoresby, Ralph. *The Diary of Ralph Thoresby*. Ed. Joseph Hunter. 2 vols. 1830.

Thornton, Alice. *The Autobiography of Mrs Alice Thornton of East Newton, Co. York*. Ed. C. Jackson. Sur. Soc., vol. LXII. 1873.

United Nations. *The Determinants and Consequences of Population Trends*. New York, 1953.

Van Gennep, Arnold. *The Rites of Passage*. Translated, 1965.

Venn, J. and S. A. (comp.) *The Book of Matriculations and Degrees . . . in the University of Cambridge from 1544 to 1659*. Cambridge, 1913.

——. *Alumni Cantabrigiensis*. 4 vols. Cambridge, 1922–7.

Verney, F. P. and M. M. (comp.) *Memoirs of the Verney Family During the Seventeenth Century*. 2 vols. New York, 1907.

Walzer, Michael. *The Revolution of the Saints*. 1966.

——. 'Puritanism as a Revolutionary Ideology'. *Hist. & Th.*, vol. III, no. 1. 1963.

West, F. 'The Social and Economic History of the East Fen Village of Wrangle, 1603–1837'. Unpublished Ph.D. thesis, 1966. Leicester University Library.

West, John. *Village Records*. 1962.

Westermarck, E. *The History of Human Marriage*. 3 vols. 5th end. 1921.

Whately, William. *A Bride-Bush: or, A Direction for Married Persons*. 1619.

Whitforde, Richard. *A Werke for Housholders*. 1533.

Whittingham, T. 'The Diary of Timothy Whittingham of Holmside'. Extracts by J. C. Hodgson. *Arch. Ael.*, 3rd series, vol. XXI. 1924.

Williams, W. M. *A West Country Village: Ashworthy*. 1963.

——. *The Sociology of an English Village: Gosforth*. 1964.

Wilmott, Peter, and Young, Michael. *Family and Kinship in East London*. Pelican edn, 1962.

Wilson, J. Dover. *Life in Shakespeare's England*. Pelican edn, 1962.

Winchester, Barbara. *Tudor Family Portrait*. 1955.

Wolf, Eric R. *Peasants*. New Jersey, 1966.

Wright, Joseph. (ed.) *The English Dialect Dictionary*. 6 vols. Oxford, 1923.

Wrigley, E. A. 'Family Limitation in Pre-Industrial England'. *Econ. Hist. Rev.*, 2nd series, vol. XIX, no. 1. 1966.

——. (ed.) 'Mortality in Pre-Industrial England: The Example of Colyton, Devon. Over Three Centuries', *Daedalus*, Spring 1968.

——. *An Introduction to English Historical Demography*. 1966.

The vital statistics of Ralph Josselin's family

Ralph Josselin: born 26.1.17; buried 30.8.83
married, on 28.10.40, to
Jane Constable: christened 26.11.21; buried 1693

Children

No.	Name	Date of birth	Interval between (months)	Date of marriage	Age at marriage years/ months	Date of death	Age at death years/ months
1	Mary	12.4.42	17½	—	—	27.5.50	8.1
2	Thomas	30.12.43	20½	—	—	15.6.73	29.6 .
3	Jane	25.11.45	23	30.8.70	24.9	—	—
4	Ralph	11.2.48	25½	—	—	21.2.48	10 days
5	Ralph	5.5.49	15	—	—	2.6.50	13 months
6	John	19.9.51	29½	-.10.81	30	—	—
7	Anne	20.6.54	33	—	—	31.7.73	19.1
8	Mary	14.1.58	43	10.4.83	25.3	—	—
9	Elizab.	20.6.60	29	5.6.77	16.11	—	—
10	Rebecka	26.11.63	41	6.5.83	19.6	—	—

NOTES
1. All dates are from the Diary and most of them are confirmed by parish register entries: here, and on the genealogical table opposite, dates are N.S., with the year commencing 1 January, and are contracted—expanded, they would read 16--.
2. The intervals are those between births, except in the first case, where it is between marriage and the first birth.

RALPH JOSSELINS KIN AND FAMILY

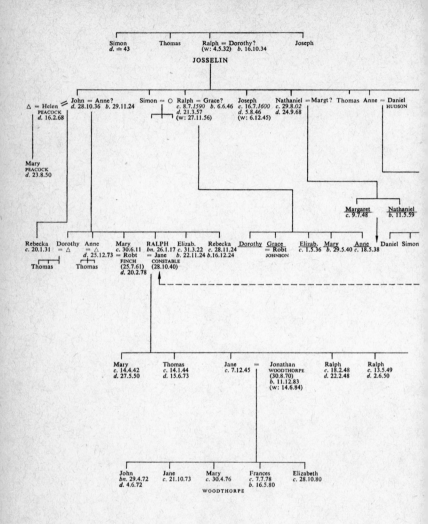

b. = buried; bn. = date of birth; c. = christened; d. date of death; (18.8.56) = date of marriage; = = married to; (w: 27.11.56) = will survives, this date of proving; △ = a male, name unknown; ○ = a female, name unknown; + = children, names/number unknown; ≏ = exact date unknown; <u>Dorothy</u> = order of birth unknown; ⌐----, = not definitely his children.

Theba

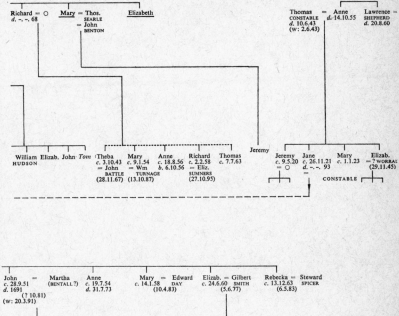

Richard = ○   Mary = Thos.   Elizabeth
d. –.–. 68   SEARLE
                  = John
                    BENTON

Thomas = Anne   Lawrence =
CONSTABLE d. 14.10.55   SHEPHERD
d. 10.6.43   d. 20.8.60
(w: 2.6.43)

William Elizab. John Tom   Theba   Mary   Anne   Richard   Thomas   Jeremy   Jeremy   Jane   Mary   Elizab.
HUDSON   c. 3.10.43 c. 9.1.54 c. 18.8.56 c. 2.2.58   c. 7.7.63   c. 9.5.20 c. 26.11.21 c. 1.1.23 = ? WORRAL
                              = John   = Wm   b. 6.10.56 = Eliz.   = ○   d. –.–. 93   (29.11.45)
                              BATTLE   TURNAGE   SUMNERS   CONSTABLE
                              (28.11.67) (13.10.87)   (27.10.95)
                                                                                                         =

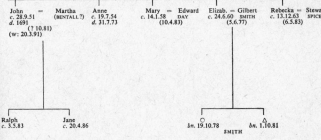

John   = Martha   Anne   Mary   = Edward   Elizab. = Gilbert   Rebecka = Steward
c. 28.9.51   (BENTALL?) c. 19.7.54 c. 14.1.58 DAY   c. 24.6.60 SMITH   c. 13.12.63 SPICER
d. 1691   d. 31.7.73   (10.4.83) (5.6.77)   (6.5.83)
(? 10.81)
(w: 20.3.91)

Ralph   Jane   ○   △
c. 3.5.83   c. 20.4.86   bn. 19.10.78   bn. 1.10.81
                                              SMITH

Index

Abbott, Henry, sen., resident in Earl's Colne, 78

Abbott, Robert, dispute of R.J. with, 63n; non-attender at church, 27n

abortifacients, 203

Act of Uniformity (1662), 28–9

Adam, William, parishioner, 31

affinal kin, 139–43

after-life, R.J.'s attitude to, 168

age-boundaries, 91

ageing, R.J.'s attitude to, 99

Ambrose, Isaac, on diary-keeping, 6–7

Anabaptist, 26

ancestors, 53, 101

Andrews, Mrs, nurse to R.J.'s grandchild, 87

angels, 180, 191

anxiety, Puritanism and, 193

apocalyptic studies of R.J., 24, 135, 190; dreams of, 185

apprenticeship: age at, 93, 206; fees for, 48, 49, 132

Archdeacon of Essex, visitation by, 29

army chaplain, R.J. as, in Civil War, 18, 38, 107

Ashmole, Elias, diary of, 204n

Ashworthy, Devon, studies of kinship and friendship in, 118, 136–7, 149, 158n

Assheton, Nicholas, diary of, 5n

aunts of R.J., 133

baptisms, 29; expenses of, 53, 89; of R.J.'s children, 88–9, 145; of R.J.'s kin, in parish registers, 217–18

Beadle, John, on diary-keeping, 7

Bentall, Lawrence, nephew of John Josselin's wife Martha, 148, 213, 214

Bentall, Widow, R.J. buys land from, 55

Benton, Jeremy, cousin of R.J., 138, 139

Benton, John, husband of R.J.'s aunt Mary, 134

Berrill, Aunt (of R.J.'s wife), 140, 141

Bible: imagery from, 24, 187, 188; reading of, 24, 186

Biford, J., parishioner, R.J. thinks innocent of being a witch, 191

births (R.J.'s children), 82, 83, 141, 199, (R.J.'s grandchildren), 85, 114, 115, 155; accounts of, 84–6; friends and neighbours at, 85, 150, 151; intervals between, 82, 200, 201–2

Bishop of London, visitation by, 29

bishops' courts, 27, 28

Bishop's Stortford, 15, 101, 131; entries from registers of, 217

Blundell, Nicholas, diary of, 4n

Blundell, Samuel, cousin by marriage of R.J., 138

Bollinghatch, Roxwell, land inherited by R.J., 60, 63, 64, 216, 219, 220

books: R.J.'s bequest of, 213; R.J.'s interest in, 15, 22–4; R.J.'s purchases of, 23, 52, 53

Borradale, Rev. John, minister at Steeple Bumpstead, 16n; persuades R.J. to remain at Cambridge, 17

Braintree, 16n, 19

Bramston, Sir John, autobiography of, 207n

breast-feeding, 83, 86, 90; see also weaning

Brewer, lessee of R.J.'s land, 68

brother-sister relationship, 129–31

Browne, Sir Thomas, 91n, 99n

building, R.J.'s expenditure on, 54

burial ground, Quaker, 27

burials, of R.J.'s kin, from parish registers, 217–18; see also funerals

Burrell, Timothy, diary of, 5n–6n

Burton, Robert, Anatomy of Melancholy by, 166n

Burton, Thomas, diary of, 9n

Bury St Edmunds, R.J.'s daughters at school at, 49

cakes, at funerals, 100

Calvinism, 110, 195; of R.J., 32, 168, 193; see also Puritanism

Cambridge: R.J. at, 16–17; son of Harlakendens at, 152

capital assets, of R.J., 57–64

Caplyn, Mr, R.J.'s loan to, 150

Castle Hedingham, R.J. preaches at, 28

cattle, 30, 69

charity dispensed by R.J., 31, 51–2

Charles I, R.J. on trial and execution of, 19

Charles II, R.J. and, 20, 188

chess, R.J. repents time spent at, 176

children: cost of maintenance of, 44–5, 46–51; duties of, to parents, 25, 82; movement of, away from home, 92–3, 112–13, 146, 205–10; see also Josselin, Ralph, children of

Christmas celebrations, 22

Church, Mrs Jane, at funeral of R.J.'s child, 100

Church, Mary, friend of R.J., 151, 155, 172, 176; legacies of (to Jane, R.J.'s daughter), 65, 151, (to R.J.), 31n, 63, 64, 151; will of, 216

Church, Mrs Rose, mother of Mary Church, 63, 151n, 216

'churching' ceremony not recorded, 88

Civil War, R.J. in, 18–19, 38, 107; R.J.'s house plundered during, 19, 151

Clarke, Rev. Mr, minister of Gaines Colne, sees a witch, 191

Clayworth, Rector's book of, 9, 204n

Clifford, Lady Anne, diary of, 199n, 201n

Coggeshall; ministers at, 29, 186; R.J. escapes to, in Civil War, 19; Quakers at, 26

Colchester: in Civil War, 19; gale at, 73; Quakers in, 27; R.J. at, 20, 29; R.J.'s daughter at school at, 91, 93, 112

collections in Earls Colne, for propagation of Gospel in New England, 22

Colne Green, R.J.'s house in, 54, 77, 212

Colyton, Devon (1560–1719): family size in, 81; intervals between births in, 201

Commonwealth, R.J. subscribes to Oath of Loyalty to, 19

communion service, 29, 30, 112, 180

Compton, Rev. Thomas, Life of, 208

conformity, Puritan need for, 194

Constable, Anne, mother of R.J.'s wife, 140, 141, 214

Constable, Elizabeth, sister of R.J.'s wife (married name Worrall), 143, 214

Constable, Jane, see Josselin, Jane, wife of R.J.

Constable, Jeremy, brother of R.J.'s wife, 133, 141, 142, 214

Constable, Thomas, father of R.J.'s wife: death of, 141; will of, 128, 214

copyholds held by R.J., 42, 220

corn, R.J.'s crops of, 70, 71

cost of living, see maintenance, cost of

courtship, 94–7

cousins of R.J., 136–9

Cranham; entries from register of, 217; R.J. takes living at, 17, 97, 98, 133, 136, 140

Cressner, George, resident in Earl's Colne, 78

Cressner, Mr, R.J. and wife lodge with, 44

Cromwell, Oliver; diary of relation of, 6, 207; prophecy about, 190; Quakers and, 26; R.J.'s references to plots against, 20; R.J. dreams about, 186

Crosfield, Thomas, diary of, 53n

Crosman, Rev. Mr, imprisoned under Act of Uniformity, 29

Crow, An, suspected witch, 191

Day, J., parishioner, 29

death-rates, pre-industrial, 163, 172

deaths: attitude of R.J. to, 155–7, 168–9; incidence of, in R.J.'s family, 164

debts owed by R.J., 55–6; see also loans

Dee, Dr John, diary of, 87n, 207

devil, the, 190–1; compared with a lapwing, 178, 188

diaries, 17th-century, 3–11

Donne, John, 169

dowries; of R.J.'s daughters, 51, 59, 93–5, 132; of R.J.'s wife, 64

dreams: of R.J., 21, 183–7; of R.J.'s children, 91, 185; of R.J.'s wife, 109, 185

Ealing, listing of (1599), 209

Earl, Mr and Mrs, friends of R.J., 150

Earls Colne: in Civil Wars, 18, 19; entries from register of, 217; R.J.'s income from living of, 34, 39; R.J. teaches school at, 34, 37, 39, 64, 76; R.J. vicar at, 17, 140

elections to parliament, R.J.'s references to, 20, 21

Elliston, Mrs Mabel, 100, 151

Elliston, Mr and Mrs, friends of R.J., 31, 78, 89, 151n

estates, R.J.'s interest in building up, 15, 34

Evelyn, John: age of, at weaning, 87n; diary of, 116, 127n, 144n, 166n

expenditure of R.J., 38–57

Eyre, Adam, diary of, 5, 9

family, extended, 146–7

family size, 81n

farming by R.J., 68–71, 188; R.J.'s expenditure on, 42–4; R.J.'s income from leasing land and, 39; wife shares in work of, 109, 171

fasting, by R.J. to save money for charity, 52

father, Calvinist view of role of, 110–11

father-daughter relationship, 111–17

father-son relationship, 117–25

Fell, Sarah, account-book of, 46n

Finch, Robert, husband of R.J.'s sister Mary, 130

food, prices of, 73, 75–6

foreign affairs, in R.J.'s annual summaries, 19–20

Forman, Dr Simon, diary of, 207

foundling hospital, cost of maintenance of children in, 45
Fox, George, Journal of, 145, 183
France, R.J.'s references to, 19, 20
Freke, Mrs Elizabeth, diary of, 204n, 207
friends, distinguished from neighbours, 149–50
funerals, 99–102; expenses of, 53n; R.J.'s sermons at, 25, 83n, 100, 107, 152, 220–2
Furse, Robert, diary of, 9

Garrod, John, Quaker, 27, 177
Gibson, Sir John, autobiography of, 210
glebe, R.J.'s, 34, 38
God, R.J.'s attitude to, 179–82, 193–4
godparents, 144; to R.J.'s children, 140, 141, 143, 145
grandchildren, R.J.'s bequest to, 213
grandparents, 127; R.J. and his wife as, 114–16, 127, 128
Greek, R.J. studies, 24
Greene, John, diary of, 87n
Greenwich, R.J. preaches at, 20
Grey, Lady Jane, age of, at weaning, 87n
guilt, R.J.'s sense of, 176

Halkett, Anne, Lady, autobiography of, 204n
Halstead, cow bought at, 69
Harlakenden, Mrs, wedding clothes of, 97
Harlakenden, Mrs Mabel, funeral of, 100
Harlakenden, Mrs Margaret, at funeral of R.J.'s child, 100
Harlakenden, Richard, lord of the manor and owner of Earls Colne living, 17, 63, 78, 191; baptism of son of, 89; contributes to R.J.'s income, 34, 35, 37, 152, 191; godparent to R.J.'s child, 145; loan to R.J. from, 55
Harlakenden, Mrs Smythee, funeral of, 25, 83n, 107, 152, 220–2
Harlakenden, Thomas, contributes to R.J.'s income, 34; godparent to R.J.'s child, 145
Harlakenden, William, 152
Harlakendens, 152; R.J.'s daughter and sister as servants to, 112, 149; R.J.'s payments to, on his copyholds, 42
harvest, on R.J.'s farm, 70–1
Harvy, Thomas, radical weaver, 26, 27
Haverill fair, R.J. buys steers at, 69
hay: cost of making, 43; crops of, 71, 180
Haynes, Mrs, gives gloves to R.J.'s wife, 150
hearth tax, 42, 77, 78, 130n
Hebrew, R.J. studies, 24
hedging and ditching, on R.J.'s farm, 43

Herbert, George, 30n, 52n, 89n, 111n, 128n, 145n, 181n
Heywood, Rev. Oliver, diary of, 9n
Hoby, Lady Margaret, diary of, 207
Holland, R.J.'s references to, 19, 20
Honeywood, Sir Thomas and Lady, of Marks Hall, friends of R.J., 100, 151, 155
hop trade, R.J. engages in, 38
hospitality; investment in, as insurance, 154, 171; R.J.'s expenditure on, 52–3
Hudson, Daniel, husband of R.J.'s aunt Anne, 134, 137, 214, 215, 219
Hudson, Tom, cousin of R.J., 137, 138
husband-wife relationship, 100–10
Hutchinson, Col., Memoirs of, 204n, 207

illnesses, in R.J.'s family, 89, 90, 155, 170–2 (bad leg), 108 (cramp), 98 (measles), 112 (sciatica), 114, 170; see also plague, smallpox
images and pictures, taken down by R.J., 22
income: of R.J., 34–9; of yeomen contemporary with R.J., 77
inheritance: dispute between R.J. and his uncle Richard about, 134, 135, 219–20; and relations between siblings, 125, 131–2
in-laws, relations with, 139–43
insecurity, constant sense of, in 17th century, 28, 171, 189
interest on loans, 55, 57n
Ireland, R.J.'s references to, 19; Worralls in, 143
Isham, Thomas, diary of, 7–8

Jackson, James, diary of, 208
Jacob, Mr, contributes to R.J.'s income, 35
'jag', measure of corn, 71
Jessop, Rev. Mr, new minister at Cogges-hall, 29
Jesus College, Cambridge, R.J. at, 16–17
Jolly, Rev. Thomas, diary of, 5n
Josselin, Anne, aunt of R.J., 216
Josselin, Anne, daughter of R.J., 82; birth of, 199; as a baby, 88, 90; learns her book, 91; as servant, 49, 93; has small-pox, 112; death of, 113, 120, 131, 166
Josselin, Anne, mother of R.J., 15, 101
Josselin, Anne, sister of R.J., 130, 131, 153, 215
Josselin, Dorothy, grandmother of R.J., 215
Josselin, Dorothy, sister of R.J., 130, 215
Josselin, Elizabeth, aunt of R.J., 216
Josselin, Elizabeth, cousin of R.J., 215

INDEX

Josselin, Elizabeth, daughter of R.J., 82;
birth of, 199; as a baby, 88; at school,
49, 93; in London, 113; sum spent on,
50; land transferred to, 60–1; marriage
of, to Gilbert Smith, 82, 93, 95–6, 113,
114; children of, 115, 116, 199n; in
R.J.'s will, 64, 65, 123, 211, 213

Josselin, Grace, cousin of R.J., 215

Josselin, Helen, née Peacock, stepmother
of R.J., 16, 126–7

Josselin, Jane, daughter of R.J., 82; birth
of, 84; as a baby, 88, 90, 91; at school,
93, 112; as servant, 112; sum spent on,
50; marriage of, to Jonathan Woodthorpe, 82, 93, 96, 97, 98, 114; dowry of,
59, 93, 95, 132; children of, 114, 115;
illnesses of, 115, 121, 155; in R.J.'s will,
64, 65, 212

Josselin, Jane, née Constable, wife of
R.J., 17, 81, 95; R.J.'s attitude to, 106–
10; pregnancies, miscarriages, and
children of, 50, 81, 83, 170, 199–204;
father's bequest to, 214; attends her
daughters' confinements, 85, 115, 116,
117, 155; in R.J.'s will, 38, 60–1, 123,
211, 212, 213

Josselin, John, 'cousin' of R.J., steward to
Harlakendens, 63, 137–9

Josselin, John, father of R.J., 15, 118,
155n, 165, 216

Josselin, John, son of R.J., 82; as a baby,
90; as apprentice, 48, 93; sum spent on,
48, 50; R.J.'s relations with, 48n, 67,
120–3; marriage of, 82, 96, 98; in
R.J.'s will, 38, 60–1, 64, 65, 66, 123,
213; pays relief on copyholds, 42; will of,
213

Josselin, Joseph, uncle of R.J., 134, 216;
will of, 214–15

Josselin, Martha, née Bentall (?), wife of
R.J.'s son John, 122–3, 213

Josselin, Mary, aunt of R.J. (married
name Benton), 134, 216

Josselin, Mary I, daughter of R.J., 82; as a
child, 89, 91; sum spent on, 50; bequest
to, 128, 214; death of, 155, 165–6, 167,
172; funeral of, 100

Josselin, Mary II, daughter of R.J., 82;
birth of, 85, 199; at school, 49, 93; in
London, 113, 132; sum spent on, 50;
dresses R.J.'s leg, 108; goes to help her
sister Jane, 115, 155; suitor of, 94, 96,
109; marriage of, to Edward Day, 82,
96; dowry of, 38, 51, 94; in R.J.'s will
61, 64, 65, 123, 211–12

Josselin, Mary, sister of R.J., servant with
R.J. and with Harlakendens, 129, 133,

148; bequest to, 215; marriage of, to
Robert Finch, 130

Josselin, Nathaniel, uncle of R.J., 16n,
135, 214, 216

Josselin, Ralph, as army chaplain, 18, 38,
107; children of (birth and childhood),
81–91, (adolescence and marriage),
92–8, (cost of maintenance of), 44–5,
46–51, (relations with), 110–25; deaths
in family of, 98–102; diary of, 10–11,
23; dreams of, 21, 183–7; early life of,
15–17; ecclesiastical career of, 17, 21–32;
as farmer, 68–78; friends and neighbours of, 149–52; marriage of, 17, 81,
95, 96, 97, 98, 106–10; mental attitudes
of, 163–82, 192–6; money affairs of,
33–4, (expenditure), 39–57, (income),
34–9, (saving), 57–67; political opinions
of, 17–21; relatives of, 126–43, 153–60;
as schoolmaster, 17, 34, 37, 39, 64, 76,
91; servants of, 44, 46, 145–8; verbal
imagery of, 187–92; will of, 31–2, 64–7,
211–13

Josselin, Ralph, grandfather of R.J., 15,
215–16, 219

Josselin, Ralph I, son of R.J., 82; dies at 10
days old, 86, 100, 165

Josselin, Ralph II, son of R.J., 82; sum
spent on, 50; dies at 13 months old,
165, 176

Josselin, Ralph, uncle of R.J., 16n, 134,
135–6; loan from, 17, 136, 149; death of
wife of, 133; funeral of, 101; will of, 215

Josselin, Rebecka, daughter of R.J., 82;
birth of, 84–5, 199; as a baby, 90; as
servant in London, 93, 113, 132; sum
spent on, 50; land transferred to, 61;
marriage of, to Steward Spicer, 82, 93,
96, 213; dowry of, 94; in R.J.'s will, 64,
65, 123, 213

Josselin, Rebecka, stepsister of R.J., 126,
127

Josselin, Richard, uncle of R.J., 134, 214,
215, 216; dispute between R.J. and,
134, 135, 219–20

Josselin, Simon, great-uncle of R.J., 215

Josselin, Simon, uncle of R.J., 135, 214,
216; involved in dispute with R.J.,
134–5, 219–20

Josselin, Thomas, son of R.J., 82, 96; as a
baby, 88, 90; at lessons, 91; as apprentice, 48, 93, 118; sum spent on, 50;
draper's shop stocked for, 48; shop
robbed, 119, 219; death of, 118, 119,
131, 166

Josselin, Thomas, uncle of R.J., 134, 215,
216

238

Kelvedon, entry from register of, 139, 217
kinship, 105–6; degrees of, 156–9
Kirkby Lonsdale, listing of (1695), 209, 210

land; dowries in, 51, 59; R.J.'s income from, 37–8, 39; R.J.'s leases of, 68; R.J.'s purchases of, 38, 54, 59–64, 149, 154; R.J.'s sales of, 39
lapwing, Satan compared to, 178, 188
Laud, Archbishop, 22
Layfield, Edward, Archdeacon of Essex, 29
Levellers, R.J. on 'quashing' of, 19
Lexden, R.J.'s daughter Jane at, 98, 114; entries from register of, 218
Litle, John, godparent to R.J.'s first child, 145
livestock, R.J.'s, 69–70
livings, incomes from (Cranham), 17, (Earls Colne), 34–7
loans: to and from R.J., 55–7, 149; from uncles, 17, 134, 135, 149; to brother-in-law, 142, cousin, 137, neighbours, 150, sister, 130
Locke, John, diary of, 9
Loder, Robert, farm accounts of, 33, 45, 71, 77
London, R.J.'s children apprenticed in, 93, 112, 113, 118, 119, 120; R.J.'s married daughters in, 98

maintenance, cost of: for children, 44–5, 46–51; for adults, 45–6
Mallories farm, bought by R.J., 60, 63, 64; leased, 68; sold, 69
Mandeville, Lord, R.J. uses library of, 23
Manningham, John, diary of, 51n
marriage, R.J.'s, 17, 81, 95, 96, 97, 98, 106–10
marriages: civil, 25; of R.J.'s children, 82, 93, 94–8, 113, 114; R.J. involved in arranging, 31; of R.J.'s servants, 147
Martindale, Rev. Adam, diary of, 50
meetings, religious, 24
mental disturbance, R.J. mentions cases of, 193
midwives, 85
Mildmay, Lady, diary of, 5n
Mildmay, Mrs Mary, godparent to R.J.'s first child, 145
Miles, Edward, cousin of R.J., 134
Miles, Thomas, maternal uncle of R.J., 133, 134
millenarianism, 185, 189, 190
miscarriages, of R.J.'s wife, 50, 83, 199, 200, 201
Moore, Rev. Giles, diary and account-book of, 6n, 49

More, Rev. John, diary of, 8n
More, Sir Thomas, 97n
Morly, H., parishioner, 30
mother-daughter relationship, 111–17
mourning, period of, 166–7

Nature, R.J.'s descriptions of, 72–3, 188
neighbours: at births, 85; at baptisms, 89; at funerals, 100; relations with, 149–52
New England, R.J. subscribes to propagation of Gospel in, 22
New Year, gifts to R.J. at, 150
Newcome, Henry, diary of, 8
Newman, Benjamin, Quaker, 27
nonconformists, R.J. on list of, 28, 30
nurses ('dry'), 85, 87

Oates, Samuel, Anabaptist, 26
Oates, Titus, 21
Olney, Buckinghamshire: entries from register of, 142, 218; R.J. curate at, 17, 140; R.J.'s in-laws at, 141, 143
omens, 189
orchard, R.J.'s, 70
ordination, R.J.'s behaviour at, 22

pain, R.J.'s attitude to, 25, 174–5
Parliament, R.J. on, 21
Parnel, James, Quaker, fasts to death, 23
Peacock, Mary, daughter of R.J.'s step-mother by previous marriage, 127
Penhacke, George, summoned as father of bastard, 191
Penhacke, John, married to Mary Potter, R.J.'s maid, 147
Pepys, Samuel, diary of, 9n, 110n, 144n
pigs, 69
plague, 119, 170, 172, 173
plate, gifts of, to children, 50, 93
Pledger, Elias, diary of, 8, 204n, 207
ploughing, 70
Plundered Ministers, Committee for, 35, 39
politics, R.J. in, 17–21
poll tax, 42
Porter, Old Mistriss, R.J.'s sermon at funeral of, 25, 222–3
Potter, Mary, maid to R.J., 147
poverty, Calvinist view of, 194–5
Powell, Walter, diary of, 6, 204n
Prayer-Book (Book of Common Prayer), 22, 25, 26, 28n, 29
pregnancies of R.J.'s wife, 81, 83, 84, 170, 199–200
Presbyterianism, 26
prices of food, 75–6; weather and, 73

procurations, paid by R.J., 29, 30
puberty, delay after, before marriage, 205; R.J.'s children leave home before, 92–3
Puritanism, 21, 95n, 193–5; see also Calvinism

Quakers, 26–7, 30, 173, 177
quarrels, R.J. as mediator in, 30–1
quit rents, paid by R.J., 42

Raleigh, Sir Walter, and his father, 117
Rawdon, Marmaduke. Life of, 208
relatives; at births, 85, 115, 116, 117, 155; at baptisms, 89; at weddings, 97; at funerals, 100
reliefs (entry fines), paid by R.J. on copyhold land, 42
Rogers, Richard, diary of, 140
Rolle, William, of Hatfield Peverel, will of, 123n
Rous, John, diary of, 5n
Roxwell, entries from register of, 129, 218; R.J. born at, 15

Sadler, John, Master in Chancery, visions and prophecy of, 191
St Paul's Cross, R.J. preaches at, 24
Sams, Rev. John, minister at Coggeshall, 186
saving: by purchase of land, 57–67, 154; by social investment, 154, 171
Sawyers, land bought by R.J., 60, 65; leased, 68
schoolmaster, R.J. as, 17, 34, 37, 39, 64, 76, 91
schools, 206–7; R.J. at, 15; R.J.'s children at, 49, 91, 93, 112
Searle, Thomas, first husband of R.J.'s aunt Mary, 134n
Seaver, works on R.J.'s farm, 43
Separatists, 26
sermons, R.J.'s, 17, 20, 24–5, 28, 124–5, 173; at baptisms, 139; at funerals, 25, 83n, 100, 107, 152, 220–2; to his children, 90, 109, 122
servants: R.J.'s, 44, 46, 145–8; R.J.'s children as, 49, 93, 112
Sewall, Samuel, letter-books of, 137
sheep, 69–70, 128, 188, 214
Shepherds, uncle and aunt by marriage of R.J.'s wife, 140, 141, 143, 145
ship money, paid by R.J.'s stepmother, 126n
siblings, relations between, 128–32
sin, R.J.'s preoccupation with personal, 177–9

Slingsby, Sir Henry, diary of, 5n
smallpox, 173; R.J.'s children ill with, 112, 113, 119, 120, 170
Smith, Gilbert, husband of R.J.'s daughter Elizabeth, 114
Socinianism, 23n
Spain, R.J.'s references to, 19, 20
Spooner, Goodman and wife, friends of R.J., 150
Spooner, 'Old', 68
Spriggs Marsh, land left to R.J., 60, 67, 211
Stapley, Richard, diary of, 7
Steeple Bumpstead, 16, 126n, 138
Stephens, parishioner, sees the devil, 191
Stourbridge Fair, 73
Stout, William, autobiography of, 46n, 48n, 49n
Stulps, land left to R.J., 60, 67, 211
suicide, R.J.'s attitude to, 169–70
Sunday observance, 22
Sunderland, R.J.'s share in vessel trading to, 38
Symonds, Mr, new minister at Colne Engain, 29

taxes paid by R.J., 42–3; ecclesiastical, 29, 30
teething, age of children at, 90
Thoresby, Ralph, diary of, 6
Thornlecke, Mr, persuades R.J. to remain at Cambridge, 17
Thornton, Alice, diary of, 86n, 202n
Thurloe, John, Secretary of State, R.J. dreams about, 186
Tibbald, lessee of R.J.'s land, 68
tithes: 'great', given to R.J. by Harlakenden, 37; R.J.'s income from, 34–5
Toke, Nicholas, farm accounts of, 46
trade, R.J.'s investments in, 38
travel, R.J. on dangers of, 171, 192
Tunbridge Wells, R.J.'s visit to, 172

uncles of R.J., 132, 133–7
Upminster, R.J. teaches at, 17

verbal imagery used by R.J., 187–9
Verneys, memoirs of, 49n

wages, of R.J.'s servants, 148n
walking, age of children at stage of, 90
Warwick, Mary Rich, Countess of, diary of, 8
weaning of R.J.'s children, 83, 87, 88; dates of, and dates of conception of succeeding children, 87, 202–3
weather: God's displeasure shown in, 175, 189; R.J.'s accounts of, 71–5, 189

Webb, William, and brother, work on R.J.'s farm, 43

weddings, expenses of, 53, 97, presents at, 98

wheat: bad harvests of, 73n; seed-, for R.J.'s farm, 70, 73

Wheatcroft, Leonard, diary of, 4n

Whittingham, Timothy, diary of, 49n

wills: of R.J., 31-2, 64-7, 211-13; of R.J.'s relatives, 123n, 128, 134, 135-6, 148, 213-16

witchcraft, 163, 165n, 177n, 189, 191-2

Woodthorpe, Jonathan, husband of R.J.'s daughter Jane, 78, 114; will of, 148, 213

words, power of, 195-6

Worrall, husband of R.J.'s wife's sister Elizabeth, 143